CAMBRIDGE STUDIES IN EIGHTEENTH-CENTURY
ENGLISH LITERATURE AND THOUGHT 3

Sterne's Fiction and the Double Principle

CAMBRIDGE STUDIES IN EIGHTEENTH-CENTURY
ENGLISH LITERATURE AND THOUGHT

General Editors: Dr HOWARD ERSKINE-HILL, Litt.D., FBA, *Pembroke College, Cambridge*
and Professor JOHN RICHETTI, *University of Pennsylvania*

Editorial Board: Morris Brownell, *University of Nevada*
Leopold Damrosch, *Harvard University*
J. Paul Hunter, *University of Chicago*
Isobel Grundy, *Queen Mary College, London*
Lawrence Lipking, *Northwestern University*
Harold Love, *Monash University*
Claude Rawson, *Yale University*
Pat Rogers, *University of South Florida*
James Sambrook, *University of Southampton*

The growth in recent years of eighteenth-century literary studies has prompted the establishment of this new series of books devoted to the period. The series will accommodate monographs and critical studies on authors, works, genres and other aspects of literary culture from the later part of the seventeenth century to the end of the eighteenth.

Since academic engagement with this field has become an increasingly interdisciplinary enterprise, books will be especially encouraged which in some way stress the cultural context of the literature, or examine it in relation to contemporary art, music, philosophy, historiography, religion, politics, social affairs, and so on. New approaches to the established canon are being tested with increasing frequency, and the series will hope to provide a home for the best of these. The books we choose to publish will be thorough in their methods of literary, historical, or biographical investigation, and will open interesting perspectives on previously closed, or underexplored, or misrepresented areas of eighteenth-century writing and thought. They will reflect the work of both younger and established scholars on either side of the Atlantic and elsewhere.

Published
The Transformation of The Decline and Fall of the Roman Empire, by David Womersley
Women's Place in Pope's World, by Valerie Rumbold
Warrior Women and Popular Balladry, by Dianne Dugaw
Sterne's Fiction and the Double Principle, by Jonathan Lamb

Other titles in preparation
Plots and Counterplots: Politics and Literary Representation, 1660–1730, by Richard Braverman
The Eighteenth-Century Hymn, by Donald Davie
The Body in Swift and Defoe, by Carol Flynn
Richardson's Clarissa *and the Eighteenth-Century Reader*, by Tom Keymer
The Muses of Resistance: Labouring-Class Women's Poetry in Britain, 1739–1796, by Donna Landry
Reason, Grace and Sentiment: A Study of the Language of Religion and Ethics in England, 1600–1780, by Isabel Rivers
Defoe's Politics: Parliament, Power, Kingship and Robinson Crusoe, by Manuel Schonhorn
Space and the Eighteenth-Century English Novel, by Simon Varey
The Rhetoric of Berkeley's Philosophy, by Peter Walmsley

Sterne's Fiction and the Double Principle

JONATHAN LAMB

Senior Lecturer, Department of English
University of Auckland

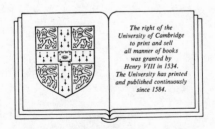

The right of the
University of Cambridge
to print and sell
all manner of books
was granted by
Henry VIII in 1534.
The University has printed
and published continuously
since 1584.

CAMBRIDGE UNIVERSITY PRESS

CAMBRIDGE

NEW YORK   PORT CHESTER   MELBOURNE   SYDNEY

Published by the Press Syndicate of the University of Cambridge
The Pitt Building, Trumpington Street, Cambridge CB2 1RP
40 West 20th Street, New York, NY 10011, USA
10 Stamford Road, Oakleigh, Melbourne 3166, Australia

First published 1989

Printed in Great Britain at the University Press, Cambridge

British Library cataloguing in publication data
Lamb, Jonathan
Sterne's fiction and the double principle –
(Cambridge studies in eighteenth-century
English literature and thought)
1. Fiction in English. Sterne, Laurence,
1713–68 – Critical studies
I. Title
823'.6

Library of Congress cataloguing in publication data
Lamb, Jonathan, 1945–
Sterne's fiction and the double principle / Jonathan Lamb.
p. cm. – (Cambridge studies in eighteenth-century English
literature and thought; 3)
Bibliography.
Includes index.
ISBN 0–521–37273–9
1. Sterne, Laurence, 1713–68 – Criticism and interpretation.
I. Title. II. Series.
PR3716.L28 1989
823'.6–dc20 89–7117 CIP

ISBN 0 521 37273 9

For my mother

Contents

Plates

Acknowledgments

This book was begun while I was a visiting lecturer at the University of Kent, and finished during a visiting fellowship at the University of Sussex; so I want to thank the Board of English Studies at Kent and the School of English and American Studies at Sussex for their hospitality and goodwill. My own University of Auckland has generously accommodated me with study leave, and the University Grants Committee of New Zealand assisted with microfilm costs in the early stages of the project. Michael Seidel's encouragement helped me (though he didn't know it) through a despondent patch and into the sunshine of a fresh start. The Bakhtin Group in the Auckland English Department constantly fed my enthusiasm for the theoretical side of fiction, and among its members I am particularly grateful to Claudia Marquis and Roger Nicholson for moral and technical support with the first draft. Without the help of my good friend Richard Winant, whose patience equals Job's, it would have been impossible to have solved problems of hardware and software.

Abbreviations used in text and notes

Letters	*Letters of Laurence Sterne*, ed. Lewis Perry Curtis (Oxford: Clarendon Press, 1935; repr. 1965)
Lowth	Robert Lowth, *Lectures on the Sacred Poetry of the Hebrews*, trans. G. Gregory (London: S. Chadwick, 1847)
MLN	*Modern Language Notes*
OM	David Hartley, *Observations on Man, His Frame, His Duty, and His Expectations*, 2 vols. (London, 1749; repr. Gainesville: Scholars' Facsimiles and Reprints, 1966)
OS	*Dionysius Longinus on the Sublime*, trans. William Smith (London, 1739; repr. Gainesville: Scholars' Facsimiles and Reprints, 1975)
PQ	*Philological Quarterly*
Sermons	*Sermons of Mr Yorick*, 2 vols. (Oxford: Basil Blackwell, 1927)
T	David Hume, *A Treatise of Human Nature*, ed. Ernest C. Mossner (Harmondsworth: Penguin, 1969)
TS	*The Life and Opinions of Tristram Shandy, Gentleman*, ed. James A. Work (Odyssey Press: New York, 1940)

Introduction

Apart from modesty, there is not much reason to make an apology for a new book on Sterne. There is no flood of essays and monographs threatening to drown it in superfluity, nor any prior brisk debate to make it seem to have missed the tide of fashionable polemic. In the ferment of the last decade, Richardson is the only male novelist of the eighteenth century to have benefited. *Clarissa* has been the object of critical and theoretical discussion whose freshness and energy have spilled over into into what used to be the deserts of eighteenth-century literature – novels by women – and made them bloom again.[1]

Sterne's failure to share in this harvest – not to mention Fielding's or Smollett's – is worth thinking about. After his rehabilitation earlier this century, his popularity and semi-canonical status in the ranks of English literature were probably bound by the nature of things to wane. More specifically, his Whiggish centrism, his weakness for sly innuendos about female sexuality, and the anti-feminist readings some of his stories will bear, have appealed less and less to readers who expect a more candid and less marginalising approach to sexual politics in fiction. *Tristram Shandy* must strike them as the sort of novel Robert Lovelace would have written, had he lived long enough to find impotence a joke. Richardson's stock has risen precisely because he dramatises the sort of conflict that develops between a female reader and Sterne. Clarissa's contempt for narrow views, bawdy talk and the sexualising arts of her lover might be echoed by Tristram's 'madam' if she had a voice of her own.

Richardson's reappropriation of this voice on behalf of women, principally by idealising the familiar letter while using it as the narrative device of his novels, has brought his work within the scope of one of the most interesting debates about eighteenth-century fiction. Jacques Derrida's *Of Grammatology* and Paul de Man's *Allegories of Reading*, both addressed to the problems of interpretation arising from Rousseau's pursuit of candour, have been

---

1 Since this book has been finished, two full-length studies of *Tristram Shandy* have appeared: Wolfgang Iser, *Tristram Shandy* (Cambridge University Press, 1988), and Ruth Whittaker, *Tristram Shandy* (Milton Keynes: Open University Press, 1988). Max Byrd's *Tristram Shandy* (London, Methuen, 1985) offers a detailed and useful survey of post-war Sterne criticism.

extraordinarily stimulating for readers who have admired Richardson's achievement while remaining sceptical of some of his assumptions about the originality and sincerity of epistolary correspondence. The question of writing's relation to identity and difference has contributed a theoretical rigour to discussions of Richardson which I (on Sterne's behalf) find enviable. Sterne's experiments in language and form, once considered so important to the formalist and modernist projects, have settled into proverbiality at the very time when the Pyrrhonist agility of poststructuralist criticism is worthy of the subtler effects of his applied scepticism. I have in mind his fondness for the undecidable in puns, propositions of identity, and storytelling, closely associated with his ability to run series and sequences in reverse, so that straightforward words came back as palindromes. Unless it is that sceptical readers need texts like Richardson's, which roundly condemn (at least at their margins) the decadence of applied doubt and so leave room for deconstructive manoeuvre, it seems both unfair and odd that Sterne should have been neglected by literary theorists. When they have given him a reading – J. Hillis Miller in his essay 'Narrative Middles' and Terry Eagleton (very briefly) in his book on Walter Benjamin, for example – the results have been exciting.

The seasonal rise and fall of literary reputations has not been altered for the better in Sterne's case by the appearance of the definitive Florida edition of *Tristram Shandy*, which came out first in two handsomely bound but critically naked volumes in 1978, followed by a volume of appended notes in 1984. Although all readers of Sterne must be grateful for the work of the Florida annotators, an unhappy result of their labours has been to re-position Sterne in a grid of borrowings, quotations and allusions that considerably restricts the freedom to read beyond the annotated pale. Melvyn New sets out these restrictions in a couple of essays where he describes the annotator's job as mediation between the uninformed reader and the potentially infinite library predicated as Sterne's source. In his rather odd image, the annotator is posted at the 'backside' of the Sternean text, reporting to an eager audience on the provenance of what passes through, and consoled for the meanness of his position by the conviction that the more he notes of this fattening stream, the more he will have to note: 'the end is nowhere in sight'.[2] The original anxiety of the annotator – that his author has read more books than he has – descends to the reader, who is staggered at the extent and detail of the reports he receives, and wonders nervously if he or she is 'getting' or 'missing' the good things that come bobbing down the current. New compares this scene of instruction to the cracking of a joke: 'some will "get" the joke; others

2 Melvyn New, ' "At the backside of the door of purgatory": A Note on Annotating *Tristram Shandy*', in *Laurence Sterne: Riddles and Mysteries*, ed. Valerie Grosvenor Myer (London: Vision Press, 1984), p. 22. See also the introduction to Laurence Sterne, *The Life and Opinions of Tristram Shandy, Gentleman*, ed. Melvyn and Joan New, 3 vols. (Gainesville: University of Florida Press, 1978–84), III, 1–31.

will not "get" it; and others, of course, will think they understand when in reality they do not'. The annotator does his duty by 'forcing all his readers to "get" a text I am certain all will miss on first reading' (pp. 15, 17). If the absolutes jostling the reader in that sentence seem at odds with the relativising tone adopted elsewhere, it is because the challenge of 'where to start, and where to stop' in the endless stream of the 'gettable' is risen to by the annotator, not by the reader. Like Toby's mediated encounter with Slawkenbergius, the reader of the annotated Sterne is expected 'to *hold* the grains and scruples of learning,——not to *weigh* them'.

I think it is a pity to strip initiatives from readers in this way, especially in view of the great lengths taken by Sterne to extend them. It is a greater pity to make the sly innuendo exemplary of the annotatable crux in his fiction, because it inflects the question of 'where to start, and where to stop' with the most unhappy blend of seductiveness and aggression. The reader is transformed into 'madam', and the scene of instruction is tilted towards the boudoir, where she will be taught to shed her prudish 'reluctance to follow the possibilities of Sterne's humour' and learn to do without punctilios 'that do seem to have something to do with delicacy' (New, 'Annotating *Tristram Shandy*', p. 16). Threatening to teach the coy reader a thing or two is a species of annotative truculence not limited to the Florida edition and its apologetics. In his essay on Earl Wasserman, Neil Hertz has very deftly handled the intonation and the drift of the classic annotative question, 'How far can I go?' And he has pointed out that in the economy of annotation at least, the bid-dable reader has no choice but to yield the power of setting limits to the doughty guardian of the nether reaches: the annotator himself.[3] The taste for having one over on the reader evidently increases with its indulgence, since W. G. Day, another of the Florida annotators, has now annotated a bibliography of recent critical work on Sterne in which he is moved to record his appreciation as follows, 'This piece has style and ideas', and 'this piece has panache' ('Annotated Bibliography', in Myer, *Laurence Sterne*, pp. 174–5).

Are we to say that Sterne's readers ask for it? – that they are stupid not to know, or to have forgotten, that to pick up one of his books is to enter into a series of tricky negotiations with other books? I think they deserve more credit for responding to the rhetorical impact (as opposed to the intentional line) of Sterne's composite texts. His borrowing Montaigne on the topic of borrowing, or plagiarising Burton's attack on plagiarism – favourite ex-amples among readers who have a fondness for Sterne's reflexive bent – shift the emphasis from borrowing as an annotatable quantum to borrowing as a trope, or a figure of rhetoric. For my part, I became fascinated by just this sort of performed pun, or pleonasm, in Sterne's fiction, and spent many an

---

3 Neil Hertz, 'Two Extravagant Teachings', in *The End of the Line* (New York: Columbia University Press, 1985), pp. 150, 159.

unprofitable hour trying to account for it. What I came up with is contained in the following pages, where I argue that this use of literary fragments is not the key to some enormously clever puzzle whose clues we go on solving in the hope of total disclosure; rather the opposite, that they are a tactical and tough-minded experiment with privation, breach, shortage and emptiness. They are 'fragments' on fragments, just like the borrowings and plagiarism committed by that notoriously incomplete autobiographer, Tristram Shandy, by way of self-supplement. This invites us to consider these exotic bits and pieces not as the language of an ultimately decipherable message, but as parts of a figurative arrangement whose efficacy lies in its unannotatable ambiguity. It will quickly become apparent that my hobbyhorse is the embroidering of the difference between figurative language which is irreducibly equivocal and the kind of joking favoured by Professor New, which disguises a literal meaning or image under a specious show of wit. The pleonasm is the best example of the first, as tautology is of the second.

It was not until I read Derrida's essay on the *pharmakon* in *Dissemination* that the range of Sterne's scepticism began to be fully apparent to me. Before that I had assumed that he was a comic platonist, recommending and even idealising the harmony of 'tune' of the eccentric proprieties of such humorists as uncle Toby, who evince the sentimental balance Richardson calls the 'consentaneousness' of thought and feeling. The discovery that this was not so, and that his fiction would stand and even reward the most unremitting of cross-grained readings, coincided with a re-reading of *A Passage to India*, and my first inkling of what Forster meant when he said that muddle ruled *Tristram Shandy*. Made to sound like a cosy platitude, his judgment is the most mordant estimate of the uncanniness and even the terror that skirts Sterne's comic enterprise. Since then I have found the Book of Job more and more important in the constellation of texts of which Sterne's form a part.

Addison's *Spectator* papers, it seems almost trite to say, have an importance out of all proportion to their size and modest bearing. It took a long time and a good deal of reflection before the immense usefulness of Addison's formulation of the double principle became apparent to me, particularly in orienting Sterne's novels towards associationist psychology and the aesthetics of the sublime. That the most complex and powerful sentiments arise from a coalition of an impression and an idea which cannot conceal the imperfection of their union, but can exploit it, is the founding premise of the following discussion, and one that Addison seems to have understood fully when he briefly outlined it in his papers on the pleasures of the imagination. In pursuing this line in psychology and aesthetics, Locke's importance in the Shandean web of relations shrinks somewhat, and Hartley's and Hume's grows much larger. I think that is a good thing on more accounts than my own. With Locke less salient it becomes easier to see how much Montaigne contributes to the structure and the reading of the Shandean sublime.

Here I am talking of authors not as influences, I hasten to add, but as possibilities of reading. Yet an instinctive preference for reading Sterne primarily through eighteenth-century texts, and largely in eighteenth-century terms, explains why Derrida's theorisation of writing remains untouched in this argument, and why Bakhtin's of dialogism is only implied and not explored. When they are handled, as I am sure they will be very soon, I hope that some aspects of this book will be found useful. In the book's latter stages I acknowledge an enormous debt to Neil Hertz's collection of essays, *The End of the Line*; and at the same point I try to assimilate his theory of the 'turn at the end of the line' to my more pragmatic notions of the pleonasm. I'm sure it could have been done less clumsily, but I believe it is a worthwhile connexion.

1

Scepticism, Job and the double principle

There is a set of sceptical commonplaces announced and exemplified in Sterne's fiction which I want to begin by enumerating. They are not especially new or interesting in themselves, but they foster experiments in characterisation, narrative and aesthetics which I hope *are* interesting because they are the subject of the following book.

Propositions and illustrations

A collection of these commonplaces, neatly summarising the assumptions of Sterne's favourite authors (especially Montaigne), is found in Hume's essay 'The Sceptic' (1741). There he maintains that all judgments about things are unstable because the value of a thing is not determined by any immutable quality belonging to it, but by the extremely varied responses it will induce in the people who encounter it. This variety is owing both to the different situations in which things may be found and to the different moods in which they will be viewed. Discourse of reason will never bring people to a consensus about things because their impressions of them (variously named sentiments, passions and tastes) are not susceptible to rational discrimination, only to the accidents, intuitions, habits and prejudices which are constantly forming and re-forming them. Hume draws two conclusions. The first is that there is never any clear relation between perceptions and things, since perceptions are neither consistent nor continuous, and since the notion of a continuous identity of things is an illusion persisting in spite of the various and interrupted views we have of them. The second is that no language will affect these perceptions which does not itself participate in the mixed cases it addresses. 'The reflections of philosophy', says Hume, 'are too subtle and distant to take place in common life, or eradicate any affection.'[1]

Tristram Shandy is littered with similar conclusions. The epigraph from Epictetus – 'It is not things, but opinions concerning them, that disturb

---

1 Hume, 'The Sceptic', in *Essays Moral, Political and Literary* (London: World's Classics, 1903), p. 175. For an authoritative commentary on the essay, as well as on Hume's scepticism generally, see Robert J. Fogelin, *Hume's Scepticism in the Treatise of Human Nature* (London: Routledge and Kegan Paul, 1985), pp. 117–22.

us' – introduces scene after scene showing that no thing is immune from the effects of its adjacent circumstances and the temper of its beholder. 'Need I tell you, Sir,' asks Tristram while his father is getting tangled up in his coat pockets, 'that the circumstances with which every thing in this world is begirt, give every thing in this world its size and shape;——and . . . make the thing to be, what it is——great——little——good——bad——indifferent or not indifferent, just as the case happens.'[2] The same scene authorises the subsequent observation that 'A man's body and his mind, with the utmost reverence to both I speak it, are exactly like a jerkin, and a jerkin's lining; ——rumple the one——you rumple the other' (*TS*, 3.4.160). When Tristram's own lining is rumpled on the way to Paris, he concludes that 'REASON is, half of it, SENSE; and the measure of heaven itself is but the measure of our present appetites and concoctions' (*TS*, 7.13.494). The importance of situation in determining what is to be thought or said of an object is most neatly illustrated in Toby's attempted distinction between the crescent-shaped siegeworks called ravelins and half-moons: 'When a ravelin stands before the curtin, it is a ravelin; and when a ravelin stands before a bastion, then the ravelin is not a ravelin;——it is a half-moon' (*TS*, 2.12.112). Mood is influenced by more factors than situation, but Tristram shows how critically the equilibrium (or otherwise) of the mind and the body bears upon our judgments. He needs only to shave his chin and put on his best suit for his writing and his temper immediately to improve; whereas Walter Shandy's awkward reaching for his left-hand coat pocket forces first his body, then his feelings and sentiments, into an irritable and combative pattern.

Shandean relativity allows nothing to stand neutral or independent. An idea needs to be animated by an impression, an object by some adjacent circumstance, or a proposition by a sentiment or case, otherwise it will never be registered. It will remain like those simple notions which 'are every day swimming quietly in the middle of the thin juice of a man's understanding, without being carried backwards or forwards' (*TS*, 3.9.167). Phutatorius' oath 'Zounds!' requires, like the chestnut that occasions it, a consideration of circumstances and impressions if it is to be assigned a value or to have its interpretation corroborated. As the heat in his breeches crosses the border between pleasure and pain, Phutatorius' imagination is incapable of staying neutral; it must fasten an image to the sensation. In fact it fastens one of a reptile's fastening teeth, and the resulting exclamation makes the same demand for extra context on the imaginations of his audience. Identity as well as neutrality is ruled out of this world. Things 'not worth a button in themselves' become

2 Laurence Sterne, *The Life and Opinions of Tristram Shandy, Gentleman*, ed. James A. Work (Odyssey Press: New York, 1940), 3.2.158, p. 158. I have decided to retain this edition, although technically superseded by the Florida edition, partly because it is more accessible to general readers and partly because I have a longstanding affection for it. Hereafter cited in brackets as *TS* followed by volume, chapter and page numbers.

serious objects when united with others – a faded uniform, for example, joined with Toby's person becomes worth looking at (*TS*, 9.2.601). Names for
which Toby wouldn't give a cherry stone are of inestimable value to his
brother. There is always some accident in the arrangement or the observation
of things to prevent them from being just themselves.

Tristram makes elaborate fun of propositions of identity. When his father
attacks his mother's motive for wanting to look through the keyhole at Toby's
courtship of Mrs Wadman, implying that it is something worse than curiosity
that impels her, Tristram remarks, 'The mistake of my father, was in attack-
ing my mother's motive, instead of the act itself: for certainly key-holes were
made for other purposes; and considering the act, as an act which interfered
with a true proposition, and denied a key-hole to be what it was——it became
a violation of nature' (*TS*, 9.1.600). This sardonic defence of the 'quidditas'
of keyholes, like the mocking tautology of his definition of nose as *nose* (*TS*,
3.31.218), serves only to emphasise the inevitability of our using things, ideas
and words in ways which destroy their simplicity and identity. People who
talk of the '*corregiescity* of *Corregio*', or gravely declare that 'nature is nature',
are either knaves or fools (*TS*, 3.12.181; 5.10.365).

In Tristram's opinion there are certain situations especially resistant to
simple ideas and univocal terms. Love is one of these, being a vortex of conflicting impressions, prescriptions and cases. It can rise as high as the galaxy and
sink as low as the devil's kitchen; the identical feeling can manifest itself as
tenderness in one breast and hatred in another, or even as an alternation between the two if the breast is as sensitive to new impressions as Tristram's (*TS*,
8.11.550; 8.4.542). Out of this confusion, where there are 'half a dozen words
for one thing', he refuses to draw even a mock definition. Instead he composes
his contradictory alphabet of love, together with a number of elaborate
metaphors, usually with a military vehicle in deference to Toby's transformation from soldier into lover. In comparing an eye to a cannon, he founds the
resemblance on the fact that 'it is not so much the eye or the cannon, in
themselves, as it is the carriage of the eye——and the carriage of the cannon,
by which both the one and the other are enabled to do so much execution'
(*TS*, 8.25.577). The conceit is picked up by Trim when telling Toby how
much women love jokes, and how the only way to find out what sort suits
which woman is to experiment 'as we do with our artillery in the field, by raising or letting down their breeches, till we hit the mark' (*TS*, 9.8.609).
Oblivious to the innuendo, Toby replies, 'I like the comparison better than
the thing itself.' 'The thing itself' is of course an unconscious addition to the
numerous equivocations on the 'hirsute and gashly' focus of all amorous
argumenta ad rem (*TS*, 8.11.550; 1.21.71); but Toby's statement of preference
is quite a complex addition to them. At a philosophical level it rehearses the
basic sceptical proposition that 'objects have absolutely no worth or value in
themselves', that our verdicts upon them embrace 'not the object simply as

it is in itself . . . but all the circumstances that attend it' (Hume, 'The Sceptic', pp. 169, 174). At the level of rhetoric it establishes the superiority of a figure over a literalism and a joke over a statement of fact. In sexual terms it is both a recommendation and an example of equivocation, faithful to Walter's written advice to his brother to 'leave as many things as thou canst quite undetermined' (*TS*, 8.34.592).

These preferences are highly esteemed by Tristram. He detests the pursuit of the thing itself, the object simply as it is in itself, on all the same grounds: philosophically, because arguments about essence and substance have 'perpetuated so much gall and ink-shed,——that a good natured man cannot read the accounts of them without tears in his eyes' (*TS*, 2.2.87); rhetorically, because he has a horror of falling into 'a cold unmetaphorical vein of infamous writing . . . like a Dutch commentator' (*TS*, 9.13.616); sexually, because concupiscence results in false abstractions, where noses, groins or a set of whiskers, in becoming the unambiguous signs of the desired thing, shed the constitutive, richly indistinct surplus of a situation, which is then viewed as insignificant rubbish – empty bottles, tripes, trunk-hose and pantofles (*TS*, 9.22.626).

Nature is the most amiable of the personifications in *Tristram Shandy* and *A Sentimental Journey*, a being 'almost as merry as she is wise'.[3] She is the source of the endless variety which, says Hume, our minds should try to equal ('The Sceptic', p. 161) and of which love, in Tristram's opinion, is the most dramatically multifarious example. She guides her followers to a spontaneous relish for the instability and uncertainty of experience. 'Whatever is my situation,' cries Yorick in an apostrophe to Nature, 'let me feel the movements which rise out of it' (*ASJ*, p. 237). In tracing the movements arising from implicit confidence in her government, Tristram exemplifies their equivocality in a telling image:

She dear Goddess, by an instantaneous impulse, in all *provoking cases*, determines us to a sally of this or that member——or else thrusts us into this or or that place, or posture of body, we know not why——But mark, madam, we live amongst riddles and mysteries——the most obvious things, which come in our way, have dark sides, which the quickest sight cannot penetrate into; and even the clearest and most exalted understandings amongst us find ourselves puzzled and at a loss in almost every cranny of nature's works; so that this, like a thousand other things, falls out for us in a way, which tho' we cannot reason upon it,——yet we find the good of it. (*TS*, 4.7.293)

As in Toby's accidental innuendo, 'obvious things' are punned to the dark edge of indecency to emphasise how hopelessly reason and analytic discourse are contaminated by sense and impulse. And just as his uncle's spontaneous

3 Laurence Sterne, *A Sentimental Journey through France and Italy*, ed. Gardner D. Stout (Berkeley: University of California Press, 1967), p. 174. Hereafter cited as *ASJ*.

pun illustrates the preferences he is trying to state, so Tristram's rhetoric is agreeable to his sentiments, inasmuch as he reproduces figuratively in the form of equivokes on the dark and crannied sides of 'things', the obscurities he mentions and values.

Whenever Tristram adopts or recommends a sceptical position, he will be found playing between extremes. Here, for example, the extremes of divinityship and dark crannies are analogous to the starry heights and 'gashly' depths which bounded his feelings about love. The same impulse to veer between ideal and carnal levels is evident in his description of what it is like to wrestle with a dilemma, where the mind is torn between two equally attractive but opposite possibilities: 'It is not to be told in what a degree such a wayward kind of friction works upon the more gross and solid parts, wasting the fat and impairing the strength of a man every time as it goes backwards and forwards' (TS, 4.31.336). The shilly-shallies of doubt are run into a lewd analogy with the rhythms of copulation, so that alternating notions and motions are equally to be derived from an act of indecent exposure Tristram calls the 'unbuttoning' of a vexation. His analysis of the sentimental element in the tender conference enjoyed by Julia and Diego after their reunion turns on two extreme hypotheses. The first is that two lovers might glance at the ceiling and knock their chins together; the other that they might stare at one another's laps and bang their foreheads. He concludes that the sentimental ingredient, which makes his own heart vibrate to Slawkenbergius' strangely suggestive phrase, 'lambent pupilability of slow, low, dry chat', is sustained by keeping eye-beams and feelings on the horizontal, much as his own are during his dance with Nanette at the end of the seventh volume, where his glance comprehends the 'heaven' of an ideal relationship and the 'lap of content' represented by the slit in her petticoat, but is seduced by neither (TS, 4.1.273; 7.43.538).

This sentimental equilibrium is not achieved by rejecting sexuality and intellectuality, but by encouraging their cooperation in the production of associated ideas and equivocal expressions. Tristram takes Swift's delight in such materialised abstractions, as 'depression' and 'gravitation'; more so when the material element is sexual, as in 'ejaculation' and 'manual effervescencies'. He regards this sort of play as not merely expressive of the psychophysiological mixtures in which we all are obliged to function, but also as an ethical obstacle put in the way of the unequivocal pursuit of 'the thing itself', whether occasioned by sexual or intellectual intemperance. The puns he makes on this phrase, 'the thing itself', blur the object of lust with the formula of identity so that the one extreme of undistracted desire mocks the other. Tristram's word-play gets brighter the further apart the extremes he negotiates: light and darkness, digression and progression, fasting and feasting, tragedy and comedy, tears and laughter. He is constantly sensitising himself and his reader to the mutuality of these opposites, not knowing, as he says, how near he may be 'under the necessity of placing them to each other' (TS, 7.19.502).

References to tragicomedy and *chiaroscuro* in particular signal that readers are being put on their mettle. The Shandy family's journey through Europe, of which only a fragment is published, is advertised as a collection of opinions 'so opposite to those of all other mortal men . . . of so odd, so mixed and tragicomical a contexture' that its varying shades and tints will be appreciated by readers till the world stands still (*TS*, 7.17.512). Being the 'tragicomical completion' of his father's prediction that he will neither think nor act like anyone else, Tristram is never very certain where to cast his shade and throw his light (*TS*, 3.23.207), and finally decides to hang up stars in his darkest passages, 'knowing that the world is apt to lose its way, with all the lights the sun itself at noon day can give it' (*TS*, 6.33.462). These stars are asterisks, of course, whose effect is not to clear but to deepen the obscurity of a sentence or paragraph. The reader's bafflement is not eased by efforts to find out what lies behind the enigma. The only resource is to imitate Tristram's flexibility amidst natural variety and be 'pleased he knows not why, and cares not wherefore' (*TS*, 3.12.182).

Readerly pleasure that cannot account for itself is not to be mistaken for mere passive receptivity. One of Walter's sounder opinions is that everything in this earthly world has two handles and that everyone has two hands; and readers are not exempt from this generalisation, in owning a public and a private ear apiece (*TS*, 7.20.503) and hands to correspond. Naturally enough, Tristram lays hands on both, demanding not only that readers apprehend ambiguities but also that they reproduce them. Pointing to the mixture of his father's opinions which causes 'sometimes such illuminations in the darkest of his eclipses, as almost attoned for them', he adds, 'Be wary, Sir, when you imitate him' (*TS*, 5.42.404). Like his earlier remarks on the dialectical nature of writing and reading, this warning outlines a high standard of reciprocal activity not limited merely to the filling up of blank spaces in the text, but stretching beyond a taste for ambiguity to a talent for ambidexterity. In Nature's world and Tristram's, there are quaquaversal arrangements of handles which it behoves readers to seize, 'of what size or shape soever' (*TS*, 7.43.536).

When mutual ambidexterity is exercised on a narrative where the characters themselves are happily seizing handles, Shandean scepticism is limitless, unbounded by beginnings, ends, plots or reasons. Instead of a pseudo-providence of achieved purposes, what is represented, recommended and practised on both sides of the text is a series of happy accidents affording every character, object and word a double appearance and a double function. As all things act and react with their circumstances, their opposites or their perceivers, there is no part of the narrative, whether scene, commentary or reading, not constitutive of the factors constituting it. Nothing has an in-dependent being; everything shares a 'double existence',[4] as Hume calls it,

---

4 See David Hume, *A Treatise of Human Nature*, ed. Ernest C. Mossner (Harmondsworth: Penguin, 1969), pp. 239–40 (I, iv, 2), hereafter cited as *T*; and Fogelin, *Hume's Scepticism*, pp. 81–3.

with its situation. The only way of tracing these coalitions is by means of analogy. In the imagined scene between Julia and Diego, for example, where glances are shared between the extremes of foreheads and laps, the relation of brain to body is suggested by a neologism – 'pupilability' – whose equivocality relies upon the same alignment of ideal and physical categories. Once imagined, the scene affects Tristram as the midpoint between his own forehead and lap; he feels 'a vibration in the strings, about the region of the heart'. Then he is able to greet the original pun with a phrase echoing its clever confusion of reason and sense: 'I felt as if I understood it.'

Curiosity and seriousness

After variety has been boundless for a while it becomes vulnerable, chiefly because it contradicts certain narrow and contracted, but nevertheless fundamental, expectations we all share about boundaries and limits. If all things mutually affect one another in ways that are endlessly analogous to each other, basic distinctions such as those between priority and posteriority, superiority, and inferiority, or cause and effect, will all be deranged. That is why Sterne's novels have very uncertain endings and beginnings, and why some of his readers have failed to be amused by such indeterminacy. No matter how well disposed towards natural variety, readers and characters alike will be tempted eventually by representations of the thing itself, whether in the form of a clear and distinct idea or a literal statement.

The Shandy brothers, Yorick, even Tristram himself, opt for plain ideas and univocal language when they start taking things too seriously. But a difference is marked between a hobbyhorsical desire for uniformity, which is held to be innocent at heart, and a more worldly desire for certainty and single terms that easily hardens into arrogance and contempt when it sets itself up as a method of intellectual, religious or social control. Almost all the fables and fragments of Sterne's two books turn on the disappointments, injustices, self-torments and dangers caused by sexual curiosity on the one hand and intellectual seriousness on the other; and they are meant as warnings to innocent enthusiasts.

Slawkenbergius' Tale, the Amours, and the fragment 'Of Whiskers' in *Tristram Shandy*, for example, and 'The Riddle' and the two fragments of *A Sentimental Journey*, are rewritings of two satires on curiosity Sterne found in Rabelais and Cervantes: the story of Panurge's pilgrimage to the Holy Bottle in the third book of *Gargantua and Pantagruel* and 'The Tale of Foolish Curiosity' in *Don Quixote*. In the first Panurge seeks all sorts of oracular assurances about the behaviour of his wife in his future marriage, even though he has not yet met a woman he wants to wed. He is mocked by the equivocal signs and prognostics of fools, mutes, poets, sibyls and astrologers, and tormented by the double advice of the sceptic philosopher Trouillagan. Not until he arrives at the shrine of the bottle, where he hears the strange, panomphean mono-syllable 'trinc' and obeys it by swallowing a bookful of wine, is his desire for cer-tain knowledge of the future assuaged. In Cervantes' story, Anselmo wishes to prove the chastity of his wife Camilla by playing pimp to his friend Lothario. The upshot is that he sacrifices himself, his best friend and his wife to an experiment so obsessively concupiscent that it can end only in adultery, despair and death.

In the Shandean versions of these stories the same frustrations and losses are sustained, but there is a sharper division between the sexes. It is the women who sink into sexual curiosity and the men who rise into schemata, rules and inventions. The lines upward and downward are, however, the same, being unindented by accident or sympathy and designed to terminate with the minimum of divagation at an unequivocal point. Tristram calls this 'the line of GRAVITATION' (*TS*, 6.40.475), and it is used by people such as Levites, cabbage planters, historiographers, flatterers and hypocrites who aim to arrive at the end of their labours as rapidly and profitably as possible. In Slawkenbergius' Tale it is the women – Julia, the trumpeter's wife and the abbess of Quedlingberg – who want proof of the fleshly reality of Diego's nose at their fingers' ends. It is the men who strain the problem 'thro' the con-duits of dialect induction——they concerned themselves not with facts—— they reasoned' (*TS*, 4.247). Both groups take their tortured curiosities out to the Frankfurt road to greet the return of the nose and the vindication of their fancies and hypotheses; and while they wait for a satisfaction that is destined never to arrive, the French army seizes their town and their liberties. Because Mrs Wadman doesn't trust Toby's offer of himself as qualified for marriage, and, like the Strasburg women, undertakes to find out what he's really made of, she loses him and her only fair chance of satisfying her curiosity. But while she is delving into the mysteries of his war-wound, all is lifted up for Toby, until, with his eyes fixed upon the ceiling, he is moved to define the elements of 'the compassionate turn and singular humanity of her character' (*TS*, 9.31.642). This idealisation ends, like her enquiry, in nothing.

The damage caused by Mrs Wadman's curiosity is largely figurative. Her love militancy and the *shock* it gives Toby is a metaphor spun out of the siege of Namur and the blow that put an end to Toby's contribution to it. The same is true of the curiosity of the women of the court of Navarre, which wounds little more than the word 'whiskers'. Similarly, the impatient appetite for 'the gross and more carnal parts' of Tristram's composition indulged by 'madam' (*TS*, 1.20.57), destroys nothing real. The intellectual curiosity of the men, on the other hand, bears heavily on bodies which come within its ambit. The legal prose of the marriage settlement, designed to thwart every imprecise accident or contingency that might 'hereafter so fall out, chance, happen, or otherwise come to pass' (*TS*, 1.15.38), is responsible partly for the flattening of Tristram's nose. So are Slop's forceps, another instrument invented to abolish casualty and to arrive as swiftly as possible at 'one single point'

(*TS*, 2.18.144). The engines of the Inquisition, the *petite canulle* of the Sorbonne doctors, and the malediction of Ernulphus all deliberately and painfully include the body in the process of ironing out irregularities. Shades of this intellectual cruelty are present in the fancy Walter takes for Caesarean section, in his frivolous treatment of his son's wounded penis, and in his referring to the system of auxiliary verbs as an engine of incredible force 'in opening a child's head'. ' 'Tis enough', replies Toby (whose own knuckles have suffered under Slop's engine), 'tò burst it into a thousand splinters' (*TS*, 6.2.409).

Like Walter in his earnest moments, lawyers, system-builders, critics and connoisseurs purge their language of equivokes. Wanting no confusion in the naming of the thing itself, they imitate the inhabitants of Pope-figland in Rabelais' fourth book, who 'call figs, figs; plumbs, plumbs; and pears, pears'.[5] Tristram mocks them with tautologies. His definition of nose as nose, his characterisation of criticism as the most tormenting of the 'cants which are canted in this canting world' and his copying out at length the redundancies of law-prose ('country seat, castle, hall, mansion-house, messuage, or grainge-house') is his way of letting ambitious accuracy turn into circular nonsense. He is careful also to note that once ambiguity is in the service of curiosity it is only a double means to a single end. Slop's weakness for bad puns, like Mrs Wadman's skill at the double entendre, is not a refuge or holiday from their set purpose of interpreting the world in one light. His crude play on the words *curtain* and *hornwork*, in common with her careful enquires and subtle intonations, is a strategic use of ambiguity designed to authorise or arrive at an unequivocal meaning which will conform to their belief that there is no altruism in sexual affairs. Under the colour of play, they go straight to the point: ' 'Tis an accent which covers the part with a garment, and gives the enquirer a right to be as particular with it, as your body-surgeon' (*TS*, 9.16.637). Stripped of this covering, Mrs Wadman's particularities are no different from a critic's or a lawyer's, since she is speaking redundantly of nothing but the thing itself: 'Was it more tolerable in bed?——Could he lie on both sides alike with it?——Was he able to mount a horse——Was motion bad for it?' (*TS*, 9.16.637).

The problem of consolation

Needless to say, systematisers of the sort mocked by Tristram never use words from inside a complex and evolving situation. They approach from outside, and aim to control what they speak of by virtue of the precision and instrumentality of their language. Like the reflections of philosophy mentioned by Hume, such words are 'too subtle and distant to take place in common life', and certainly they never eradicate any affection. It isn't solely the curious

5 *The Works of Francis Rabelais MD*, trans. Sir Thomas Urquhart and Peter Motteux, 5 vols. (London: John Hart, 1750), IV, 303.

and the serious, however, who run into this problem. There are exigencies which reduce even the most ambidextrous equivocators to awkward silence. A *Sentimental Journey* ends half-way through a sentence because the situation has become too unambiguous for words. So it has when Walter leans over Toby's coffin, his systems baffled by his sorrows and his only sentiment a forlorn gesture. Confusion, sudden disappointment, and death seem to cause either a loss of words or a torrent of them. Walter's silent walk to the fish-pond contrasts with the loquacity of his complaint for the death of a child, just as Toby's quiet reception of Trim's explanation of Mrs Wadman's motives contrasts with the eloquence of his apology in defence of his bowling green sieges. In the latter cases, the words are usually remote from what they want to handle, especially when they are addressed vicariously to a sorrow in the form of consolation. Time and again in Shandean crises, words of comfort fail to touch the 'affection' of grief they are meant to eradicate.

In the scene where Walter is trying to rise literally and figuratively out of the prostration into which the loss of his son's nose has thrown him, Toby positions himself to give comfort but is under no illusion about the difficulties he faces. Tristram explains what these are in an image whose topography is based on the familiar mediation between extremes.

Before an affliction is digested,——consolation ever comes too soon;——and after it is digested,——it comes too late: so that you see, madam, there is but a mark between these two, as fine almost as a hair, for a comforter to take aim at: my uncle Toby was always either on this side, or on that of it. (*TS*, 3.9.216)

Before Tristram thinks of the scene at his own deathbed, where comforters will be making him feel ten times worse than he is already, he sets up an equally familiar distinction between 'the mode and manner of this great catastrophe' and 'the catastrophe itself' (*TS*, 7.12.492). The double apprehension of object and situation, and of one extreme and the other, is evidently as critical in scenes of distress as it is in those of natural variety. And since equivocal language generally accompanies the response to nature's hidden things, it is consistent to suppose that the successful language of consolation will be double talk of some sort.

Support for this assumption is given by the sequel of Toby's readying himself as comforter. No sooner has Walter raised himself from the bed to talk metaphorically of the lashes he has received, than Toby fells him with a recollection of literal floggings in the Flanders regiments. When they get on to the stairs, Walter changes his metaphor and asks his brother to calculate the odds of the 'chapter of chances' that have afflicted him. In another literalising move, Toby once again wounds the man who is asking for consolation, but the accident produces an opportunity for the right words to be uttered:

I know no more of calculations than this balluster, said my uncle Toby, (striking short of it with his crutch, and hitting my father a desperate blow souse upon his shinbone)——'Twas a hundred to one——cried my uncle Toby,——I thought, quoth my father, (rubbing his shin) you had known nothing of calculations, brother Toby, ——'Twas a meer chance, said my uncle Toby——Then it adds one to the chapter ——replied my father.

Tristram adds, 'The double success of my father's repartees tickled off the pain of his shin at once' (*TS*, 4.9.280).

A quick glance at other scenes of distress shows that pain is successfully treated by an equivoke, or joke, which expresses a double sense of it. This is why Tristram assigns such a high value to the tragicomic. Faced with Eugenius' hopeless optimism, Yorick dies cracking jokes out of *Don Quixote*. It is only because he has been telling a joke that Death himself turns away from Tristram's door. The pathos of Maria's madness is tempered by the witty parallel Tristram discovers between himself and her goat. And the account of the death of Le Fever is exquisitely ambivalent. Corporal Trim's remarkable speech on mortality has jokes on the fringes, and the best of them shows how consolation wanes when the double appeal to the consolee becomes single:

Are we not like a flower of the field——a tear of pride stole in betwixt every two tears of humiliation——else no tongue could have described Susannah's affliction——is not all flesh grass? . . . What is the finest face that ever man looked at!——I could hear Trim talk so for ever, cried Susannah,——what is it! (Susannah laid her hand upon Trim's shoulder)——but corruption? —— Susannah took it off.   (*TS*, 5.9.364)

At the height of his speech, when he asks, 'Are we not here now, and are we not gone! in a moment', punctuating the question with the dumb eloquence of his falling hat, the appeal is made simultaneously to the minds and senses of his audience. In Hume's terms, Trim wins their belief because the idea of death's suddenness is sharpened by an impression drawn from its circumstances. The hat 'fell dead' not because the essence of death or of hats has been touched on, but because of the double and necessarily figurative relation Trim has brought them into.

If a loss of double appeal and equivocal language is the effect of consolation's failure, is it possible to specify the cause? We get some hints from Sterne's own life, which frequently overlapped his fiction. For example, he highly regarded Yorick's kind of death, where you died with a joke on your lips; and he promised to be numbered on 'le liste de ces Heros, qui sont Morts en plaisantant'.[6] After an especially bad bout of illness, he wrote to John Hall Stevenson, 'If God, for my consolation under [my miseries], had not poured forth the spirit of Shandeism into me, which will not suffer me to think two moments upon any grave subject, I should else, just now lay down and die—die——' (*Letters*, p. 139). This spirit is the force of heterogeneity which

---

6 *Letters of Laurence Sterne*, ed. Lewis Perry Curtis (Oxford: Clarendon Press, 1935; repr. 1965), p. 416. Hereafter cited as *Letters*.

leads Sterne to celebrate the instability of his circumstances and the inconsistency of his own self, and to contrast these lively symptoms of difference with those of deadly sameness by means of the contrast between the pun on 'grave' and the bare iteration of 'die—die'. In the event, he was not to imitate Yorick. 'My spirits are fled,' he wrote in his last letter, ' 'tis a bad omen'; and John Macdonald, who saw him die, reported that his last words were not a joke but a statement of fact: 'Now it is come' (*Letters*, p. 419 and n. 3).

Apart from the pangs of terminal consumption, what would account for the disappearance of his spirits? After all, when his spirits were up, Sterne could make a joke out of a haemorrhage: 'I have had my menses thrice this month, which is twice too often' (*Letters*, p. 290). Part of the answer is contained in a quotation from the Book of Job he sent, when very sick, to Eliza Draper: '*Skin* for *Skin*, nay all that a Man has, will he give for his Life' (*Letters*, p. 336). He indicates that fear and the sheer desire not to die exclude those extra circumstances called by Tristram the 'mode and manner' of the catastrophe, and concentrate the mind solely upon the 'catastrophe itself'. The consolation offered by the spirit of Shandeism is impossible when this feeling is so strong it cannot be distracted by adjacent circumstances or blend with a different mood. Fear or grief swelling with this pressure cannot be reached by a pun; it speaks in an insistent, repetitive, imminently tautological form: 'die—die', 'skin for skin', 'catastrophe itself'.

Consolation which focuses the mind of the sufferer on this or any related catastrophe, rather than distracting it, helps wear away the spirits. When he was prostrate with bleeding lungs, Sterne received a visit from an acquaintance who roared in his ear, 'Z—ds, what a fine kettle of fish have you brought yourself to, Mr S!' (*Letters*, p. 392). Toby gets this sort of comfort from his surgeon, who tells him it is a great happiness that his wound at Namur was caused by the gravity of the stone fragment rather than its velocity. As far as Toby is concerned it is a distinction without a difference, altering neither the pain in his groin nor his understanding of it. It is an example of 'mode and manner' failing to contextualise a catastrophe and therefore simply helping to affirm that it is one. In his second sermon on Job, Sterne gives another. A Roman emperor was consoled in his misery by the assurance that it could not be helped, and replied that 'this was so far from lessening his trouble——that it was the very circumstance which created it'.[7] Hume

---

7 Sterne, *Sermons of Mr Yorick*, 2 vols. (Oxford: Basil Blackwell, 1927), I, 175. Hereafter cited as *Sermons*. Similar stories are to be found in Montaigne. 'Solon, being importun'd by his Friends not to shed powerless and unprofitable Tears for the death of his Son: It is for that Reason, that I the more justly shed them, said he, because they are powerless and unprofitable': *Essays of Montaigne*, trans. Charles Cotton, 3 vols. (London 1711), II, 383–4. Hereafter cited as *Essays*. In his sceptical phase, Fielding's Billy Booth says that people who have lost lovers or children are not easily consoled for this reason: 'Do you really think, that any Mediations on the Shortness of Life will soothe them in their Afflictions?' *Amelia*, ed. Martin C. Battestin (Oxford: Clarendon Press, 1985), p. 350). His point is endorsed in *Joseph*

gives several variants of the same failure of philosophical reflection to reach the troubles of common life, of which this comes closest to Tristram's: '*Your sorrow is fruitless, and will not change the course of destiny.* Very true; and for that very reason I am sorry' ('The Sceptic', p. 177). This is the mockery Job himself complains of when the description of his specific case is turned into a prescription by his comforters, who then recite it back to him as an inducement to patience. 'I also could speak as ye do', he reproaches them, 'if your soul were in my soul's stead, I could heap up words against you' (16:4).

There is another branch of failed consolation where the motives of the suffering party are impugned. One of Sterne's early critics objected to his transformation of Dr Richard Mead into the perverse Kunastrokius, but consoled him for the necessity of having to write such scandal with a fair prospect of paying readers. 'The consolation you give me', replied Sterne, 'is very unconsolatory – to say nothing of how mortifying' (*Letters*, p. 88). When Walter consoles Toby for the loss of his hobbyhorse after the Treaty of Utrecht, he looks to motives too, and discovers that there is no altruism in Toby's grieving for the lost war, just private frustration. 'Never mind, brother Toby, he would say,——by God's blessing we shall have another war break out' (*TS*, 6.31.458). All the attention directed by Mrs Wadman at Toby's wound, mistaken by him for the sublimest comfort, is motivated by the belief that Toby has motives of his own for keeping the extent of the damage secret.

Yet another failure is detected in the same letter answering the criticisms of his treatment of Mead, which have evidently been listed under the heading *De mortuis nil nisi bonum*. Examining the precept, Sterne confesses, 'I can find nothing in it, or make more of it, than a nonsensical lullaby of some nurse, put into Latin by some pedant, to be chanted by some hypocrite to the end of the world, for the consolation of departing lechers.' Here the fault of the consolation lies in the arbitrariness or disingenuousness of what it proposes, disguised by repetition so that it gains the familiarity (and to that extent the authority) of a popular maxim. The meaningless cry of the starling in *A Sentimental Journey*, 'I can't get out', is of this order because it attracts pathos only by virtue of iteration. So is the comfort offered by passers by to the remains of a Yorick they never knew: 'Ten times in a day has Yorick's ghost the consolation to hear his monumental inscription read over with such a variety of plaintive tones as denote a general pity and esteem' (*TS*, 1.12.32). It would be a patient spirit that would fail to detect symptoms of inanity or mockery

Andrews when the hero consoles Parson Adams for the loss of his child by repeating his preceptor's much-touted doctrine of Christian submission, only to be told by the stricken father not to talk of impossibilities: *The History of the Adventures of Joseph Andrews*, ed. Douglas Brooks (Oxford: Oxford University Press, 1971), pp. 277–9. Having just been the recipient of the sort of comfort Toby is given by his surgeon, Sancho Panza responds bitterly, 'Was the cause of ailing so hard to be guessed, that you must tell me that so much of me was sore as was hit by the weapon?' *The History of Don Quixote de la Mancha*, trans. Peter Motteux and John Ozell, 4 vols. (Glasgow, 1757), III, 227. Hereafter cited as *DQ*.

in the endless bandying of the three unoriginal words, 'Alas, poor Yorick!' Walter's remarkable effort of self-consolation belongs to this category too. His repetition of the standard fragments of ancient consolation is so exact and lengthy that it erases the reason for their recollection, the death of his son Bobby.

The failures of consolation, then, form three branches of mockery. There is the mockery of impertinence, where consolation is little more than a description of the case masquerading as an explanation of it. Then there is the mockery of the mongered motive, arising from the fancied detection of the 'real' source of pain. finally, there is the mockery of the echo or refrain, which comes about when formulae supplant an encounter with what is going on. This threefold mockery is invariably owing to the appalling confidence with which consolers handle the diffidence and confusion of suffering people. The opposite of sceptics, they have no doubt about the short- and long-term ends to which events of the world are directed, or about the privileged station they enjoy vis-à-vis those events. They are quite certain of who they are, and they have entire confidence in language as a clear medium of the ideas they choose to express. Bristling with these certitudes, they endeavour to hold instructive discourse with folk prone to ask why they were born, or 'What is man?' or 'Where am I, or what?' or 'Why is light given to a man whose way is hid?'

Translating Job

It isn't hard to see how the Book of Job matches the range of Sterne's defence of scepticism. On one side there is Job himself, inhabiting the extremes of doubt into which Walter Sandy occasionally falls ('wondering why he was begot,——wishing himself dead;——sometimes worse' (*TS*, 5.13.370)) – the same doubt experienced by Sterne as the fear of death, and which Hume describes as 'inviron'd with the deepest darkness, and utterly deprived of the use of every member and faculty'.[8] On the other side stand the three comforters, who jointly illustrate every failure to which consolation and philosophical reflection are susceptible. In his efforts to show why their words are mockery, Job turns repeatedly to the topic of language, estimating its power to wound and its uselessness for communicating the terror of an unaccountable suffering. So urgent are his complaints that Ephraim Chambers (like Robert Burton, one of Sterne's reservoirs of recondite information) reported that, 'Some have even charged Job and Solomon with *scepticism*, from their proposing a great number of questions, without deciding any of them.'[9]

8 T. p. 316.
9 Ephraim Chambers, *Cyclopaedia, or, An Universal Dictionary of the Arts and Sciences*, 2 vols. (London, 1741), article 'Scepticism'. An anonymous German author went further, tracing the genealogy of scepticism back, via Job, to the devil. See Richard H. Popkin, *The High Road to Pyrrhonism* (San Diego: Austin Hill Press, 1980), p. 72.

Sterne had a double interest in Job. As a clergyman he had preached and published two sermons on his story ('Job's Account of Life' and 'Job and his Wife'), and another on the sublimity of scriptural poetry which drew largely on the Book of Job for its illustrations ('Search the Scriptures'). As a novelist he had intended his first book to include 'an allegory . . . run upon the writers on the Book of Job'.[10] The sermons dealing with Job's afflictions offer rather wooden, not to say perverse, readings of the text aimed at extracting the orthodox lesson that the dispensations of providence are to be endured without repining. Job's 'heroic cast' comprises the patient endurance of suffering, says Sterne, compounded with an optimistic temperament that keeps him 'cheerfully holding up his head, and entertaining his hard fortune with firmness and serenity' (*Sermons*, I, 175). The reading is forced so close to the edge of parody in order to secure its moral, it is hard to think he was blind to its improbability. He has twice borrowed Eliphaz's words of consolation in vindicating the ways of God to his congregation: 'Man is born unto trouble, as the sparks fly upward (*Sermons*, I, 123, 172; Job 5:7). Underneath the piety of his public exercise, Sterne is exploring the paradox of all positive readings of Job, which condemns the commentator to repeat the error of the comforters. Here is the germ of his interest in the strains that doubt puts upon language, to which Job contributes not cheerfulness but two useful hints. One is his brief analysis of the perversity of positive propositions, paraphrased in the sermon, 'The Pharisee and the Publican': 'If I justify myself, mine own mouth shall condemn me; if I say, I am perfect, it shall also prove me perverse' (Job, 9:20; *Sermons*, I, 75). The other is his rebuke to those guilty of this perversity: 'How hast thou counselled him that hath no wisdom? and how has thou plentifully declared the thing as it is?' (26:3). Here in its most ancient form is doubt expressed of the thing itself, and suspicion of those who are certain of their grasp of it and of the language in which they promise to deliver it.

The allegorical plan was to be Sterne's contribution to a wide-ranging debate upon the Book of Job which reached its hottest in a dispute between Robert Lowth and William Warburton about the origin and interpretation of the text.[11] Exactly how Job's two hints are fertilised by Lowthian aesthetics to produce the Shandean sublime is discussed in chapter 5; all I want to assert here is that it depends, like Hume's scepticism, on the displacement of attention from

10 Letter of 15 April 1760, first published in the *St James Chronicle*, April, 1788; reprinted in Alan B. Howes, *Sterne: The Critical Heritage* (London: Routledge and Kegan Paul, 1974), pp. 58–9. For a different account of the Book of Job and *Tristram Shandy* see Everett Zimmerman, '*Tristram Shandy* and Narrative Representation', *The Eighteenth Century: Theory and Interpretation*, 28:2 (1987), 131–3.

11 See Martin C. Battestin, *The Providence of Wit* (Oxford: Clarendon Press, 1974), pp. 199–203; and Melvyn New, 'Sterne, Warburton, and the Burden of Exuberant Wit', *Eighteenth-Century Studies*, 15:3 (1982), 245–74.

the thing itself (which can never be plentifully declared) to its situation. Without this double sense of what generates an idea or a passion, words will attenuate into silence or thicken into platitude, the two extremes of the failure of consolation. Having heard himself silence Job's suffering in the interest orthodox prescription, Sterne decides in his fiction to restore elements of ambiguity and instability to scenes of consolation. He does this by packing ancillary detail around sentiments, just as Lowth re-animated Job's complaints by tracing in their images and metaphors to the historical circumstances in which they were uttered; and in this way suffering is removed from a prescriptive economy of single, moralised meaning to a much more fluid and intense set of relations. For example, the generalisation of the first Job sermon, 'Consider slavery, – what it is – how bitter a draught, and how many millions have been made to drink of it' (*Sermons*, I, 122), is transformed in *A Sentimental Journey* because Yorick is unable to hold such an allegorical idea in his head. 'I could not bring it near me', he confesses; so instead, 'I took a single captive, and having first shut him up in his dungeon, I then look'd through the twilight of his grated door' (*ASJ*, p. 201). The same transformation, or translation, is effected when Tristram turns Sterne's gloss on Job ('with how quick a succession, do days, months and years pass over our heads?——how truely like a shadow that departeth do they flee away insensibly, and scarce leave an impression with us?' (*Sermons*, I, 118–19)) into his apostrophe to Jenny: 'The days and hours of [Life], more precious, my dear Jenny! than the rubies about thy neck, are flying over our heads like light clouds of a windy day, never to return more' (*TS*, 9.8.610). When the sentiment is localised it leaves a strong impression because the adjacent circumstances work metonymically and metaphorically. Like Trim's hat, their salience adds to the illusion of historical or biographical accuracy at the same time as it disturbs and refreshes a trite reflection with a figurative parallel.

Best of all are unconscious or accidental translations. Trim's quotation of Job's parallelisms, 'He cometh forth like a flower, and is cut down: he fleeth also as a shadow, and continueth not' (14:2), is splendid because he does it unconsciously: 'Are we not, continued Trim, looking still at Susannah——are we not like a flower of the field?' (*TS*, 5.9.364). He is able to arrive at this translation, of course, because he has already circumstanced the bare sentiment which on its own, as Tristram points out, is in peril of becoming jejune: 'Are we not here now,——and gone in a moment?' And he goes on adding circumstances, increasing the tension between notions of mortality and his immediate situation, until Susannah's feelings are thoroughly mixed.

Our feelings are likely to be just as mixed because translations like these can rarely avoid giving the tragic a comic aspect. Here it is Job, a patriarch and a scriptural byword, who keeps stooping to the level of the everyday. Walter frequently compares himself with Job when he is the victim of a ludicrous accident. 'By heaven, brother Toby! you would try the patience of a Job,' he shouts, when Toby tries to imagine why Mrs Shandy doesn't want Dr Slop to attend her, 'and I think I have the plagues of one already' (*TS*, 2.7.101). 'What plagues!' he cries, as he is being pestered by Obadiah for some yeast in a scene that duplicates the delivery to Job of the messages of his ruin (*TS*, 5.2.238). When he is quoting Socrates after Bobby's death, Mrs Shandy mistakes the speech for one of her husband's habitual paraphrases of Job. His disappointments are also comparable in a comic way: he thinks himself mocked by his comforter, he cries out in his Lamentation that his days are past, his purposes broken off: and he is forced to compare himself unfavourably with those whose 'bull gendreth and faileth not, [whose] cow calveth' (Job, 21:10; *TS*, 9.33.647). If Walter were always immune to real distresses, and never endured the dark incomprehension that goes with a real and unexpected loss, these parallels would be no more than a burlesque of Job. As it is, the sense of the serious is sharpened by the trifling addition that situates and images it, tangling the feelings of the characters and the audience alike.

Since the language of these tangles cannot be a plentiful declaration of the thing as it is, and must in some way be equivocal if the pattern of analogies outlined above is to hold, I want to end this section by suggesting what it is. There is a generalisation in 'Job's Account of Life' which keeps reappearing, without the benefit of localisation or comic additions, in all Sterne's subsequent work; and that is his characterisation of the language of Job as 'the words of that Being, who first inspired man with language, and taught his mouth to utter; who opened the lips of the dumb, and made the infant eloquent'. It is repeated in 'Search the Scriptures', and it forms an invocation at the end of Tristram's sketch of his uncle's funeral to those 'Gracious powers! which erst have opened the lips of the dumb in his distress, and made the tongue of the stammerer speak plain.' In *A Sentimental Journey* it makes part of Yorick's prayer for fit language, addressed to the 'powers which touch the tongue with eloquence in distress' (*Sermons*, I, 112; II, 227; *TS*, 6.25.452; *ASJ*, p. 137).

Although there are speeches, for example, Toby's Apology and Walter's analysis of love and war, which are eloquent, and sometimes unexpectedly so, I don't think this is what Sterne means. I suspect instead it is language that is still very close to silence, either because of the unpractised tongue that speaks it, or because of a shock or accident that impedes it. At that primitive frontier between dumbness and darkness on one side and the light of articulate words on the other, Shandean puns originate. The epochal transition from imbecility to utterance is not made, as Sterne the preacher suggests, by looking on the bright side; it is a specific conversion of accident into a limited design. Job calls this 'breach upon breach' (16:14), a sort of second-order disaster of which I shall have more to say later, and for Sterne the novelist that entails using the effects of ruin in order to represent it: taking the fragments to circumstance and figure havoc that otherwise would remain unspellable and beyond consolation. In Tristram's joke about the stars he hangs up in dark places, it means using obscurity upon obscurity – asterisk upon shadow – to compound for the terrors of the night. The doubling up of imperfection into a pleonastic remedy lies at the root of all other Shandean doublings. If the symptoms of Maria's distraction can be read as a sort of tragicomic reproof of lechery, then the ruins of her mind are not as baffling and silent as they might be. Because Job does not refrain his mouth and swallow up his words, and elects instead to speak in the anguish of his soul, he makes a complaint whose sublimity is owing to a dialectic of mean circumstances and noble metaphors.

The double principle

A rather clearer picture of how Sterne's scepticism branches into analogous experiments with double arrangements and double effects may be had by pointing (as rapidly as possible) to the theories he uses to illustrate or justify what he is doing. Tristram's first discovery, made while he was trying to draw his uncle Toby's character, is that a story can be written digressively and progressively at the same time, and he is half tempted to compare this double motion in the machinery of his work with the double rotation of the earth, simultaneously circling the sun and turning on its axis. The image is one of many allusions to Dryden's criticism in *Tristram Shandy* and is designed to recall his approval of tragicomedy in 'An Essay of Dramatic Poesy'. There Dryden compares the double motion of English subplots to that of the planets, which turn both in their own circles, and that of the *primum mobile*: 'If contrary motions may be found in Nature to agree; if a Planet can go East and West at the same time . . . it will not be difficult to imagine how the under Plot, which is onely different, not contrary to the great design, may naturally be conducted along with it.'[12] Dryden is made to speak on behalf of all wits who, in Yorick's words, reconcile incompatible movements (*TS*, 1.10.20), and against 'their *gravities*' (including Locke) who have made a '*Magna Carta* of stupidity' by trying to divide and define them.

Having already discovered the principle of double motion in his narrative, Tristram adapts it for the structure of the story of Toby's Amours by running the Trim and Bridget underplot simultaneously with the main action. He proudly declares there is no comparison 'betwixt a single amour, and an amour thus nobly doubled, and going upon all four, prancing throughout a grand drama' (*TS*, 3.24.209). The rudiments of the technique are evident

---

12 'Of Dramatic Poesy: An Essay', in *The Essays of John Dryden*, ed. W. P. Ker, 3 vols. (Oxford: Clarendon Press, 1900), I, 70.

from the first introduction of Trim, whose function has always been to supply the comic counterweight to the seriousness of the Shandy brothers. From his invention of war games to his speech on death, he reveals a largely un-conscious talent for making comic tropes out of destruction. So the purpose of double plots, that 'scene of mirth mixed with tragedy', which, Dryden says, 'has the same effect upon us which our music has betwixt the acts, [and] which we find a relief to us' ('Essay of Dramatic Poesy', I, 70), is largely met in Trim. Walter has a portion of this talent. His rapid alternation of com-plaint and joke in the coach between Stilton and Grantham is so 'truly tragic-comical, that [my mother] did nothing but laugh and cry in a breath . . . all the way' (*TS*, 1.16.42). After the accounts of how the news of Bobby's death was received are complete, Tristram performs an *entr'acte* on his fiddle to 'the grave man in black' – the first hint of the figure of Death himself who will appear two volumes later – in a hopeless attempt to find some comic buoyancy by acting out Dryden's similitude (*TS*, 5.15.371).

Putting all of this together, we can see how Dryden is used to gather analogous examples of Shandean double motion under the heading of tragicomedy. A digressive narrative that still contrives to get forward, a dou-ble plot, a synthesis of the comic and the serious, the mixture of laughter and tears, the talent for making something out of ruin, and the *non plus ultra* of greeting Death with a joke, are all keyed to the poetics of the English drama.

English painting is used in the same way, with Hogarth as both its representative and theorist, to make a collection of analogies conforming to a double principle. The first time he hangs up some stars in the dark, apropos Toby's doubtful sentence about his sister-in-law's aversion to Slop, Tristram turns to Hogarth's *Analysis of Beauty* as his authority for leaving four asterisks to mark what might have been the point of its interruption. 'Just heaven! how does the *Poco piu* and the *Poco meno* of the Italian artists;——the insensible MORE or LESS, determine the precise line of beauty in the sentence, as well as in the statue!' (*TS*, 2.6.100). *Il poco piu* is Hogarth's term for the exquisite extra turn of the chisel, brush or pencil which catches and exercises the viewer's imagination. *Il poco meno* is Tristram's own addition, but it alludes to the same combination of excess and absence when, with a more extensive flourish, a line gestures at what isn't there. Hogarth locates this effect most decisively in his reflections on the serpentine line – the line of beauty in three dimensions – which, he says, 'by its waving and winding at the same time different ways . . . may be said to inclose (tho' but in a single line) varied con-tents; and therefore all its variety cannot be express'd on paper by one con-tinued line, without the assistance of the imagination'.[13] The twisting of the line serves to spur the imagination to fill the emptiness it describes. When Tristram puts this principle to use after his experiment with the stars, he

13 Hogarth, *Analysis of Beauty* (London, 1753; repr. Menston: Scolar Press, 1971), p. 39.

riddles his text with holes and demands the reader fill them in: 'Let the reader imagine then . . . Let him suppose . . . Let him imagine' (*TS*, 2.11.109).

In his battles against the uniformity of 'gravity and solemn looks' and the 'strong prejudices in favour of straight lines' (*Analysis*, pp. 131, viii), Hogarth wears as his badge of variety the picture of an eel encircling a cone. In verses he composed about himself for Hall Stevenson's *Crazy Tales*, Sterne chooses peristalsis and the corkscrew for his device:

> For to this day, when with much pain,
> I try to think strait on, and clever,
> I sidle out again, and strike
> Into the beautiful oblique.
> Therefore, I have no one notion,
> That is not form'd, like the designing
> Of the peristaltick motion;
> Vermicular; twisting and turning;
> Going to work
> Just like a bottle-skrew upon a cork.[14]

The broadness of the conceit doesn't obscure the emphasis laid by Sterne and Hogarth on motion, the actual turning of the line. At its best this produces what Hogarth calls the '*joint-sensations* of bulk and motion', and 'our usual feeling, or joint-sensation, of figure and motion' (*Analysis*, pp. 69, 79), when outline and emptiness stand in their most dynamic relation to each other. Then it is possible for him and his Shandean imitators to enjoy the representation of a limited sexuality, composed of transient and incomplete gestures: an erotic elegance, 'too alluring to be strictly decent', whose intricacies the eye wantonly reconnoitres (*Analysis*, pp. 24–35).[15] Tristram's eye behaves like this when it follows Nanette, with a slit in her petticoat, as she capriciously bends her head and dances up to him 'insiduous' (*TS*, 7.43.538).

Hogarth's preference is for a coalition of lightness and curve, when 'many waving and contrasted turns . . . ravish the eye with the pleasure of pursuit'. The image he chooses is of 'wanton ringlets waving in the wind' (*Analysis*, p. 28). It is the same image Tristram manages to conflate with Sterne's paraphrase of Job, when he situates Jenny's curls in the winds of transience and watches while they turn grey round her fingers.

Whilst thou art twisting that lock,——see! it grows grey; and every time I kiss thy hand to bid adieu, and every absence which follows it, are preludes to that eternal separation which we are shortly to make. (*TS*, 9.8.611)

This is turn on turn, a remarkable self-consolation accomplished in a traverse

---

14 John Hall Stevenson, *Crazy Tales* (London, 1762), pp. 117–18.
15 The most adroit discussion of the sexual possibilities of 'this wandering celibate line' is J. Hillis Miller, 'Narrative Middles: A Preliminary Outline', *Genre*, 11 (1978), 375–87. A reading of Hogarthian double entendres is included in New, 'Annotating *Tristram Shandy*', pp. 15–23.

of wantonness and mortality, using the frailest picture of serpentine equilibrium to figure the lightening of the darkest emptiness.[16]

The difference between the analogies herding under Dryden's principle of double plotting on the one hand, and Hogarth's principle of joint-sensation on the other, is not very great. The serpentine or corkscrewing line is obviously designed for more erotic ambiguities than the digressive–progressive one. The joint response to a figure and the space it turns in is, as Hogarth repeatedly observes, a voluptuous one, with the eye, like the line it follows, trying to roll itself round a hidden dimension. On a par in this respect is his *Strolling Actresses in a Barn* and Tristram's description of La Fosseuse, who takes her bodkin and traces 'the outline of a small whisker, with the blunt end of it, upon one side of her upper lip' (*TS*, 5.1.347). The oblique line goes on to absorb the digressive one, at the end of the sixth volume, into a series of polemical oppositions between its own libertine grace and the straight line of gravity.

The sexuality of the waving line is, however, necessarily incomplete; and to that extent it joins the comedy of genital imperfection which, in turn, belongs to the doubling up of infirmities into compensatory representations. The basic figure in this branch of rhetoric is the aposiopestic break, which represents every variety of interruption, including sexual ones. The aposiopesis is also expressive of that impeded speech, so close to silence, to which infant eloquence and the oriental sublime both belong. Tristram seems to have adapted all of these analogies to a Hogarthian image in the scene where Jenny's curl fades, which is far richer in joint-sensations than the crude farce of his fiddle-playing after Bobby's death. This indicates that the oblique line of grace is a more versatile principle of ambiguity and double effects than tragicomedy, which tends to fail Tristram (and Sterne) when in a real emergency they try to make a joke out of death.

Addison, who both invented the term 'double principle' and disliked tragicomedy and double plots, helps to authorise this distinction in favour of Hogarth. His *Spectator* papers on 'The Pleasures of the Imagination' (Nos. 411–21) provide Sterne with a compendious theory of double effects, all originating in a set of sceptical propositions remarkably like those shared by Hume and Sterne. Addison argues that we cannot reason upon our feelings because we are ignorant of what causes them; we can give no account of why identical objects should produce different responses among their observers, or why one person's imagination is stronger than another's; therefore perceptions must be distinguished from objects.

16 In an argument that begins with Hogarth and then, via Hume, compares the aesthetics of mourning in the pictures of Joseph Wright of Derby with that of the death scenes in *Tristram Shandy*, Ronald Paulson suggests that the play on emptiness and fullness informs them both – 'The Aesthetics of Mourning', in *Studies in Eighteenth-Century British Art and Aesthetics*, ed. Ralph Cohen (Berkeley: University of California Press, 1985), pp. 148–81.

This last proposition is the one most carefully augmented by Addison, partly because it gives him the opportunity of isolating and then applying the double principle, and partly because he wants to evade the tyranny of the thing itself. This makes its appearance in No. 412 as the sublime prospect, 'stupendous works of nature' that exceed the capacity of the imagination and fling us into a 'pleasing astonishment at such unbounded views'. In No. 418 it is the horrid object, a public execution or torture, where 'the object presses too close upon our senses' and obscures the faculty of reflection. The sublime object and the horrible object oppress the mind in the same way, for in overwhelming and immobilising the soul they are antithetical to Addison's preferred landscape, 'an image of liberty, where the eye has room to range abroad' (No. 412). Although he blurs this antithesis by calling astonishment 'pleasing', it is clear from what follows that objects filling the mind to the exclusion of all other impressions and reflections constrain the soul, and deprive it of the subtle pleasures that come of comparing different things.

Addison's maxim being that 'pleasure still grows upon us, as it arises from more than a single principle', he places the aesthetic object in every relativising light he can think of in order to show how it may 'afford the Mind a double Entertainment' (No. 412). Objectively our view of it may be doubled by various other objects, and by the accompaniments of movement, colour, novelty and surprise. Subjectively, it is doubled by the ideas the object excites, these being 'different from any thing that exists in the Objects themselves' (No. 413), and by any ideas in the memory and imagination which may be associated with them. Thriving between these two points is the objectified subjectivity of representation, whether in statues, pictures or words, and here pleasure is complicated by a doubling of the double principle; for as well as any double entertainment to be derived from the ideas associated with the object, there is now the added amusement of comparing them with the ideas provoked by the representation of it (particularly vivid if this is a description).

Consistent with his doubts about the thing itself, Addison suggests that in comparing representations with objects we always favour the former; for even in objects that are not vast, horrid or disgusting, there is still 'some defect' which the artist mends by imitation (No. 418). The mind's chief delight is to oscillate as rapidly as possible between the perceptions of the same thing as both natural and artificial, as real but defective, and as whole but copied; hence his celebrated remark on gardening, that 'a man might make a pretty landscape of his own possessions' (No. 414) by carefully mingling the effects of natural irregularity with those of pastoral utility. The same oscillation is produced by the 'accidental landscapes' perceived in veins of marble, and in the moving landscapes projected on to the wall of a *camera obscura*. In these cases 'our pleasure rises from a double principle' because the same objects may be represented to our minds 'either as copies or originals'. It rises from the same source when we locate 'the effect of design, in what we call the works of chance' (No. 414).

The complex modifications of pleasure resulting from the alternation and mutual intensification of different ideas may be illustrated by elaborating Addison's example of a painting of a woman. 'It is pleasant to look on the picture of any face where the resemblance is hit, but the pleasure increases if it be the picture of a face that is beautiful, and is still greater if the beauty be softened with an air of melancholy or sorrow' (No. 418). The pleasure has two distinct sources: the design and colours of the copy and the presence of the original. It begins to be compounded when the mind starts oscillating between the set of ideas appropriate to each. As the mind delights in 'all the Actions and Arts of Mimickry' (No. 416), the ideas of the copy will be full and perfect, but those of the original will be marked by the defects of the real. The temptation will be to sink the ideas of defectiveness either by turning exclusively to the copy or by establishing an identity between it and the original; and in either case the oscillation ceases. If it is to be preserved, the difference between the two must be sustained, and this is managed by representing the ideas of pain (associated with defects) and pleasure (associated with perfections) in the expression on the woman's beautiful countenance. Her melancholy glance becomes the image of the oscillation she has caused, which is now more intense because the viewer is implicated in it on two counts. The picture dramatises the relation between artefacts and objects the viewer is at present experiencing at the same time as it objectifies in an acceptable form the deepest anxieties of the mind, those secret 'Apprehensions to which the Mind of Man is naturally subject' (No. 419). One need only imagine a legend or poem beneath the picture, heightened by some surprising metaphor ('a description often gives more lively ideas than the sight of things themselves' (No. 416)), to see how the oscillation could reach a very high frequency indeed. For this reason the Gothic novelists are fond of weaving their stories round pictures of beautiful women whose faces betray signs of mysterious woe and melancholy.

At its fullest stretch, then, the double principle sets up a complex reaction between immediate ideas, or impressions, and remoter ones stored in the mind, in which vividness is not an index of an idea's proximity of a thing but of its resemblance to another idea. Addison is aware how close this is to the operation of wit, and he remarks that puns and quibbles are the language sometimes annexed to it. He is also aware that allegory, being a transcription of 'Ideas out of the Intellectual World into the Material' (No. 421), formalises the intense moment of reaction when old ideas take shape as the cause of new impressions; and that is why he values it.

Despite his hostility to them, double plots fit easily into the economy of Addison's double principle. In inviting a comparison between different sets of ideas whose disparity inevitably causes an oscillation between feelings of pain and pleasure, they are analogous to Addison's picture. The joint-sensation of Hogarth's serpentine line is not so instantly compatible, but that Addison understands its dynamic is evident from the reason he gives for the pleasure we take in viewing convex surfaces: 'In such bodies the sight must split upon several angles, it does not take in one uniform idea, but several ideas of the same kind' (No. 415). The fancy is provoked to supply the absent parts, but never arrives at the full stop of an entire conception of the thing itself. What is missing from a representation – the reason for the melancholy expression of the beautiful woman, for example – is at once evidence of natural imperfection and a sign of the intensity of our response to its represen-tation. This mixture is very close to Sterne's Hogarthian treatment of Jenny's greying curl.

The development of Yorick's friendship with Mme de L*** at the beginning of *A Sentimental Journey* amounts to a dramatisation of Addison's brief example of the picture of a woman. Holding hands with her but unable to see her face, Yorick invents for her the head of a goddess, a shape like an angel of light (*ASJ*, p. 92). When he catches sight of the original, he observes, 'It was not critically handsome, but there was that in it, which in the frame of mind I was in, which attached me much more to it – it was interesting; I fancied it wore the characters of a widow'd look, and in the state of its declension, which had passed the two first paroxysms of sorrow, and was quietly begin-ning to reconcile itself to its loss – but a thousand other distresses might have traced the same lines' (*ASJ*, p. 94). Here there is no oscillation between the copy and the original; the original instantly translates its real defects into representative marks – 'the characters' – of mixed feelings which, in mir-roring her companion's initial disappointment, now authorise a rising interest in mysteries (absence of explanations) that have supplanted defects (absence of beauties). This shift is possible only if Mme de L***'s figure represents ideas in which Yorick literally has an interest, namely his own. It is at its most intense when it is scarcely possible to tell who is representing whom. As Yorick sees her walking 'with her cheek half resting upon the palm of her hand – with the slow, short-measur'd step of thoughtfulness, and with her eyes, as she went step by step, fix'd upon the ground' (*ASJ*, p. 106), he realises that her gestures not only mimic the ones he has just made, but that they are signs of the identical thoughts he has just been thinking. This sets up a delicious oscillation between copies and originals that are both made of flesh and blood.

At the heart of his scene there is a transformational technique which is found everywhere in Sterne's fiction. It sometimes appears as the conversion of accident to advantage, where the unexpected or inconvenient thing – a broken chaise, news of a death, a story that is going backwards, a wound to the groin – turns out to be a peculiar felicity. Closely related to this is the conversion of chance into design, upon which all of Tristram's boasted im-provements in the art of autobiography depend, together with his frequent challenges to the reader to distinguish between natural, spontaneous variety and the cunning reproduction of it. Most important of all, the technique provides the only effective consolation available in the Shandean world, the translation of real imperfections and loss into representations which complicate feelings and associate ideas. These representations are almost always attended with the puns and quibbles Addison mentions; and despite Sterne's suspicion of allegory he is fascinated by the confusion of the intellectual and the material worlds that comes about when words straddle the border between figurative and literal meanings. Like the transformations it accompanies, this wordplay enacts a repudiation of the thing itself. In the following chapters I want to trace Sterne's experiments with the double principle in the fields of associationism, narrative and the sublime; but first I want to see how it affects his treatment of comic originals.

2

Originality and the hobbyhorse

When Sterne invented the Shandy family and its satellites he broached a set of dilemmas that tormented the eighteenth century. Whether they were posed in economic, political, moral, Christian or philosophical terms, these amounted to the impossibility of reconciling notions of primitive innocence with the facts of civilised society. As Britain developed ever more sophisticated patterns of financial and social relations, the opportunity of locating any point of coincidence between the satisfaction of private appetites and the fulfilment of public duties became correspondingly remote. J. G. A. Pocock's influential analysis of this rift turns on the conflict between the values associated with the ethos of civic humanism, 'in which the ego knew and loved itself in relation to a *patria*', and the evidence of the progress of corruption, 'a chaos of appetites, productive of dependence and loss of personal autonomy, flourishing in a world of rapid and irrational change'.[1] The writing of these disturbing times is filled with complaints against the symptoms of degeneracy, such as the growth of London and the increase of metropolitan vices, interspersed with pictures of embarrassed or exiled virtue. Very often these pictures idealise as well as explain the marginal condition of characters who have chosen to preserve their integrity against the odds, as in novels like *Clarissa*, *The Vicar of Wakefield* and *Humphry Clinker*, or a poem like *London*.

When the idealisation of marginal virtue is done in the discourse of civic humanism, it becomes especially difficult to order the language of praise and blame. If the essence of civic virtue is its devotion to public duties and ends, and if the only available virtue is isolated and private, how can it be esteemed? Being merely noncorrupt, negatively defined by a depraved public sphere it can never enter, the isolated ego lacks its authenticating *patria*. To itself and to similar isolated examples of virtue, it may stand as a reproach to a polity which has no use for innocence, but it cannot represent to the times what the times lack. By its nature *singular*, it can in fact represent very little; and while there is a degree of integrity in being like nothing but itself, such singularity verges on eccentricity and oddity, neither of which is far removed from the

---

1 J. G. A. Pocock, *The Machiavellian Moment* (Princeton: University of Princeton Press, 1975), p. 486.

indulgence of caprice and private fancy which civic discoursers take to be a prime symptom of the general loss of public spirit. Samuel Richardson runs into these problems at the end of *Clarissa*, where he wants to recommend to the world the exemplary quality of Clarissa's inimitable, isolated virtue at the same time as he resolves to preserve it from contamination by removing it forever from that very world. The closer she gets to the pitch of integrity (interpreted by the audience round her deathbed as a sort of angelic oddity) the less of an example she becomes, and Richardson ends the novel unable to decide whether her lesson lies in a life of virtuous resolution that *ought* to have represented the best to which the world can aspire, or in a death so singular it transcends all human competence.

In *Tristram Shandy* the baffling nature of local virtue is examined from a number of points salient in the debate about public spirit and civic humanism. There is no doubt that members of the Shandy circle feel a duty to the public, although they generally try to fulfil it in private, behind a hedge or in a study. In the barricaded secrecy of the bowling green Toby is working hard 'for the good of the nation' by taking his sword in his hand 'to keep the ambitious and the turbulent within bounds' (*TS*, 3.22.206; 6.32.462). Walter has brought the bulk of his theories to publishable form 'for the public good' (*TS*, 1.18.44). Every Sunday Yorick speaks to the public about what most concerns its moral and spiritual health. For his part. Tristram expects 'all the *world*' to profit from the publication of his life and opinions (*TS*, 1.13.36). Hand in hand with these benefactions go some fairly brisk estimates of the shortcomings of the public. Yorick's sermon dramatises the manifold seductions that lie in wait for a good conscience, and then shows how viciously prostituted consciences will react to innocence. Tristram's narrative of Yorick's unhappy life is a case in point: the destruction of a virtuous man 'to gratify a private appetite' masquerading as a public duty (*TS*, 1.12.29). Several of Walter's set speeches are given on the topic of corruption, political and personal (see, for example, *TS*, 1.18.46; 2.19.146).

Of course the world inhabited by these public-spirited men is only the 'world', a miniature disc four miles wide situated in a bye-corner of the kingdom. They are obscure individuals who have either retired from public life or given up any hope of rising in it. Apart from Yorick's pulpit, they have no public platform from which to issue challenges or enter pleas. When Toby suggests the infant Tristram be exhibited at the market cross in order to contradict rumours of his castration, his brother knows better: ' 'Twill have no effect (*TS*, 6.14.433). As a result, the Shandies are driven further into the privacy of the study, the parlour and the bowling green, places that become the courtyards of minds as eccentric as they are private, and from which no public project can be launched that is not a fantasy. The questions then arise whether this privacy is the guardian of naive and ingenuous characters who are valuable despite their irrelevance to the world, whether it gives cover for capricious and unsteady behaviour that contributes its mite to the 'chaos of appetites' and claims a part in the 'world of rapid and irrational change', or whether the discourse of civic humanism is inappropriate to the characters and effects of Sterne's fiction.

Hints are scattered on all sides. The qualities of impetuousness, candour and sincerity – especially Toby's guilelessness, the simplicity and singleness of his heart – are contrasted with a world that is, as Tristram says, 'ashamed of being virtuous' (*TS*, 8.27.580). So detestable does he find those who ply the 'ceremony of slow chicane', like Phutatorius and Didius, and so attractive those who wear their hearts on their sleeves, that his apostrophes to Toby and Trim come close to idealising their singularity. In the vision of Toby's funeral, Tristram's exclamation and Walter's gesture unite in a powerful salute to Toby's unparalleled virtue: 'The first——the foremost of created beings . . . in what corner of the world shall I seek thy fellow?' (*TS*, 6.25.452). Sterne was tempted to follow suit. He likened his Latin to Toby's *Lillabulero*, 'being not understood because of its purity', and he confessed, 'So much am I delighted with my uncle Toby's imaginary character, that I become an enthusiast' (*Letters*, pp. 179, 143). This enthusiasm has often been caught by Sterne's readers; Hazlitt, for example, thought Toby's character one of the finest compliments ever paid to human nature.

It is an interesting exercise to set Toby's history alongside that of a man not prone to compliment human nature in any form, namely Swift. Like Toby he takes a special interest in the War of Spanish Succession, the Treaty of Utrecht and the subsequent negotiations over the demolition of Dunkirk. His pamphlets, 'The Conduct of the Allies' and 'The Character of Richard Steele' are devoted to these issues, and it is surprising how far these models of civic humanist discourse depart from the views summed up by Toby in his 'Apolegetical Oration'. For Swift the war was a conspiracy of venal soldiers, who fought not for honour but for gold, and of corrupt politicians who served their turns in a conflict that could never benefit England; the Treaty was a monument to the public spirit of his friend Viscount Bolingbroke; and the Dunkirk negotiations were a fiction invented to countenance rearguard Whig propaganda. All Toby's self-esteem is founded on his belief in the justness of the war and its betrayal by the Treaty; the negotiations are the lingering sad last farewell he bids the business of his life. Subsequent analysis, much of it produced by Bolingbroke himself,[2] gives weight to Swift's opinions. Standing armies, paid auxiliaries, national debt and the flight from the traditional values of land and gold into the speculative medium of paper credit were the inheritance of a war which cost the nation its solvency and integrity. To the ambitious and the turbulent, whom Toby's war was aimed at restraining, it offered unparalleled opportunities for pelf and political manipulation.

2 For an account of Bolingbroke's contribution to the line of political thought represented by Machiavelli and Harington, see Isaac Kramnick, *Bolingbroke and his Circle: The Politics of Nostalgia in the Age of Walpole* (Cambridge Mass., Harvard University Press, 1968).

Pursuing this line of enquiry turns up quite a lot of evidence of Shandean involvement in activities opprobrious to civic humanists. A former merchant, Walter sees no contradiction between the investment of his time in reading and of his money in the Mississippi Scheme. He finally decides to invest Dinah's legacy not in land, but in the bodiless good opinion of the world that travel brings. Like the nation, Toby runs himself into debt to fight his battles, raising cash not against solid pledges of land, but against a pension and an annuity. Tristram goes into chapter-debt with his readers; Yorick issues 'promissory' looks of repentance. In *A Sentimental Journey* and the *Journal to Eliza* the exchange of money and sentiments, or cash *for* sentiments, literalises the metaphor of travel-as-bargain, which Sterne coined first for his sermon on the prodigal and refurbished for the 'Preface in the Desobligeant': 'Conversation is a traffick; and if you enter into it, without some stock of knowledge . . . the trade drops at once' (*Sermons*, I, 237). The two sentimental tales Yorick tells in Versailles are both about trade. The *Journal* is like a piece of scrip, everywhere inscribed with memorials of debt and payment all stemming from Yorick's opening offer to buy Eliza from her husband for five hundred pounds (*Letters*, p. 313). The uncanny blend of low finance and sentiment culminates in this invitation: 'Eliza what say you, Eliza! shall we join our *little capitals together?*' (*Letters*, p. 348).

Although there are strong lineaments of Scriblerian satire in Tristram's account of the hobbyhorse, especially in his first volume where it includes the unscrupulous appetites of Didius and Kunastrokius as well as the amiable eccentricities of his uncle, there is no point in treating Toby as Swift treats Sir Richard Steele: identifying in him a culpable mixture of self-interest and self-delusion. At the beginning of his second volume Tristram repudiates all interpretations of Toby's actions which judge them to be inconsistent or foolish. At the same time, neither Toby's altruism nor that of his circle is ever mistaken for the real thing. How can 'public spirit, and a thirst of glory' (*TS*, 6.32.461) be satisfied on a bowling green? When Toby tells Walter that his war-debt doesn't matter, 'so long as we know 'tis for the good of the nation', Tristram carefully ascribes his father's smile to 'the generous (tho' hobbyhorsical) gallantry of my uncle Toby' (*TS*, 3.22.206). The kind of adjustment being made here between public sentiments and private contexts (analogous to Tristram's own decision to address the *world* in *confidence* (*TS*, 1.13.36)), would not be possible if a covert idealisation of civic virtue were being maintained beneath the burlesque. We have to assume that Sterne's hatred of deceit and hypocrisy did not lead (as it did with many civic humanists) to the enshrinement of an ideal of absolute personal integrity that somehow survives corruption to sustain what is left of the *patria*.

Reasons for making this assumption don't lie merely in the hobbyhorsical qualification attached by Sterne to Shandean virtues, or in his unabashed use of commercial themes, metaphors and suggestions. It is evident from an important letter already quoted on p. 18 (*Letters*, p. 88) that he had little time for Bolingbroke. He ends a set of antithetic doublets ('our angels and our devils . . . our Sydenhams, and Sangrados, our Lucretias, – and Massalinas') with 'our Sommers, and our Bolingbrokes' (*Letters*, p. 88), indicating a judgment of patriots and patriotism not far removed from Johnson's. Not that Sterne shares Johnson's brand of Toryism. A Whig realism seems to lie behind his mockery of utopian prospects and nostalgic retrospects; so when Tristram refers to the past as the 'sweet aera in the life of man' to which belongs 'the simplicity which poets sing of in better days' (*TS* 7.31.520; 7.43.537), he has in his eye the dreams of Gothic integrity *The Craftsman* was so fond of ornamenting.[3] More specifically, the Gothic antecedents of the primitive dialectic of Walter's beds of justice, and his habit of interrogating corruption in a *sorites* ('Why? why are we a ruined people? ——Because we are corrupt' (*TS*, 2.19.146)), make fun of the favourite themes of patriotic rhetoric.[4]

In Bolingbroke's tireless emphasis on wholeness and uniformity lies the reason for this satire. The man who belongs to the *species liberalis* must, in his opinion, exhibit invariable consistency. 'A certain propriety of words and actions, that results from their conformity to nature and character, must always accompany him, and create an air and manner, that run uniformly thro' the whole tenour of his conduct and behaviour' (*Letters on Patriotism*, p. 198). Such a character is like a work of art, where the superior intention is evident 'through the whole piece'. Defects are not to be palliated: 'They may be hid, like spots in the sun, but they are spots still' (p. 202). The defects he has in mind are 'the uncertain and irregular motions of the human mind', never so obvious as when we cease to '*fix* our minds [on] *virtuous objects*' and retire to some private spot, there to sink into 'trifling amusements and low cares' (pp. 124, 20). To put it mildly, there is no doubt principle here. The public object is the thing itself, pursued by a man who is at all times like himself; even spots, as Homenas would put it, are spots.

John Barrell has shown how the same severe algebra of private and public integrity dominated the aesthetics of Sterne's contemporary and portraitist, Sir Joshua Reynolds, until he was beset by a change of mind. In a quest for the 'universal pattern' that checks 'frail caprice', he praised abstraction, uniformity and clarity, and blamed singularity, ambiguity and circumstantiality. Then in his 'Ironic Discourse' and his unfinished essay on Shakespeare, he seems to rediscover the double principle of Dryden and Addison, arguing that the mind is naturally averse to uniformity because it

---

3 Kramnick calls them 'sweet memories of a nobler and simpler age that had been forever lost' (*Bolingbroke and his Circle*, p. 172); see Pocock, *The Machiavellian Moment*, p. 482.
4 Compare Bolingbroke on the character of the political knave: 'From whence has such a man his strength? From the general corruption of the people.' *Letters on the Spirit of Patriotism, the Idea of a Patriot King, and the State of the Parties* (London: A. Millar, 1749), p. 20.

'always desires to double, to entertain two objects at a time'.[5] Sterne doesn't have to make this shift, but in drawing his characters he is constantly aware of the tautological forms of 'universal patterns' with which they might be confused or contrasted. After all, he himself felt tempted to idealise Toby's singularity as unparalleled purity. So he works his way carefully through the familiar positions concerning ancient virtue, British originality, and consistency of character, handling each with an ambidexterity I will be contrasting from time to time with the classic civic discourse of Adam Ferguson.[6]

The old English plainness and sincerity

The phrase is Tillotson's, from his sermon 'Of Sincerity towards God and Man' which is quoted at length no less than three times in *The Spectator*. His theme is 'the great Corruption and Degeneracy of the Age wherein we live', all owing (and the metaphor is significant) to 'a Trade of Dissimulation' driven by Frenchified metropolitans (see *The Spectator*, Nos. 103, 352, 557). This has cost the country not only the good coin of unadorned language but also the genuine English character, 'that generous Integrity of Nature, and Honesty of Disposition, which always argues true Greatness of Mind'. Since Addison's double principle is the foundation of Sterne's sceptical response to this sort of plain talk, it is worth canvassing his (and Steele's) opinions of what constitutes a good character.

They evolve three types of humorism or singularity out of Tillotson's desideratum. At the highest level stands a man like Cato who, refusing to pass his life in opposition to his own sentiments and principles, ceases to observe the standards of his society. 'Singularity in Concerns of this Kind is to be looked upon as heroick Bravery, in which a Man leaves the Species only as he soars above it' (No. 576). The lowest level of singularity is occupied by the unhappy gentleman of the same paper who has a commission of lunacy taken out against him for having followed the dictates of reason at the expense of fashion, form and custom. In between these two is a singularity neither heroic nor lunatic that belongs to Sir Roger de Coverley, whose departures from social norms are only 'as he thinks the World in the wrong' (No.2). As this middle area provides the seedbed of all subsequent experiments with English humorism, including Sterne's, and as it is also rendered highly problematic by

5 Cited by John Barrell, *The Political Theory of Painting from Reynolds to Hazlitt* (New Haven: Yale University Press, 1986), p. 160. See also pp.78–136.
6 I have chosen Ferguson for this purpose chiefly because of his importance in the debate about civic humanism, and the significance attached to his work by Pocock in *The Machiavellian Moment*; also because he was writing at the same time as Sterne, entering a debate about civic virtue and selfish excess which was particularly vigorous during the 1750s and 1760s. See John Sekora, *Luxury: The Concept in Western Thought, Eden to Smollett* (Baltimore, Johns Hopkins University Press, 1977), pp. 88–131.

the extremes of private obsession and public spirit at its borders, it is worth approaching Sterne's humorists via the ambiguities and inconsistencies of Addison's old-fashioned Englishman.

Sir Roger's neglect of common forms is apparent in church, where he stands up to count the kneeling parishioners, delivers strident amen's to prayers he approves of, and lengthens out the last note of a psalm after everyone else has stopped singing. On the bench he gives a long speech that nobody can understand, and whenever he talks of the widow who broke his heart he becomes especially irregular (Nos. 112, 122, 113). There are, however, three distinct responses to Sir Roger, corresponding to the three levels of singularity Addison and Steele have outlined. There are those who think he is mad; those who find a kind of heroic bravery in his oddity; and those who interpret his behaviour as the sign of a good heart.

He appears mildly insane when he enters the public domain of London, where he is both unrecognised and unrecognising. So when he calls a coach and then begins to interrogate the driver about the strength of his axle and his taste in tobacco, when he goes aboard a riverboat confiding. 'I never make use of any Body to row me that has not either lost a Leg or an Arm', or when he orders a waiter at the Spring Gardens to carry some hung beef 'to the Waterman that had but one leg' (No. 383), there is manifest danger of sauciness and contempt. On these occasions Mr Spectator mediates between the knight and the public by articulating the ideas that have been fore-shortened by Sir Roger's laconic way of talking (his distrust of London vehicles, for example, his intention of visiting a tobacconist's shop, his desire always to employ an ex-serviceman if he can, and so on).

It is chiefly to himself that Sir Roger appears heroic. He talks in the highest terms about political integrity, and concerning individual conduct (which must include his own) he is quite explicit: 'I lay it down for a Rule, That the whole Man is to move together; that every Action of any Importance is to have a Prospect of publick Good . . . without this, a Man . . . is hopping instead of walking, he is not in his intire and proper Motion' (No. 6). In those key phrases about the wholeness, entirety and propriety of a public man's initiatives, the Tory squire anticipates Bolingbroke, the Tory philosopher. Johnson's admiration for the squire, seasoned with impatience at the author who could despatch such a fine character to the grave, is the echo of his own *amour propre*: 'The irregularities in Sir Roger's conduct seem not so much the effects of a mind deviating from the beaten track of life . . . as of . . . that negligence which solitary grandeur naturally creates.'[7] It seems that Addison is faintly tempted to contribute to this praise when he adjusts Steele's introductory qualification of Sir Roger's character, 'more beloved than

7 Samuel Johnson, *The Lives of the English Poets*, in *Works*, ed. Arthur Murphy, 12 vols. (London, 1810), X, 88.

esteemed', to 'beloved and esteemed' (Nos. 2, 122); but even when he allows propriety to the man's actions, thoughts and speech, declaring them to be 'particularly his', he points out that imperfections are harmonised with virtues in Sir Roger's character by force of extravagance, not heroism (No. 106).[8]

Captain Sentry's judgments on his kinsman are the soundest. He allows the moral superiority of 'a Man of a warm and well-disposed Heart with a very small Capacity' (No. 544). He also emphasises the importance of modesty in such a character, those absences and reticences he has already interpreted (No. 350) as 'the certain Indication of a great Spirit'. Sentry understands that it is what is missing from Sir Roger – the absence of order, connexion and ceremony in what he does and says – that allows us to interpret his actions and speech as the signs of a great heart. Without his imperfections he would not be readable; his defects are the characters or marks of an amphibian virtue that can be apprehended only as a paraleipomenon, half absent. The same imperfections allow Mr Spectator to be the public translator, as well as protector, of Sir Roger. His translations get more interesting the further back he delves into the history of the man's extravagance, particularly the story of the alluring but cruel widow whose hand made such an impression on Sir Roger thirty years before, and whose rejection of his suit caused time to stop for him. His old-fashioned habits are not mere caprice, but evidence of a heart that was fine enough to break; just as his broken speech in praise of the hand that ruined him is bewilderment with a touch of the sublime (No. 113). In Sir Roger, Addison finds the solution to a problem of representation which he poses like this: 'There are many silent Perfections in the Soul of a good Man, which are great Ornaments to Humane Nature, but not able to discover themselves to the Knowledge of others; they are transacted in private, without Noise or Show, and are only visible to the great Searcher of Hearts' (No. 257). The answer is, *pace* Bolingbroke, to pay attention to defects and trifles. Virtues are made visible by spots.

Because Adam Ferguson has scant interest in the middle ground occupied by characters like Sir Roger, he assigns these representational spots either an heroic or a vicious function. 'A matter frivolous in itself', he points out, 'becomes important, when it serves to bring to light the intentions and

---

8 Compare William Duff: 'Sometimes the character may be so amiable, that its little peculiarities, instead of lessening our esteem or affection, increase the former, and conciliate the latter; provided, however, those peculiarities are innocent in themselves, and indicate or imply genuine excellence. Of this kind is the character of Sir Roger de Coverley.' *An Essay on Original Genius* (London, 1767; repr. Florida: Scholars' Facsimiles and Reprints, 1964), p. 50. The best account of the growing tendency to idealise the singular character is found in Stuart M. Tave, *The Amiable Humorist* (Chicago: University of Chicago Press, 1960). For the representation of heroism, see *The English Hero 1660–1800*, ed. Robert Folkenflik (Newark: University of Delaware Press, 1982), and Edgar Wind, *Hume and the Heroic Portrait*, ed. Jaynie Anderson (Oxford: Clarendon Press, 1986), pp. 1–52.

characters of men.' This is not the case with the 'frivolous occupations' of the modern nobility, who have arrived at that period 'when men, being relieved from the pressure of great occasions, bestow their attention on trifles; and having carried what they are pleased to call *sensibility* and *delicacy* . . . as far as real weakness or folly can go, have recourse to affectation in order to enhance the pretended demands, and accumulate the anxieties, of a sickly fancy, and enfeebled mind'.[9] By the first sort of frivolity Ferguson means those low circumstances in which, much to the embarrassment of politer critics of the eighteenth century, Homer's heroes were occasionally found: cooking and making beds. 'In all these particulars we perceive the vigour of spirit, which renders disorder itself respectable' (p. 107). By the latter sort he means those virtuoso tastes listed by Tristram as 'a maggot, a butterfly, a picture, a fiddle stick——an uncle Toby's siege——or an *any thing*' (*TS*, 8.31.584). Ferguson further characterises this difference as one between originality and imitation. The original poet or hero 'delivers the emotions of the heart, in words suggested by the heart', while the modern trifler is obliged to rest 'on what may be learned in retirement, and from the information of books' (pp. 173, 30).

Sterne's thoughts on this head take the same route as Addison's. In his sermons he refers frequently to the rarity, silence and vulnerability of truly good people who carry their hearts in their hands.[10] He also points out that all human characters, good and bad, are hard to decipher and require some sort of parabolic representation if we are to appreciate them properly (*Sermons*, I, 227; II, 248). The best and the worst actions are performed in secret, and even if the action comes to light, it is attended with 'numbers of circumstances . . . which can never come to the knowledge of the world' (*Sermons*, II, 250). Were they to be visible, these circumstances would be more likely to strike the observer as 'inadvertencies . . . starts . . . trifles, light as air' (*Sermons*, II, 250–2) than the genuine marks of sterling character. These are the problems Tristram confronts when he chooses to draw his uncle Toby's character not from the reports of 'Fame' or 'Rumour', nor from the precise images of the pentagraph or *camera obscura*, but solely from his hobbyhorse. He knows his uncle's inadvertencies, and the trifles they have given rise to, are as likely to suggest muddleheadedness as modest worthiness. Walter's bagatelles and Yorick's horse are open to the same range of interpretations. He also knows that a mixture of modesty, privacy and obsessiveness prevents a character on a hobbyhorse from ever giving a publicly intelligible account of what he is doing. Toby will use no other defence of his hobbyhorse than that of simply mounting and riding it; Yorick will give any reason but the true one for being astride his. But like Sir Roger, they all reckon to have a clear 'Prospect of the

9 Adam Ferguson, *An Essay on the History of Civil Society*, ed. Duncan Forbes (Edinburgh: Edinburgh University Press, 1966), pp. 32, 256. Hereafter cited as *Essay*.
10 See for example 'Hezekiah and the Messengers', in *Sermons*, I, 201.

publick Good'. Objectively they behave like Ferguson's frivolous moderns, passionate about trifles which they discover in books and pursue by means of imitation and mimicry. Subjectively, they are in their proper motion and quite at home, their deeds and speech of a piece with their thoughts and feelings. The problem is to assign a representational function to singularities that threaten to be self-subsistent: spots that are nothing but spots.

Origins in accidents

The first step Sterne takes towards making his characters readable, so that their defective outsides will signify (like Socrates') something of greater worth within, yet not so great as they conceive it, is to supply them with a past. The repetition in Trim's and Toby's histories of portions of Sir Roger's – Toby's bootless passion for a widow, Trim's fond memories of a lovely hand – indicates that Sterne was alert to the importance of attaching trains of associated ideas to inadvertencies so that they might not appear simply arbitrary or futile. The pressure on Tristram to supply this sort of corroborative biography for all his characters is responsible for the unconscionable postponement of his own birth. The term 'hobbyhorse' embraces the relation between present trifles and past misfortunes; for Shandean singularity, like Sir Roger's extravagance, has its origin in a painful mischance. The histories of Yorick's bad luck with horses, of Toby's misfortune at Namur and Trim's at Landen, of Walter's difficulties with his grandmother's jointure and his aunt's reputation, supply genealogies of their oddities and whims that make them intelligible if not exactly admirable. These accounts of inadvertent and trifling behaviour form the larger account of Tristram's own obliquities, which are traced back to the first of the 'embryotic evils' to afflict him – the momentous interruption in which he was conceived.

Once an aetiology of eccentric or trifling behaviour has been established, patterns of reconciled contraries start branching from the basic union between the painful impression at the beginning of the biography and the customary forms of thought and activity deriving from it. For example, Yorick's absurd taste for riding a broken-down horse through his parish, or Walter's extravagant theory of Christian names, are less capricious if they are seen as palliative replays of an original experience of loss and pain. Once this is understood, Shandean oddity, just like Sir Roger's incoherences, may be interpreted as a mode of laconic or foreshortened recollection. Toby's wish that Dr Slop, imminently to lament the manifold difficulties of delivering babies, had seen what prodigious armies took the field in Flanders (*TS*, 2.18.144), is probably the finest specimen of this. Slop is in the position of Sir Roger's coachman, astounded by the sheer nonsense of such a wish, at such a time, being made on his behalf; Walter and the reader are in the position of Mr Spectator, enabled to supply the missing bits of a nicely dry observation which, like most of Toby's, is based on the scene of his greatest disaster.

The mediation between the apparent nonsense of the present and the seriousness of the past involves an appreciation of how strange things can become familiar, how chances can reveal patterns that look like destiny, and how an original thought or gesture is really a copy of another. But the reader discovers this in a sequence quite the reverse of that followed by the characters. For them, the original impression of a bare, painful and shocking chance comes at the beginning of their story and it is made familiar and providential by the various repetitions out of which the hobbyhorse will eventually be formed. For the reader or observer it is their first sight of the hobbyhorse which is shocking, peculiar and (in the sense of unprecedented) original. Hence the paralysis of Yorick's parish as it beholds him on horseback: 'Labour stood still as he pass'd,——the bucket hung suspended in the middle of the well,—— the spinning-wheel forgot its round,——even chuckfarthing and shuffle-cap themselves stood gaping till he had got out of sight' (*TS*, 1.10.19). Total surprise is diminished the further one investigates the first springs, as Tristram calls them. The flush of recognition, whether it is owing to the reader's backward glances or the character's strengthening grasp of future possibilities, is the moment of maximum pleasure and keenest sympathy. This is when the element of caprice (in Toby's whistling of *Lillabulero*, for example) is precisely matched by an intuition of its propriety, or when the sense of loss just begins to turn into the promise of excess. Either way, as the reader's perception of singular nonsense or as the character's experience of singular pain, these spots of deficiency start signifying richer, nobler alternatives.

Another sign of the crossing from singularity to recognisability is a word or phrase which, like the spot, will bear a double meaning. The shocked silence following an accident in *Tristram Shandy* is always broken by an equivoke, or by an exclamation that isn't quite spontaneous. Susannah's cry after the sash-window has fallen, 'Nothing is left', is perfectly equivocal, embracing the related states of her charge's penis and her own options (*TS*, 5.17.376). Similarly, Tristram's 'Out upon it!' after the ass in Lyons has torn his breeches, doubles up as a cry of alarm and a description of the consequences (*TS*, 7.32.524). It is never decided whether Walter's 'Pish!' after the christening is 'an interjection of contempt or an interjection of modesty' (*TS*, 4.14.288). The puns Yorick delivers from the saddle are rather more achieved reconciliations of mortality and festivity. Wilder punning on words such as 'lash', 'train', 'siege' and 'mortar' accompanies the collisions of Walter's and Toby's hobbyhorses. Walter's equivocation on the phrase 'chapter of chances' is exemplary, being caused by an unexpected pain which it names and eases. These are local instances of an equivocalising shift necessary to hobbyhorse-riders: an ability to see something (like a Turkish tobacco pipe, for instance) in a double relation, and to comprehend in a word like 'puff' the ideas of smoking and bombardment. This is how Walter starts on Christian names and noses, adding figurative possibilities to literal terms until, like Toby's bowling green at the end of the war, those possibilities harden into literalisms, leaving no difference between the symbol and what it symbolises.

In this unhappy tendency to excessive confidence, the reverse symmetry of the hobbyhorsical character and the Shandean reader holds good. Once the character has learned to interpret the marks of woe as equivocal signs of pleasure, and to convert pure chance into a limited design, he begins to desert history in favour of present self-fulfilment unalloyed by memories of pain. In Ferguson's terms he begins to occupy fully the ground of modern trifling; but in his own eyes he has become a patriot whose contribution is unique, made possible by an original turn of mind that skirts the corrupt institutions of the state and then thwarts them. His emphasis on originality exactly coincides with his announcement of civic virtue because it is only by shedding the past and becoming as it were a self-created inventor of new ideas that the hobby-horsical patriot acquires the unspotted, unequivocal stamp of competent virtue. When this point is reached, simply to ride the hobbyhorse is sufficient justifica-tion of the value of the activity, for deeds are perfectly continuous with inten-tions and speech is a transparent medium of the heart. When they are suffici-ently dislodged from these positions of self-confidence to have to justify them, members of the Shandy circle jointly gesture at the unparalleled novelty of their schemes and at the purity of their motives for undertaking them. In his Apology, Toby begins the vindication of his original mode of warfare by affirming the unspotted transparency of his being and energetically rejecting his brother's attempt to read obliquely from siege to motive: 'I have concealed no one action of my life, and scarce a thought in it . . . such as I am . . . you must by this time know me' (*TS*, 6.32.460). Yorick responds in the same way to Didius' attempt to 'read' his burning of the sermon he has just preached, explaining that it is a comically original defence of transparent language. Walter is never *driven* to self-justification because polemical argument is his usual style of hobbyhorse-riding, but his defence of the good character of his bull is a displaced affirmation of self-evident, unequivocal integrity.

Reading depends on signs that are not continuous with their meaning, so it is no wonder that hobbyhorse-riders, especially when they are at an extreme of virtuous originality, should be wary of it. Nevertheless, it is possible to read back to a point of historical origin and locate there a form of primitive integrity not unlike the hobbyhorse-rider's perception of his own originality. This is possible when the spot, the sign of deficiency erased in the modernising move, is expanded by the reader into a tragic primal scene where the afflicted hero exhibits Cato's heroic bravery, or the magnanimity of Ferguson's Epaminondas, who cries, 'Draw this javelin from my body, and let me bleed' (*Essay*, p. 39). Instead of being transcended, loss is studied and idealised. Eugenius reads the last lambent stream of fire in Yorick's eyes as the faint copy of his former merriment and therefore as a sure sign of his broken heart;

at which point he weeps not for a friend or a clown, but for a hero whose tragic destiny was inscribed in the first joke he ever cracked. Similarly, Walter's reading of the lacquered plate on Toby's coffin produces an idea of excellence that is unparalleled because death has removed it to the past, ensuring its originality in the senses both of priority and uniqueness. Tristram accords Toby and Trim the same reading when he interprets the grand desideratum of the siege of Lille not in the light of its comic supplement but as a hole expressive of the grave in which master and man are already buried, and which therefore authenticates Trim's 'genius' and Toby's absolute priority: 'first and foremost of created beings' (*TS*, 6.15.451–2). In her efforts to interrogate the map of Namur so as to 'get at my uncle Toby's groin' Mrs Wadman herself strikes into this sort of reading, when 'with tender notes playing' she leads him 'all bleeding by the hand out of the trench, wiping her eye, as he was carried to his tent' (*TS*, 9.26.637). Again, Walter is not quite so prominent in this historicisation of originality, and we have to read him reading before he fits into an heroic past.

Despite the distinctions drawn by Ferguson and Addison between ancient and modern originals, it begins to be clear that they aren't very different. The sentry-box into which Toby retires in order to fight the battle of Lille is remarkably like his coffin to the extent that in the one he can take the representation of a battle for a battle indeed, and that in the other he can be read (by his brother and nephew at least) as a man comparable to himself alone, unfellowable. The tendency among hobbyhorse-riders to purge their speech of ambiguity and equivocation is equally evident among idealising historians. Eugenius is deliberately blind to the tragicomedy of Yorick's last joke. The refusal to countenance ambivalence not only reproduces the hobbyhorsical error of confounding a representation with what is represented, it obliterates the middle ground on which eccentricity thrives and continues to be readable.

That is why Tristram, poised between the coffin-reading and the sentry-box, wakes up to what is happening with an unoriginal cry of alarm. His warning to Toby, 'Don't go into the sentry-box!' echoes Sancho's to Don Quixote as he prepares to enter the Cave of Montesinos: 'Good sweet sir, consider what you do. Do not venture into such a cursed black hole!' (*DQ*, III, 178). The allusion is particularly apt, for in the cave Don Quixote is as unrestricted in the invention and realisation of his peculiar ideas of chivalry as Toby intends to be with his ideas of siege warfare in the box. This adventure of the cave, witnessed and narrated entirely by Don Quixote himself, is destitute of readerly discontinuities: its grotesqueries reveal no enigmas, no occult significations. What they are is what they represent. This self-subsistent continuity between narrator and narrative is claimed subsequently by Cid Hamet Benengeli as soon as his hero has been placed in the other black hole of the grave. It is hard not to compare his apostrophe to his pen and to his dead hero with Tristram's joint-apostrophe to his uncle's corpse and his own powers of narration. Possibly, as Johnson suspected, this was Addison's reason for killing off Sir Roger, since next to the excitement of inventing an original character who walks in a motion proper and peculiar to himself, is the delight of declaring with absolute certainty that his like will never walk the earth again. It is a temptation evidently difficult to resist; but the reading most frequently called for by Tristram does resist it.

Originality and imitation

We have seen Adam Ferguson distinguish between a primitive integrity, animated by what he calls 'the living impressions of an active life', and a decadent immobility which uses the knowledge of books as a substitute for 'the inquisitive or animated spirit in which they were written' (*Essay*, pp. 30, 217). In a book published in the same year as the first two volumes of *Tristram Shandy*, Edward Young tries out an adjusted formula in which ancient virtue and modern originality are combined in a powerful alliance against imitation. In effect Young excludes the readerly talents of resistance which treat even the most original phenomena as representational signs – 'a sort of *Manufacture* wrought up by those *Mechanics*, *Art* and *Labour* out of pre-existent materials not their own' – in favour of a simple originality that embraces the oldest and newest in British life: 'Something new may be expected from *Britons* particularly, who seem not to be more sever'd from the rest of mankind by the surrounding sea, than by the current in their veins; and of whom little more appears to be required, in order to give us *Originals*, than a consistency of character, and making their compositions of a piece with their lives.'[11]

In the work of a novelist like Richardson, who actively promoted these views, the coincidence of literary originality and politico-moral integrity is achieved by letting the heroine or hero reflect and be reflected in the excellent novelty of the work in which they appear. Indeed it is always important to Richardson to sustain the illusion that the novel is the genuine product of his characters' hands, not his. Clarissa's scornful rejection, therefore, of compositions that are nothing but '*notes* and *comments* upon other people's *texts*', illuminates equally her moral inimitability and Richardson's assessment of her story as 'something that never yet had been done'.[12] When literary originality extends even further to a story of unique male virtue, the chorus

---

11 Edward Young, *Conjectures upon Original Composition* (London, 1759; repr. Scolar Press, 1966), pp. 12, 76. William Duff makes the same point even more succinctly, defining an original writer as one who 'instead of tracing the footsteps of his predecessors, will allow his imagination to range over the field of invention, in quest of its materials, and, from the group of figures collected by it, will strike out a character like his Genius, perfectly Original.' *Essay on Original Genius*, p. 132.

12 Samuel Richardson, *Clarissa: or the History of a Young Lady*, 4 vols. (Dent: Everyman's Library, 1932; repr. 1965), IV, 495, 553.

in praise of the hero's moral orginality is insistent. Jeronymo tells Sir Charles Grandison, 'This is like you. It is you yourself.' Harriet Byron refers to her lover as 'the man of men'; and the man of men informs the world that he lives not to it, but 'to himself and his own heart'.[13] Resisting self-division in Italy, where he manages to escape heart-whole from a passion that has more in common with a theorem than a tragedy, he vindicates the Machiavellian maxim, translated by Ferguson as, 'The fortune of a man is entire while he remains possessed of himself' (*Essay*, p. 228). Grandison's cultivation of some rather grave singularities, such as dining earlier than is customary and refusing to have the tails of his carriage horses docked, is not intended to be read as modern eccentricity denoting secret magnanimity; these are the clear effects of Catonic heroism, not spots at all, and only mistaken for blemishes by the corrupt world Sir Charles does not live for. His consistency of character is of a piece with his composition, likewise misunderstood by 'the greater vulgar' who burlesque virtue and refuse to attend to wisdom unless 'we shew her with a Monkey's Grin'.[14]

When this ideal comes under strain, fragmentation – the breaking down of structures that are all of a piece – and imitation – the incorporation of exotic material as a supplement to works and to characters that are no longer entire – are inevitable dangers faced by these originals. For example, the conflict between Clarissa's inimitable originality and her imitable example is focused in the extraordinary use she makes of the Book of Job, transcribing apt fragments into her meditations and quoting others at her tormentors. In an equally extraordinary perception of what she is doing, Lovelace estimates her originality with a quotation from the same source: 'Miss Clarissa Harlowe, indeed, is the only woman in the world, I believe, that can say, in the words of her favourite Job (for I can quote a text as well as she): *But it is not so with me*' (*Clarissa*, IV, 135). Between them, Clarissa and Lovelace unstitch the simple seam dividing originality from imitation in Young's and Richardson's formula, and replace it with a much more complex overlap in which singularity is both achieved and announced in fragments from other texts. The double nature of this new order of originality can be apprehended only in terms of the ruin of the combined ideal of individual integrity and literary novelty. Clarissa is what she is because she is no longer what she was: her story is unique because it is supplemented with quotations from another narrative. Don Quixote approaches these paradoxes from the other side when, in an unparalleled act of madness, he decides carefully to imitate the madness of Beltenebros. In both cases the act of imitation produces the effect of originality, for character and author alike. Because it is then impossible

13 *Sir Charles Grandison*, ed. Jocelyn Harris, 3 vols. (Oxford: Oxford University Press, 1972), II, 189; III, 75; I, 137.
14 *Selected Letters of Samuel Richardson*, ed. John Carroll (Oxford: Oxford University Press, 1964), pp. 87, 129.

to separate the elements of artifice and design from those of accident and chance, this copied originality obeys the laws of the double principle, and its characters fall into the middle area defined by Addison and occluded by Young.[15]

In the opening chapters of *Tristram Shandy* originality is carefully scrutinised under several different headings. Tristram mentions proudly the 'air of originality' in his dedication and the narrative of the 'original journey' he took with Mr Noddy's eldest son (*TS*, 1.9.16; 1.11.24). On the other hand he laments the misfortune that has condemned him to think and act like no-one else, and in his history of Yorick the 'extravagance of his humour' (despite his being 'originally of Danish extraction') is blamed for his downfall. But when he gets to Toby, Tristram sheds his diffidence and enters this testimony in favour of his uncle and his family:

His humour was of that particular species, which does honour to our atmosphere; and I should have made no scruple of ranking him amongst one of the first-rate productions of it, had not there appear'd too many strong lines in it of a family-likeness, which shewed that he derived the singularity of his temper more from blood, than either wind or water, or any modifications or combinations of them whatever: And I have, therefore, oft times wondered, that my father, tho' I believe he had his reasons for it, upon observing some tokens of excentricity in my course when I was a boy,——should never once endeavour to account for them in this way; for all the SHANDY FAMILY were of an original character throughout.   (*TS*, 1.21.65)

But this is a self-undoing assertion. The familiar alliance of character and composition under the banner of originality, joined to the customary observations on the British temperament, which is then modified by an exception against climate in favour of blood, leaves the Shandy family original to the degree that they are all alike. No matter how far Tristram goes in declaring and exemplifying the singularity, oddity and unexpectedness of his family's proceedings and character, he ends up with the contradiction of a derived singularity, an originality that has already occurred in the family and been identified in other books.

---

15 Sir Roger gives a sample of this sort of originality in the theatre, where his spontaneous approval of the playwright's decision to have the bloody work of Pyrrhus' death transacted offstage is an unconscious quotation of Horace's rule (*The Spectator*, No. 335). The confusion of originals and copies is treated more satirically by Smollett in *Humphry Clinker* when Matthew Bramble, himself an 'original', tries to cultivate fellow originals in London. Among the manifold corruptions and sophistications of the place are knaves whose originality is nothing but a mask: 'If you pick up a diverting original by accident, it may be dangerous to amuse yourself with his oddities: he is generally a tartar at bottom; a sharper, a spy, or a lunatic.' The most ironic misuse of originality occurs in *Ferdinand Count Fathom* where Sir Stentor Stiles and Sir Giles Squirrel impersonate bluff country squires of the de Coverley and Western breed in order to lure card-players to their destruction. Smollett's usage is interesting. He is the only author I know of who uses the word 'original' as a noun synonymous with 'eccentric', 'humorist', and so on. The quotation is from *The Expedition of Humphry Clinker*, ed. Lewis M. Knapp (Oxford: Oxford University Press, 1984), p. 123.

This contradiction can come about in fairly obvious ways. Walter's maxim of originality, 'that every man's wit must come from every man's own soul,——and no other body's', introduces an account of how he cobbles a theory of childbirth out of other men's books. Modern editing shows how his borrowings from the Prignitz and Scroderus are themselves borrowed from Chambers' articles on 'Brain', 'Soul' and 'Sensory' (*TS*, 2.19.147). Although it is Toby's library that is compared with Don Quixote's, Walter and Yorick exhibit a greater reliance on books than he, involving a greater need to imitate and plagiarise. The equivalent of Amadis in Walter's life is Socrates, whose words he quotes and whose gestures he mimics; in Yorick's it is Yorick his Shakespearean ancestor, Don Quixote and, just before he dies, Sancho Panza.

Assuming that an author does not share Richardson's and Young's investment in originality for its own and the nation's sake, the best way s/he can preserve a double sense of the copy-in-the-original and vice versa is to let it speak for itself, without commentary. It is owing to this autonomy that Lovelace's discovery of Clarissa's originality in a quotation is so surprising, despite his author's clear adherence to a contrary position. In Sterne's fiction a common technique is to let an original sentiment run as it were accidentally into quotation; or the reverse of that, to let a formal quotation be interrupted by an accident. Walter quotes Shakespeare's Cassius, for example, without being aware of it: 'Forgive, I pray thee, this rash humour which my mother gave me' (*TS*, 2.12.115; compare *Julius Caesar*, IV, iii). But when he quotes Socrates deliberately, 'I have three desolate children', Mrs Shandy breaks in, 'Then you have one more, Mr Shandy, than I know of' (*TS*, 5.13.370).

Ernulphus' malediction is the reference point for this sort of imitation because it supposedly contains every oath, in every form and permutation, that we might deliberately or spontaneously pronounce in the course of our lives. Tristram's theory is that Ernulphus has invented, like a Fergusonian primitive, all the oaths in his document; that ours are all copies of these and, 'like all copies, how infinitely short of the force and spirit of the original'. Walter on the other hand will not allow Ernulphus to be an original, rather a learned and faithful collector of all known oaths and modes of swearing (*TS*, 3.12:183). The corollary of Walter's theory is that imprecations ought to be used with great presence of mind so that they match the exact 'size and ill intent of the offence'; but all of his oaths, from his first '*Good G—*' to his wishing the whole science of fortification at the devil, are sworn in an absence of mind almost as great as Phutatorius' enigmatic 'Zounds'. At moments like these he deserts the corollary of his 'singular and ingenious' theory by swearing with a fervency that contradicts, at the same time, Tristram's theory about the faintness of copies. The conflicts here between theory and theory, and theory and practice, combine to show that originality cannot be determined by degrees of priority but by the sudden and mutually constitutive encounter of a living impression with an established form of expression.

The equivocal relation between the pretext and the pre-text for swearing is repeated in the strange parallels formed by Walter's *Tristrapaedia* and Tristram's own *Life*. Walter's document, incomplete but enjoying the advantage of chronological priority, ought to be the original text from which both life and *Life* derive as a species of enlarged quotation. At the crisis of the circumcision, therefore, Tristram duly refers to the chapter on sash-windows in the *Tristrapaedia* foretelling it, 'the most original and entertaining one in the whole book' (*TS*, 5.26.383). Inscribed there is a story which infant Tristram believed was his own to tell, except that it was told by Susannah to Jonathan, by Jonathan to Obadiah, and finally by Obadiah to Walter who replies, as if he did indeed already know it, 'I thought as much.' It transpires, however, that Tristram has inserted the chapter at a later date, repossessing his own story by tampering with the authenticity of the text in which it is supposed to have first appeared. Whether in the *Tristrapaedia* or Tristram's own *Life*, therefore, the claim for that story's originality can be made only on the grounds of its falseness.

There is a turn, or 'dedoublement', in this confounding of copies with their originals that Tristram finds irresistible, and it depends on a supererogatory resemblance between the two. The celebrated example is Tristram's attack on plagiarism at the beginning of the fifth volume, plagiarised from Burton's *Anatomy of Melancholy*. The extra element of fidelity derives from Burton's plagiarism of the passage from Jovius, so that instead of a relatively straightforward contrast between an original and a copy there is a pleonasm: a plagiarism of a plagiarism on the topic of plagiarism. The copy includes the defect of the original and finds a 'genuine' community with it in terms of defectiveness. It is this sort of community that Lovelace finds Clarissa and Job sharing, one where the fragmentations of words, texts and bodies follow so closely on one another that quotation becomes the necessary and the only authentic form of speech.

Walter's last speech, on hearing the reason for Toby's termination of his Amours (as usual before the principal party has had time to tell it), is an attack on sexuality borrowed from Charron's *Of Wisdom*, itself largely borrowed from Montaigne's essay 'Upon Some Verses of Virgil'.[16] Here the supererogatory resemblance isn't founded on the defect of plagiarism, but on an apparent loss of direction in the original. Montaigne suddenly stops his satire on sex to denounce such blackguarding of human nature as he has been impersonating: 'Fanatick People! who think to honour their Nature by denaturing themselves; that value themselves upon their Contempt of themselves, and grow better by being worse' (*Essays*, III, 129). Walter reproduces this switch when his attention is distracted by the accoutrements

16 For detailed notes on this and other borrowings, consult *The Life and Opinions of Tristram Shandy, Gentleman*, ed. New.

of war, and his indignation at the instruments of reproduction is diverted towards those of destruction, 'Nay, if it be but a *scoundril* cannon, we cast an ornament upon the breech of it' (*TS*, 9.33.645). By accident he returns the element of fortuitousness to Montaigne's digression which Montaigne, in imitation of his highly esteemed Plutarch, was carefully replicating as a strategic version of an 'inform and irregular way of speaking' (*Essays*, II, 467). On account of its genuine defect Walter's copy equals itself to its original, discovering by chance the same rhetorical swerve it gained by design.

To work properly the theme of these pleonasms of deficiency – defect upon defect, fragment upon fragment – has to be incompleteness: a child who has been diminished by a sash-window, gossip about the wholeness or otherwise of Toby's groin, and (in the case of Ernulphus) the cutting of Slop's thumb and the cursing to pieces of Obadiah. The figure of the pleonasm emerges at the point in the implementation of the double principle where the Bolingbrokian 'spot' (often incarnated as a wound) is deployed not simply as readable sign but also as a component in figures of double infirmity. The copying or quotation of a text already imperfect, where fidelity depends upon the reproduction of lacunae and damage rather than of primordial integrity, extends the community of mixed originals and copies to all characters and stories ready to acknowledge their infirmities. Once this is established, opportunities of using imperfection upon imperfection in various reconstitutive moves begin to multiply.

It becomes important to be able to distinguish, therefore, between the ideas and expressions of identity which Richardson, Ferguson, and overconfident hobbyhorse-riders make use of, and the pleonastic representation of imperfections which can easily seem to resemble them. A hero who is like himself, in possession of himself, a man of men, belongs to a category of the inexpressible constantly attempted in the heroic tragedies of Dryden, Lee and Otway, and as constantly mocked in Scriblerian parody. In Pope's *Art of Sinking*, the line 'None but Himself can be his Parallel' is compared for bathos with the showman's boast, 'This is the greatest Elephant in the World, except *Himself*.'[17] When Tom Thumb is asked what his conquered giants are like, and grandly replies, 'Like nothing but themselves', Fielding's commentary shrewdly estimates the problem of such locutions: 'It will be necessary that we comprehend every Man to contain two Selfs.'[18] In fact he anticipates Wittgenstein's observation on the sentence, 'A thing is identical with itself': 'There is no finer example of a useless proposition, which yet is connected with a certain play of the imagination. It is as if in imagination we put a thing into its own shape and saw that it fitted.'[19]

17 Alexander Pope, *The Art of Sinking in Poetry*, ed. Edna Leake Steeves (New York: Russell and Russell, 1952), p. 31.
18 Henry Fielding, *The Tragedy of Tragedies*, ed. L. J. Morrissey (Berkeley: University of California Press, 1970), p. 78 n.
19 L. J. J. Wittgenstein, *Philosophical Investigations*, trans. G. E. M. Anscombe (Oxford: Basil Blackwell, 1968), 216, p. 84e.

The fact that language is resistant to any notion of identity, and splits it along the lines of imitative originality we have just been looking at, explains why Shandean pleonasms seem to be founded on tautologies of perfection. Consider the example of Toby, whose originality is said to centre in the characteristic of 'a most extream and unparallel'd modesty of nature' (*TS*, 1.21.66). It turns out that this modesty is not entirely natural, having been acquired by a blow he received in a trench called a *parallel*. His consolation is to imitate the Duke of Marlborough's campaigns in miniature, running the first parallels of his fortifications parallel to the Duke's (*TS*, 6.21.444). The idea of unparalleled virtue decomposes, as it does in the *Art of Sinking*, into parallel upon parallel. Pleonasms such as these are different from Harriet Byron's 'man of men' because they are always made in respect of phenomena which cannot be intensified, owing to the fact that they are incomplete in themselves. Plagiarism upon plagiarism will never result in plagiarism itself; nor will parallel upon parallel, defect upon defect, or copy upon copy ever bring themselves to identity. To make the slightest effort towards a self-affirming statement in this context leads instantly to the replication of fragments and the doubling of words.

Yorick on his horse is a kind of pleonasm that gestures, like Toby's unparalleled modesty, at the unique while actually disintegrating into resemblance. On the horse's back, says Tristram, 'he could unite and reconcile every thing', because 'they were, centaur-like,——both of a piece' (*TS*, 1.10.19–20). The animal and the man, however, do not supply one another's wants, they repeat them, being as lean, bony, tubercular and impotent as each other. Defect mounted on defect can be 'of a piece' only to the extent that they are neither of a piece, that is, whole. This is like the 'VEXATION upon VEXATION' of the seventh volume. The first vexation is an ass that symbolically castrates Tristram, leaving him less than entire; the second is a commissary to whom Tristram identifies himself in the virtuous formula 'I am I' (*TS*, 7.33.525); then he lets the tautology unstitch itself: '——And who are you? said he.—— ——Don't puzzle me; said I.' Two volumes later Tristram drives another tautology of integrity beyond its limit. His recommendation for a flagging writing is to shave and then to dress in his finest clothes, 'so that he has nothing to do, but take his pen, and write like himself' (*TS*, 9.13.617). The shaving, however, requires a man to sit 'overagainst himself', to consult his own image first in terms of the reduction of its natural consistency – the beard – and then in terms of adding the artificial – the new suit. Such a writer can write like himself only if, as Fielding would say, 'we comprehend every Man to contain two Selfs'.

The interplay of fragmented identities and de-originalised compositions reaches its height in *A Sentimental Journey*, where Yorick gives Count de B**** a lesson in responding doubly to characters who double up as originals and copies. Pointing to his name in *Hamlet* and then to himself, Yorick sets up the same relation between a text and a situation as an Ernulphian imprecation, for it is at once the name most proper to the scene and yet not of it. The Count fails signally to understand the distinction that underwrites the resemblance between 'the idea of poor Yorick's skull' and 'the reality of my own' because, being a Frenchman, he conceives better than he combines. Like all poets and readers who take phrases such as 'He is like himself' to refer to the impregnable identity of the heroic individual, the Count is incapable of that 'certain play of the imagination' mentioned by Wittgenstein. To his proposition, 'Vous êtes Yorick', Yorick replies, 'But there are two Yoricks.' To which the Count imperturbably rejoins, ' 'Tis all one' (*ASJ*, pp. 221–3). The scene illustrates the hendiadys – a figure *Hamlet* abounds in – because it consists in the conveying of 'a dual perception of a dual phenomenon . . . the perception . . . of each idea in turn and then of their combination or fusion'.[20] The hendiadys is closely allied to the pleonasm in demanding that the original and the copy be viewed not as a relation of the perfect to the less than perfect, but as repetitions of the same sort of imperfection – here the peculiar boniness of head – which despite the closest resemblance can never be of a piece or all one – boniness itself. The resemblance is controlled, empowered and limited by a difference between fragments and wholes that prevents any two fragments from being confounded entirely with one another. The figures of hendiadys and pleonasm belong to the field of the double principle. They stimulate the alternation between resemblance and difference that allows the same words or characters to be represented to the mind 'either as Copies or Originals' (*The Spectator*, No. 414), and they indulge the mind in its desire, as Reynolds puts it, 'to double, to entertain two objects at a time'.

Defective archetypes

It has been observed already that the hobbyhorse, although traversing this field of the double principle, does not stop long to graze there but climbs to the higher ground of patriotic originality where its suffering, spots and scars are forgotten. Although a self-idealising original ought strictly to be independent of all libraries and models, to the extent that he uses them they must reflect his own integrity. When Walter chooses to transcend his grief for Bobby's death by inhabiting the stoical commonplaces of the ancients, he secures his immunity to misfortune with what he takes to be their heroic disdain of accidents, especially that of Socrates, about whom he has written a book. But it is plain by now that the texts and heroes out of which hobbyhorses are

20 See George T. Wright, 'Hendiadys and *Hamlet*', *PMLA*, 96 (1981), 168. Geoffrey Hartman discusses how the figure emerges in Smart's poetry in terms germane to this argument in 'Christopher Smart's *Magnificat*: Towards a Theory of Representing', *ELH*, 41 (1974), 429–54. For paradoxes like this one proposed to the Count by Yorick see Thomas McFarland, 'The Originality Paradox', *New Literary History*, 5 (1974), 447–76.

composed are inevitably as defective as their imitators, otherwise the supererogatory resemblance so dear to Sterne – the resemblance founded on the failure of identity – would not be possible.

To look back at these archetypes through Sterne's perspective is to find that the defects of hobbyhorse are never forgotten, nor the combination of privation and play he associates with its most successful moments. Montaigne, for example, remembers Socrates as the man who used 'to play at Cob-nut [and] ride the Hobby-horse with the Boys' (*Essays*, III, 356). Dryden's 'Life of Plutarch', which leans as heavily on Montaigne as Montaigne leans on Plutarch, praises the historian's faithful rendering of trivial details: 'Here you are led into the private Lodgings of the Heroe: you see him in his undress, and are made Familiar with his most private actions and conversations. You may behold a Scipio and a Lelius gathering Cockle-shells on the shore, Augustus playing at bounding stones with Boyes; and Agesilaus riding on a Hobby-horse among his children.'[21] We cannot assume with Ferguson that even such a primordial hobbyhorse is a thing 'frivolous in itself' which brings to light the heroic 'intentions and characters of men' (*Essay*, p. 32). It may be a sign of goodness of heart and of modesty not unparalleled, but if it is a hobbyhorse it cannot represent the integrity of civic or heroic virtue; it must be restricted by some infirmity or limitation. Agesilaus and Socrates are not heroes because they ride the hobbyhorse, but in spite of it; indeed, the hero who behaves unlike himself by seizing the ridiculous substitute of warlike status can scarcely be said to be a hero at all.

In the case of Socrates, these limitations are ignored by Walter but heavily underscored by the authors Tristram uses. Rabelais begins his *Gargantua* with a comparison between his book and the uncouthness of Socrates' appearance. In his essay 'On Physiognomy' Montaigne reports that everyone, including Socrates himself, thought he had the countenance of a thief, and that it was only by strenuous remodelling of his nature that his life was able to contradict his looks. Montaigne builds on this contradiction to show how conventional words, as well as conventional appearances, were alien to Socrates' feelings and thoughts. In the face of death Socrates' singularity is to turn away from the familiar pieties, and to seek no consolation beyond the bounds of the experience (*Essays*, III, 61); this is why his Apology strikes Montaigne as sublime incompetence, at once 'inferior to common Contrivance' and above art: 'innocent childish Pleading of an unimaginable Loftiness' (*Essays*, III, 377–9). Both of these notable defects make their way into the speeches of the Shandy brothers by accident. Walter is most like Socrates when his wife's interruption jolts him out of the quotation of the Apology and into the bare acknowledgment that he has lost a child ('By heaven! I have one less'). Toby's defence of his bowling green wars on the ridiculous grounds that they were in the national

21 'The Life of Plutarch', *The Works of John Dryden*, ed. Samuel Holt Monk (Berkeley: University of California Press, 1971), XVII, 275.

interest is to be compared in sheer naivety with the request made by Socrates to his judges that he be awarded a state pension instead of the death penalty.

Mikhail Bakhtin considers the coexistence of the ridiculous and the admirable in Socrates' character to be the earliest sign of the comic, or 'novelised' hero, as opposed to the epic hero. Like an integer of civic virtue, the latter always 'coincides with himself, he is absolutely equal to himself', whereas his laughing double breaks the shell of conventional expectations, he is the ordinary man for whom 'all existing clothes are always too tight'.[22] In his ramillie wig and his blue and gold, which 'had become miserably too strait for him, that it was with the utmost difficulty the Corporal was able to get him into them' (*TS*, 9.2.601), Toby strides, albeit somewhat stiffly, right into Bakhtin's metaphor to show that he does not coincide with a military, heroic self. On his forehead Nature may have written 'GENTLEMAN', but that sign depends for its readability on the uncurled, tarnished, ill-fitting and generally incongruous appearance his uniform makes in the *tout ensemble*.

Older than Socrates, Job exhibits in much less genial form the same irrelevance in the public sphere, similar bodily afflictions, and an inability to use, or patiently to hear, the common discourse of consolation. The 'heroic cast' assigned him in Sterne's sermons can't apply to any public standard of integrity, only to his way of experiencing private disintegration. No matter how nobly he conducts himself in this plight and how sublimely he speaks of it, his cannot be construed a public success. The four men who hear him belong to the world that no longer attends to Job. Their incomprehension and his own lack of access to a public discourse torment him more than the plague in his body: 'Oh that my words were now written! oh that they were printed in a book' (19:23). Because his prayer is answered and they do appear in a book, just as Socrates' childish pleadings appear in Plato's *Apology*, a limited success, a success based on the representation of human limitation, comes about. It is achieved because a reader can interpret the 'mark' and 'byword' Job insists he has become as a representational sign of an unrepresentative case, instead of assuming, like his live audience, that he is a clear example of the impenetrable extent of divine power. The reader has the opportunity to appreciate, like Montaigne in his reading of Socrates or Lovelace in his reading of Clarissa, a privacy that communicates itself by signs of privation; and once the double principle is operating, it comprehends the hendiadic scope of announcements like this: 'It is not so with me.' Clarissa's quotation of the phrase from Job (9:35) locates the common element in her singular distress and the copiable words of her unique complaint, without which it would remain noise on the far side of silence, unheard, unprinted, unread and unquotable.

22 Mikhail Bakhtin, *The Dialogic Imagination*, trans. Michael Holquist and Caryl Emerson (Texas: University of Texas Press, 1981), p. 37.

Don Quixote occasionally exhibits a capacity to read and quote with the same supererogatory doubling of the original. In his unimproved state he is of course like Job and Socrates, physically grotesque and of no account in the world. He claims public attention by quoting and imitating the texts he thinks the world believes in, offering himself as the embodiment and agent of the values it esteems. Here, where it is reading and quoting that emphasises the isolation of the singular individual, the scenario of incommunicability is taken one step further; for the closer the knight adapts his life to these master texts, the more insane he is taken to be.

This is especially so in the Sierra Morena where he decides to imitate the best original in the annals of knight errantry, by going mad for love in exactly the same manner as Amadis, who did penance on the Poor Rock under the *nom de manie* Beltenebros. Accordingly, he strips himself naked in order to cut 'twenty or thirty mad gambols' which he wants Sancho to witness and report to Dulcinea: 'He tumbled with his legs aloft [and] discovered such rarities, that Sancho even made haste to turn his horse's head, that he might no longer see them, and rode away full satisfied, that he might swear his master was mad' (*DQ*, I, 236). The scene exemplifies Sancho's maxim, 'Who but a madman would have minded what a madman said?' (I, 220). To imitate such mad actions requires a degree of madness in the imitator hardly distinct from that of the original. But there being no such thing as madness itself, for during the fit one is 'beside oneself' or 'less than oneself', madness is most suited to appear as a copy, that which is not itself. Moreover, the representation of this copied madness, as Cervantes' enthusiastic readership proved, was more exquisite than any original. Madness on madness is the arch-pleonasm of defectiveness, authorising a multitude of Cervantine copies of copies in a century dogged by the myth of the self-coincident hero. In this pattern of imitations there is finally no original, just moments when supererogatory resemblance can make the product of fragments multiplied into themselves seem more than a fraction.

The reflection of the Shandies in their archetypes, and of their archetypes in them, is a shimmering of difference and resemblance whose tendency is to mitigate but not abolish the defects they mirror. Like the picture of the melancholy woman in Addison's example, which converts real blemishes and disappointments into an image which softens defectiveness by reflecting the beholder's response to it, the image of Socrates, Job and Don Quixote supply the consolation of representing loss, and of representing the representation of loss. They yield a solace like that which Toby enjoyed when he found a way of telling the history of his wound in a manner guaranteed to 'beguile the pain of it'. The substitutive play of the hobbyhorse is beguiling and useful not because of an heroic constituent its frivolity obliquely announces, but simply because of its ability 'to canter it away from the cares and solicitudes of life' (*TS*, 8.31.584). Only when it canters too far, to the stage where it forgets that cares and solicitudes exist and that substitutes are no more than consolations, does it cease to be useful. Then, as Ernst Gombrich puts it, it deserts the proper place of the substitute, 'that narrow ledge that lies between the lifeless and the uncanny', and starts to risk death or compulsive repetition.[23]

The discourse of civic humanism mocked by this endless comic doubling is sustained, as we have seen, by a conservative desire for uniformity and a nostalgia for the primitive magnanimity that 'renders disorder itself respectable' (Ferguson, *Essay*, p. 107). It arises from the fear that disorder may be unrespectable, and trifling pernicious, when associated with the 'excentrick, unnatural, and unaccountable' motions of trade and credit (Pocock, *The Machiavellian Moment*, p. 454). Adam Ferguson, whom Pocock believes to have been mourning in suitably coded form the extirpation of the Scottish clans, advocates a virtue that perhaps never existed and certainly will not exist again. Hume, a Scotsman with a less romantic view of history and one whose work provides the focus for Pocock's immense study,[24] is responsible for a psychology of unrespectable disorder. How far such a psychology is consistent with the eccentricities of Sterne's characters and narratives is what I now want to find out.

23 Ernst Gombrich, *Meditations on a Hobbyhorse* (London: Phaidon, 1963), p. 8.
24 'It might be imprudent to draw too close a connexion – though a connexion of some kind must exist – between the concern which Hume felt as a philosopher with the relation of reason to passion and the interest which he displayed as a historian of England in the relation of land to commerce and of the executive to the legislative.' *The Machivellian Moment*, p. 493.

3

Associationism

When Locke's influence on Sterne's fiction began to be canvassed fully, roughly forty years ago, critics assumed that the disorderly narrative of *Tristram Shandy* was a fictional demonstration of Locke's account of the association of ideas. But owing to Locke's cursory and disapproving treatment of the topic, there was little leeway for the reader beyond taking the hobbyhorse for a comical example of 'this sort of unreasonableness . . . this sort of madness'.[1] James Work was not unusual in claiming that 'the most important structural device is the principle of the association of ideas upon which the whole progression of the book is based' (*TS*, p. xlix). When John Traugott dismantled this assumption in what remains one of the most authoritative studies of Sterne, and one of the most detailed considerations of Locke's effect on Sterne's fiction, he observed that Sterne's 'history of the mind is not Locke's history, but it is one informed by the contemporary development of Locke's notion of association-of-ideas madness into an epistemology such as Hume's'.[2] The reason Traugott's hint in Hume's direction has been so seldom improved is that evidence of Sterne's reading of Locke litters both his novels, whereas there is little in the way of verbal echo or allusion to link him distinctly to any of the associationist philosophers.[3] But if Locke's polemical afterthought to his third edition of the *Essay* is assumed to provide the model for the depicted and depicting hobbyhorses of *Tristram Shandy*, then there is little choice but to see them as involuntary deviations from normative patterns of thought and speech.

1 Locke, *An Essay Concerning Human Understanding*, ed. John W. Yolton (London: Dent, 1961), II, xxxii, 3. Hereafter cited as *ECHU*.
2 John Traugott, *Tristram Shandy's World: Sterne's Philosophical Rhetoric* (Berkeley: University of California Press, 1954), p. 48.
3 Among the pro-associationists are Francis Doherty, 'Sterne and Hume: A Bicentenary Essay', in *Essays and Studies, 1969*, ed. Francis Berry (London: John Murray, 1969); Howard Anderson, 'Associationism and Wit in *Tristram Shandy*', *PQ*, XLVIII (1969), 27–41; and my 'Language and Hartleian Associationism in *A Sentimental Journey*', *ECS* 13 (1980), 285–312. For the Lockean orthodoxy see Helen Moglen, *The Philosophical Irony of Laurence Sterne* (The University Presses of Florida, 1975). The issue is cautiously raised in *Tristram Shandy*, ed. New, III, 16–17; and even more gingerly in W. G. Day, '*Tristram Shandy*: Locke may not be the Key', *Laurence Sterne; Riddles and Mysteries*, ed. Myer, pp. 75–83. A useful survey is supplied by Martin Kallich, *The Association of Ideas and Critical Theory in Eighteenth Century England* (The Hague: Mouton, 1970).

I hope it is already clear that 'REASON', being half of it 'SENSE' in the Shandean scheme of things, is as subject to the force of circumstance as the body, susceptible to that 'kind of ATTRACTION, which in the mental world will be found to have as extraordinary effects as in the natural'.[4] It isn't just the peculiarity of accidental alliances of ideas that the hobbyhorse illustrates. The complex relation of ideas to impressions, passions, words and circumstances, the infinitely mobile actions and reactions of sentiments and situations, are what Tristram and Yorick are implicated in and what, as far as possible, they love to describe. Although they may point to the fallibility of hobbyhorses, they never exempt themselves from the conditions which make riding them inevitable. The talent for serendipity, of turning accident into design, requires a pliancy of mind learned only in the eddies of this gravitational field, not from extrinsic standards of what is right and proper. In this chapter I mean to refashion Work's conclusions about associationism by expanding Traugott's hint.

It is reason which distinguishes Locke's 'sort of madness' from associationism. As far as he is concerned the greatest faculty of the mind is its ability to reflect upon its own operations. The most useful ideas (mixed modes or ideas of reflection) arise from the operation of that faculty, and the most useful words (those susceptible to a clear and full definition) are the signs of those ideas. 'Though these complex ideas or essences of mixed modes depend on the mind and are made by it with great liberty, yet they are not made at random and jumbled together without any reason at all' (*ECHU*, III, v, 7). On the contrary, the judgment measures and the reason assembles the various ideas that comprise the complex idea of justice or gratitude, for example, and this idea is communicable in proportion as one mind may trace the work of reason in another. Only in complex names of substances are the ideas combined according to a natural union, and even then the understanding has some latitude in the arrangement of them. Farthest from the liberty of mixed modes are the names of simple ideas, which 'are perfectly taken from the existence of things and are not arbitrary at all' (III, iv, 17).

There are a number of occasions in *Tristram Shandy* when this valorisation of mental self-reflection is mocked or undermined. The clearest example is the Preface, where Locke's attack on wit – another irrational combination of ideas – is denounced as stupidity. Tristram builds on that opinion when he insists that it is judgment, not wit, that has deceived him in his life (*TS*, 5.11.367), when he parodies definitions, jeers at dictionaries, calls Locke 'the great reasoner', and laughs at any complex idea not founded on experience and practice. Uncle Toby helps to focus this mockery, first of all in being the victim of the mixed modes of calculus, which have threatened his life, not cleared his head. Such words and ideas are shown to be a false remedy for

4 *ECHU*, p. 60.

Toby's condition of inarticulate frustration, because they have exacerbated
feelings which they can never express. Action or exclamation is the proper
response to distress – a sudden gesture or an oath 'falls out for us in a way,
which tho' we cannot reason upon it,——yet we find the good of it' (*TS*,
4.17.293).

The more Toby deserts the terms of mathematical demonstration for the
expressive alternation between doing and saying what he pleases, the more
he finds health and what passes for common sense in the 'world' he inhabits.
In a number of scenes where Walter is battling for mastery of abstract concepts in monologues that become more obscure by the second, Toby's inter-
jections return the discourse to the level of the concrete. When Walter gives
his brother an account of duration by paraphrasing Locke, and Toby puts an
end to the analysis of 'TIME and ETERNITY' by comparing his own mind to
a smoke-jack; or when in the abstract regions of nose-theory, the conduct of
his pipe is compared, in another paraphrase of Locke, to the operation of the
medius terminus, the joke is against the self-reflective capacity of the mind, for
none of the collections of ideas in Toby's bears any resemblance to the
workmanship of the understanding (*TS*, 3.18.191; 3.40.238).[5]

Ungoverned by reason, and in Toby's case made more ungovernable by
the language of reason, these collections derive from the arrangements of
things in space or of experiences in time which, on account of their
resemblance, contiguity, causation or contrast, end up as allied ideas in the
brain. Resemblance is the province of wit and sexual innuendo. The association of the ideas of Dutch silkmills and English families, mortgagers and
jesters, spouts and penises, whiskers and testicles, broken bones and sexual
satisfaction, etc., exhibit some of those 'degrees of consanguinity and alliance'
catalogued by Rabelais in his account of Ennasin, to which Tristram directs
his reader while negotiating the tricky relations of noses (*TS*, 3.32.219). Contiguity is responsible for Mrs Shandy's association of copulation and
clockwinding, Obadiah's of a child and a calf, and Mrs Wadman's of a husband and her household furniture. The relation of cause and effect is more
complex: it is owing either to a conjunction of ideas that is subsequently
arranged as a sequence, or to the arbitrary association of different ideas
which then manifests itself as a necessary connexion. Of the first sort is the

---

5 In trying to correct the emphasis on Locke, it doesn't do to make him sound like Tristram's
   straw man. He is admired for the sceptical groundwork of his philosophy, of which the most
   congenial part as far as Tristram and Yorick are concerned is that dealing with the natural
   defects of the mind, not the part outlining the cure. Locke's contribution to the scepticism
   discussed in the first chapter may be gauged from a proposition such as the following: 'Our
   faculties carry us no further towards the knowledge and distinction of substances than a collection of those sensible ideas which we observe in them' (*ECHU*, III, vi, 9). I fancy Sterne liked
   to think of Locke and Newton as a modern composite of Job, Newton asking, 'Canst thou
   bind the sweet influences of Pleiades, or loose the bands of Orion?' and Locke demanding,
   'Shall vain words have an end' (38:31; 16:3). The point about both questions is that they must
   stay rhetorical.

resemblance between the careers of the biblical Dinah and the Shandy Dinah, out of which Walter develops the theory of *nomen est omen*; of the latter is Tristram's belief that he was doomed by marriage articles to have his nose squashed. Whenever Fate, Destiny or the Artillery of Heaven are invoked as causes of accidents, we are being treated to the exemplification of this Shandean maxim: 'When great or unexpected events fall out upon the stage of this sublunary world——the mind of man . . . naturally takes a flight, behind the scenes, to see what is the cause and first spring of them' (*TS*, 4.27.323).

Association-by-contrast is at once the most 'unreasonable' and the most fundamental mechanism of the Shandean mind: ideas of light and darkness, weight and buoyancy, joking and dying, continuity and interruption, and, as we have just seen, originality and imitation, are mingled both in the action and the narrative of the book. Ten years before it was written, Fielding claimed to have pioneered the 'vein of contrast', demanding, 'What demonstrates the beauty and excellence of anything, but its reverse?'[6] Sterne mines it for the slightest evidence of the mind's fondness for extremes and for fixing an idea in terms of its opposite. This is what the scullion does when she responds to the news that Bobby is dead with, 'So am not I' (*TS*, 5.7.360). Tristram does it in his preface when he tries to show how things are by showing how they aren't; when he gives a lengthy account of the causes of confusion Toby's did *not* spring from: and again when the word *gay* puts him in mind of the word *spleen* (*TS*, 7.19.501).

The alliance rarely takes places between ideas on an equal footing. Typically of eighteenth-century unions, a well-connected idea meets and grows fond of an energetic parvenu. When Mrs Wadman beholds Toby in her own house, he presents a fresh and as it were naked idea in a context of old familiar ones, until 'by reiterated acts of such combinations, he gets foisted into her inventory' (*TS*, 8.8.546). Similarly, when the shocking novelty of death enters the Shandy house, it is assimilated to the familiar ideas of the inhabitants: Walter incorporates it into his reading, Trim associates it with battle, Obadiah can conceive of it only on a coachbox, and Susannah thinks it most natural in bed. The familiar idea belongs to the congeries of tastes and customs which constitute the history of the individual mind. As long as the new idea isn't so astounding as to break habitual associations, it takes its place in the mental terrain, forming one of the many fissures, defiles and tracks reconnoitred by the animal spirits in the processes of recollection, thought and feeling.

The circular 'tracks of happiness' imprinted on Toby's bowling green perfectly correspond to those in his brain: one military item inevitably introduces another, and all the new ideas that enter there – of haste, bridges,

---

6 Henry Fielding, *The History of Tom Jones*. ed. Fredson Bowers (Oxford: Clarendon Press, 1974), p. 212.

love, and so on – are duly militarised to fit. The hobbyhorse is only the most eloquent example of how the residues of experience are used to colour and familiarise accidental events. Everyone, even Phutatorius and Dr Slop, operates in the same way. Each sensation contributes to the pattern of previous sensations which make it intelligible, enforcing the old Epicurean axiom which provides the starting point of Locke's philosophy as well as Montaigne's, Hume's and Hartley's: 'Nihil in intellectu quod non fuit prius in sensu.'

Early associationisms

Among the associationist thinkers known to Sterne there is considerable variation in the interpretation of this axiom. Hobbes and Addison both believe the order of ideas is determined by the order of experience, rather like the pattern of Locke's simple ideas. Even though the sequence of ideas may be compressed, 'We have no Transition from one Imagination to another', Hobbes asserts, 'whereof we never had the like before in our Senses.'[7] Addison argues that a well-supplied mind, prompted say by an idea of gardening, will despatch the animal spirits along associated traces until 'the whole Sett of them is blown up, and the whole Prospect or Garden flourishes in the Imagination' (*The Spectator*, No. 417). Montaigne can't be certain even of this relation between his experience of the world and the operation of his mind, only that custom has given a form to his life and that this form changes for reasons he can never identify. Thus it has been his 'particular Opinion and Fancy' to dislike radishes and white wine, then late in life to start enjoying them (*Essays*, III, 445–6).

Before looking further into these different accounts of the association of ideas, I shall offer a simple model that suits all of them except Locke's. First an impression, or sense perception, is registered upon the nerves and carried to the brain, or sensorium. Secondly, it achieves the status of an idea by attaching itself to an idea, or train of ideas, already lodged in the brain. Thirdly, the energy generated by this conjunction activates the animal spirits which, when impelled down the trace formed by these associated ideas, illuminates them or, in Addison's metaphor, blows them up. Whether the mind is occupied with thinking, remembering or dreaming, these traces will be patrolled continually by the animal spirits, prompted either by the force of casual impressions, or by the vividness of certain blown up ideas which, gaining the impact of impressions themselves, keep the animal spirits in agitation. Out of this motion are formed the 'little gusts of passion or interest' that stir the thin juice of the understanding (*TS*, 3.9.167). Although a trace is partly formed and illuminated by the arrival of an impression, it is a mistake

---

7 *Leviathan*, ed. Michael Oakeshott (Oxford: Basil Blackwell, 1946), p. 13.

to think (as Locke and Coleridge do) that the contents of the mind are just the residue of these impressions and the traces merely the vestiges of the sequences in which they occurred. The impression triggers a tendency in the mind itself to combine ideas – Hume's 'gentle force which commonly prevails' (*T*, p. 58) – that usually operates conjointly with the patterns of outward impulses but can, in reveries and dreams for instance, declare its independence and superior power. To this extent association is always a case of what of what Hartley calls 'the Association of Associations'.[8]

Hobbes' notion of ideas patterned according to the sequence of their original impressions gets some support in *Tristram Shandy* when Trim finds it impossible to recite the fifth commandment without giving the previous four; but generally ideas in a sequence will develop an equality which allows for the substitution or omission of intermediate steps. Mrs Shandy has lost her sense of sequence when she asks her husband the question about the clock, and in almost every hobbyhorsical activity an illusory notion of cause and effect is established as soon as the relics of real experience are effaced or transposed. Rather than stay in the order in which they first arrived, ideas develop simultaneity or reversibility. Hobbes admits as much when he talks about the short-circuiting of ideas, such as the man in the Civil War who put the question, 'What is the value of a Roman penny?' and invisibly combined the ideas of Charles' betrayal and Christ's. He also gives an intriguing account of how the symptoms and origins of certain emotions are interchangeable, so that heat may be both the effect of anger and its causes (*Leviathan*, pp. 11, 14). Toby's wish that Slop had seen the Flanders armies splendidly short-circuits his refutation of Slop's opinions on the difficulties of childbirth; and when Walter reaches his left hand into his right coat pocket, there is such a suffusion of blood in his face that there is no time to decide whether it is the cause, effect or merely the appearance of rage (*TS*, 2.18.144; 3.5.162). It is Hobbes' brief hint about 'the motion from the brain to the inner parts, and from the inner parts to the brain being reciprocall' (p. 11) which is to provide the basis of the most intriguing speculations of eighteenth-century associationism and of the most complex scenes in Sterne's fiction.

Addison's spatialisation of the memory, rendering it as a garden ready to bloom or a landscape about to unfold its prospects, has a powerful influence both on the imagery and the theories of subsequent associationists. Of course Addison has simply elaborated Locke's bare metaphor of the 'smooth path' or 'track' into a garden walk, which is exactly what Tristram does too. As nothing is easier in associative thinking than to transpose the literal and figurative elements of a proposition, it is a short step from the garden walk to landscaping proper. Pope's and Shenstone's gardens are expressions in

8 David Hartley, *Observations on Man, His Frame, His Duty, and His Expectations*, 2 vols. (London, 1749; repr. Gainesville: Scholars' Facsimiles and Reprints, 1966), I, 67. Hereafter cited as *OM*.

soil, stone, foliage and water of individual sets of associated ideas and tastes. Shenstone called The Leasowes the 'perfect picture of his mind',[9] and by analogy the larger plan of an estate such as Stowe constitutes a national memory and psychology. Likewise, in Gothic and early Romantic literature the chasms, peaks and torrents of mountainous prospects half-resemble and half-create the sublimer reaches of the soul. In all of these landscapes the human figure functions like the animal spirits, moving up and down the tracks and defiles and generating new images and sensations at every turn. If that figure happens to be the same individual whose mental landscape is responsible for the contours he traverses – a Pope, a Shenstone or a Wordsworth (in *Tintern Abbey*) – then each move redoubles an established train of thinking, and each surprise is wonderfully familiar. This would constitute an example of the association of associations; it would also exemplify a kind of reflexive or infoliating turn typical of associationism.

The landscaping of associations is a device that fully exploits the analogy explored by Hume between the physical and mental worlds. Sterne is fascinated by this. When Tristram recalls his eccentric meanderings through the plains of Languedoc, he declares, 'The traces of it . . . are all set o'vibrating together this moment' (*TS*, 7. 43. 536); and it is clear that the *trace* forms a map on his brain that matches, squiggle for squiggle, the winding tracks he followed through the plains of Languedoc. The same equivalence between physical and mental topographies is evident whenever Tristram pores over a map, for what he is tracing is the geography of a thought; and as each turn of his finger lights up an association in his brain, it becomes clear that moving and thinking are entirely reciprocal activities. That is why he can trace the wanderings of his mind in the maps he draws at the end of his sixth volume. Toby's garden, according to the same principle of equivalence, is as perfect a picture of his mind as The Leasowes is of Shenstone's; and as he walks up and down its borders he simultaneously promenades along the tracks of his mind, redoubling his pleasure as he deepens the trace. Once embarked on his sentimental journey, Yorick finds it easy to substitute a trace of thinking for a trace of travelling. Although he never makes the trip to Brussels to hear Mme de L***'s story, he informs the reader that he already has 'the traces thro' which my wishes might find their way to her, in case I should never rejoin her myself' (*ASJ*, p. 107).

The first attempt to deal with the association of ideas in the systematic way later attempted by Hume and Hartley, rather than in the incidental manner of Locke, Hobbes and Addison, was the Reverend John Gay's 'Dissertation Concerning the Principle and Criterion of Virtue and the Origin of the Passions', prefixed to Edmund Law's translation of Bishop King's *Essay on the*

---

9 Quoted by John Dixon Hunt, *The Figure in the Landscape* (Baltimore: Johns Hopkins University Press, 1976), p. 191.

Origin of Evil (1732).[10] It seems likely that Sterne owned a copy and that it may have given him his first inkling into the humorous and narrative possibilities of associationism. Briefly, Gay's argument is that the pursuit and approval of virtue can be owing neither to innate ideas nor to reason, but must depend originally upon the association of certain ideas with personal pleasure and happiness. That virtue is apparently followed for its own sake may be explained, Gay argues, in terms of that short-circuiting of ideas already noted by Hobbes. Just as a miser will transfer the pleasure of an end or purpose to the means of obtaining it, and be happy merely assembling the cash he will never spend, so the virtuous person finds as much happiness in the pursuit of virtue as in the accomplishment of virtuous purposes. In both cases the original impulse is hedonistic, and self-denial is only the garment worn by self-enjoyment. Once association has contrived this shift from ends to means, its power becomes so great 'as not only to transport our Passions and Affections beyond their proper bounds . . . but also to transfer them to improper Objects' (law, *Origin of Evil*, p. lv).

Tristram's first associationist set-piece – uncle Toby and the Fly – indicates how well Sterne understood these basic propositions. The scene turns on an improper object, as if Tristram were responding to Montaigne's boast that he could write an essay on anything, even a fly (*Essays*, III, 125). Tristram's fly, however, is used to open up a view of his uncle's moral character and to inculcate a lesson in philanthropy. In the first instance this is managed by curtailing the train of ideas that connects the liberty of flies to the liberty of human beings. Toby is like the miser with his money or the Civil War gentleman with his question about Roman pence. The pleasure softening his gestures ('a tone of voice and harmony of movement, attuned by mercy' (*TS*, 2.12.114)) is communicated to his nephew, setting his 'whole frame into one vibration of most pleasurable sensation'. Included in this vibration are the mixed modes, or abstract ideas of 'philanthropy' and 'universal good-will'. Their presence in the scene is plausible only if the infant Tristram is understood to have associated the pleasant experience of harmony with a variant of Toby's short-circuited analogy: as to flies, so to me, so to people. Although such an association is easily expanded into a general notion of good-will, Gay is right to insist that it is unsusceptible to the kind of definition Locke would expect, because in the end it consists of nothing but a pleasurable impression allied to ideas of personal safety and enlargement. The

10 Although it isn't entirely to be trusted, the sale catalogue of Todd and Sotheran contains the quarto (1731) and octavo (1732) editions, numbers 583 and 1237. Their *Catalogue of a Curious and Valuable Collection of Books* (York, 1768) is advertised as containing the library of the late Laurence Sterne. With a preface by Charles Whibley it reappears as *A Facsimile Reproduction of a Unique Catalogue of Laurence Sterne's Library* (London: James Tregaskis, 1930). My references are to the first volume of *An Essay on the Origin of Evil and A Dissertation Concerning the Principle and Criterion of Virtue and the Origins of the Passions*, trans. Edmund Law, 2 vols. (London, 1732).

rest of Tristram's story is remarkably faithful to these original associations. Awkward or turbulent gestures (such as those Walter has just performed with his pipe) always threaten or preface cruelty of some sort. In the ninth volume, when Toby is placed once again in the vicinity of ideas of imprisonment and liberty and cruelty and benevolence, he hears of 'a poor negro girl, with a bunch of white feathers slightly tied to the end of a long cane, flapping away flies——not killing them' (*TS*, 9.6.606).

Hartley and Hume

Gay's resistance to Locke's conception of the mixed mode as the product of the mind's self-consciousness anticipates the fundamental revisions of Lockean sensationism undertaken by Hume and then Hartley. Although no two thinkers could operate more differently – Hume reasoning inductively and sceptically, Hartley proceeding deductively from Newtonian proposition to psychological corollary – they begin by restoring the close connexion beween ideas of sensation and ideas of reflection that was broken when Locke introduced a class of idea that had nothing directly to do with sensation. In the complicated opening argument of his *Treatise of Human Nature* (1739) Hume aims to reappropriate the word 'idea' as a term for all our perceptions ('I had rather restore the word to its original sense, from which Mr Locke had perverted it' (p. 50n.)) and to apply the word 'impression' to an effect produced by an object upon the senses. Every idea, then, is a copy of an impression, fainter and less vivid; and it is subsequently bound to other ideas not by the workmanship of the understanding but by the force which binds ideas together on grounds of resemblance, contiguity, cause and effect and contrast. In his *Observations on Man* (1749) Hartley is equally determined to reassert the homogeneity of all our ideas. 'It appears to me', he says, 'that all the most complex Ideas arise from Sensation; and that Reflection is not a distinct Source, as Mr Locke makes it' (*OM*, I, 360). A sensation, in his view, consists in a vibratory motion imparted to the nerve-ends by an object. The vibration passes up the nerve (a solid capillament whose pores are dilated with Newtonian ether) to the medullary substance of the brain where it is afterwards stored as a miniature vibration, or vibratiuncle, which will echo the original vibration whenever a charge of energy passes down its trace. Hume would not dare to be so specific about the generation of ideas and the mechanics of their association, but he and Hartley are agreed that all thought is a species of sensation. ' 'Tis not solely in poetry and music, we must follow our taste and sentiment, but likewise in philosophy' (*T*, p. 153). Hartley looks forward to a time when the art of analysis will be subtle enough to reduce 'all that vast Variety of complex Ideas, which pass under the Name of Ideas of Reflection, and intellectual Ideas . . . into the simple Ideas of Sensation, of which they consist' (*OM*, I, 76).

The episode of the fly shows that such complex ideas as philanthropy arise in the Shandean mind from accidental impressions, more specifically from 'vibrations' of pleasurable sensation. The process can easily be reversed. When Tristram sets himself to elucidate the meaning of Slawkenbergius' hard words, 'lambent pupilability of slow, low, dry chat' (*TS*, 4.1.273), he experiences a 'vibration in the strings, about the region of the heart' that assures him he *feels* he understands them; but he doesn't *know* what they mean because his brain supplies him with no ideas. Here and in all analogous difficulties, Tristram follows his taste and sentiments down vibrationary traces where the sublimest ideas are joined to the lowliest sensations.[11] There are very few situations in Sterne's two novels that don't develop a reciprocal play of sensations and ideas corresponding either to Hartley's scheme of vibrations or Hume's of gravitational pull; and despite the simplicity of these basic propositions, the subtlest redoublings of Shandean wit and wordplay are owing to them.

I shall begin a selection of associationist readings of Sterne's fiction with Hartley's clearest statement about the mechanism of mind: 'Every Action, or bodily Motion, arises from previous Circumstances, or bodily Motions, already existing in the Brain, i.e. from Vibrations, which are either the immediate Effect of Impressions then made, or the remote compound Effect of former Impressions, or both' (*OM*, I, 501). The simplest demonstration is a case where nervous vibration produces a single reaction from the brain that brings the sequence to a close. It is likely this would be a painful case because pleasure extends and complicates these reactions. The warmth of the chestnut in Phutatorius' breeches soon turns into painful heat, and Phutatorius is at a loss until his mind supplies the idea of a biting reptile to go with the unaccountable sensation in his groin. With all respect to Tristram, it is only then, when the impression has an associated idea, that the reaction from Phutatorius' medullary substance delivers a huge charge of nervous energy and effects the convulsive removal of the chestnut. These sudden and violent

11 The literary history of vibrations, and the musical metaphors which often accompany it, is long and not yet very clearly defined. For summaries of Sterne's familiarity with the idea of the vibrating sensorium, see Gardner D. Stout's edition of *A Sentimental Journey*, pp. 274 n., 353; and Melvyn New's edition of *Tristram Shandy*, III, 162–3. Hartley says he has taken the idea from Newton's *Opticks* (*OM*, I, 13–21). Hume uses the metaphor of the stringed instrument ('after each stroke the vibrations still retain some sound' (*T*, p. 487)) to explain how passions, as opposed to ideas, overlap and mingle with each other. Sterne's most likely source for the development of scientific ideas of vibration is Chambers, *Cyclopaedia*, articles 'Brain', 'Sensation', 'Sensory,' 'Vibration'. He has of course a source in satiric literature in Swift's *Tale of a Tub*, where so many associationist scenarios are despatched before they are fully conceived, particularly in the 'Digression on Madness'. Recent work on this and related topics includes Mark Loveridge, *Laurence Sterne and the Argument about Design* (New Jersey: Barnes and Noble, 1982), pp. 71–93; Jerome Christenson, 'Philosophy/Literature: The Associationist Precedent for Coleridge's Late Poems', in *Philosophical Approaches to Literature*, ed. William E. Cain (Lewisburg: Bucknell University Press, 1984), pp. 27–47; John A. Dussinger, 'The Sensorium in the World of *A Sentimental Journey*', *Ariel* 13 (1982), 1–16; and Valerie Grosvenor Myer, 'Tristram and the Animal Spirits', in *Laurence Sterne: Riddles and Mysteries*, pp. 99–112.

movements, Hartley avers, 'contribute most to remove or asswage the Pain' (*OM*, I, 113), as they are seen to do once again when Tristram hurls his wig around the room or Walter destroys pipes and pincushions. They are sallies 'of this or that member' that soonest terminate *'provoking cases'* (*TS*, 4.17.293). Violent motion may, of course, initiate the case, as in Walter's awkward reaching for his handkerchief or in Yorick's unpleasant experience in the chaise at Nampont. A rumpled body can cause as well as register a rumpling of the mind.

If the sequence is to exceed the bare triad of impression, association and response (bearing comparison with the proposition, reply and rejoinder of Walter's beds of justice), neither the pleasure of sensations nor the motion of the body ought to become extreme. This moderation is evident in the regular cycles of involuntary or semi-voluntary movement, such as the beating of the heart or the respiration of the lungs. Hartley accounts for this regular contraction and expansion of muscles in terms of vibratory exchange between the mind and the body in which excitations are alternately absorbed and resisted. A contracting muscle, for example, will simultaneously despatch a vibration upwards to the medulla while shutting itself off from the one coming down. By the time the upward vibration fetches a further downward response, the muscle will have relaxed and be ready to receive a new impulse. Then it will contract once again, and the sequence is repeated, endlessly, (*OM*, I, 90–112). No matter how crudely mechanical this principle of alternation may seem, it accounts, as far as Hartley and Sterne are concerned, for the subtlest and the grandest passages of life as well as the simplest. This is how Le Fever dies, the muscle of his heart flickering its last responses to the waning impulses from the brain; and it is how Yorick makes love, the muscles of his hand alternately tightening and loosening to the rhythms of his excitement (*TS*, 6.10. 426; *ASJ*, pp. 91–106). Often in Sterne's stories an alternating glance or gesture indicates an aroused sensibility, alert to an interesting situation without any desire to end or improve it.

I look'd at the gloves, then to the window, then at the gloves, and then at her – and so on, alternately.   (*ASJ*, p. 168)

Maria look'd wistfully for some time at me, and then at her goat——and then at me—— and then at her goat again, and so on, alternately——.   (*TS*, 9.24.631)

Mechanism and love fruitfully combine in those scenes where the pulsations of the arteries convey, by the medium of a finger's palp, the internal telegraphy of one organism to another so that passion is registered, caught, sustained and measured in the regular throbbing of a heart.

More exquisite and brief are encounters where accumulation replaces alternation. 'The Temptation. Paris' intensifies itself to a point of collapse because alternation ('I held it ten minutes with the back of my hand resting upon her lap – looking sometimes at the purse, sometimes on one side of it') and repetition ('she passed her hand in silence across and across my neck in the manoeuvre') (*ASJ*, p. 236) leave no room for resistance, but mount excitements on top of one another until a 'combustion' takes place.[12] The scene begins with a notable example of 'association of associations', suitable for a case of rising passion. The red window curtain heightens both the glow of the setting sun and the rosiness of the fille de chambre's cheek, producing a compound impression which Yorick associates with the idea of blushing. 'The idea of it made me blush myself – we were quite alone; and that superinduced a second blush before the first could get off' (*ASJ*, p. 234). Yorick's virtuous reflections upon the half-guilt of this double blush produce a delicious sensation in his nerves, and the scene is set for 'The Conquest'; but in the meantime there has been a rousing traffic between his impressions and his ideas. Three times they have reacted upon each other, generating that 'Mixture of vivid real Impressions among the Ideas' which Hartley takes to be a symptom of 'the Irritability of the medullary Substance' (*OM*, I, 80). In this state vibratiuncles achieve the power and vividness of impressions, and exert such pressure that 'by rising higher and higher perpetually . . . they come at last to border upon, and even to pass into, disagreeable Vibrations' (*OM*, I, 394). This is what happens after Yorick loses his balance and falls on to the bed with the fille de chambre, or when Tristram's health suddenly fails in a sexual encounter with Jenny, or when Amandus and Amanda die at the moment of their reunion. These are sexual instances with a basic structure – recurrent motions which bring excitement to the point of self-extinction – and the appropriate figure *seems* to be the pleonasm – association upon association leading to one thing on top of another – although we will discover that the tautology is more aptly applied to the self-destructive intensities of association.

Here I want to emphasise the connexion developing between these basic associationist scenarios and the evolution of the hobbyhorse described in the last chapter. There a distinction was marked between the hobbyhorse in its representational or imitative state, and the condition of self-sufficiency it disappears into when it begins to take representations for the things themselves. The same difference exists between ideas and impressions that act and react according to 'the same perpetual Recurrency of Vibrations' and those that combust 'by rising higher and higher perpetually' (*OM*, I, 397, 394). The endless alternation between ideas and impressions is like the alternation between copies and originals that constitutes the hobbyhorse and our perception of it; both of which correspond to the double principle. But the mounting of idea upon impression until no differences exists between them, destroying in the process the representational film that divides feelings from objects, is to ensure a shock or interruption. So the pleonasm is the figure that

---

12 See *Letters*, p. 391.

belongs to perpetual recurrency, where the doubling and alternating of impressions and ideas sustains a minimal difference between the two. But when that difference is obliterated by higher rising and they become 'all one', as the Count de B**** puts it, associationist perceptions have entered the region of identity, where things are nothing but themselves.

Hume dwells more carefully than Hartley on the reciprocal relation of impressions, ideas and passions because he obliges himself to offer a purely psychological account of it. We have already seen in the first chapter how carefully he divides the thing itself from our perception of it. For him there is only an analogy between the world of objects and that of ideas, not Hartley's direct mechanical linkage of matter and mind via Newtonian vibrations; therefore the degree of an idea's vividness depends less on mechanical factors such as recurrency than on the nature of belief. 'Belief', he writes, 'causes an idea to imitate the effects of the impressions . . . and is nothing more but a more vivid and intense conception of any idea' (*T*, p. 169). As associated ideas are in the first place copies of impressions, exactly representing them (*T*, p. 52), the moment of belief is a species of reverse mimesis in which the copy starts copying the original and briefly achieves a force comparable to it. Again, this is a proposition already aired in the two previous chapters in the context of Addison's portrait of a lady, and examples of supererogatory resemblance. The analogy between scenarios of mutual reflection, where an image or a text embodies the idea of what its beholder feels, and Hume's notion of belief, where an idea enters into a reflexive relation with an impression, will run the length of this chapter. At the moment I want to broach Hume's theory of belief under his own rather complex device of the 'double relation'.

In the case of sympathy, 'A cheerful countenance infuses a sensible complacency and serenity into my mind; as an angry or sorrowful one throws a sudden damp upon me.' This is owing to the fact that the idea of cheerfulness or anger, aroused by the signs of these feelings in the faces of the company, 'is presently converted into an impression, and acquires such a degree of force and vivacity as to become the very passion itself, and produce an equal emotion, as any original affection' (*T*, p. 367). Such affable or spirited responses are the result of neither negative capability nor altruism, but the effect on the self of ideas sharpened to impressions by means of one or more of the four modes of relation: causation, contiguity, resemblance and contrast. That is to say, if there is an evident cause of someone's cheerfulness, and she or he is physically close to us as well as being a friend or blood-relation, it is proportionately easier to see oneself at first concerned and then reflected in the emotions they exhibit. It is the addition of self that constitutes the extra circuit of the double relation. If an object impresses agreeable or unpleasant sensations which abut upon the relation of the self to that object (like Tristram and the fly), then feelings of pride or humility will ensue because the sensation excites an *idea* of the sensations of the emotion, and then the emotion itself. By this time the impulse from object to self is echoed by another from self to object; or as Hume puts it, 'When an idea produces an impression related to an impression, which is connected with an idea, related to the first idea, these two impressions must be in a manner inseparable' (*T*, p. 341). A fine house, for example, is pleasing to the eye; if it also belongs to the owner of the eye, the sense of aesthetic pleasure and the feeling of pride lend each other mutual assistance until they are quite intense and hard to disentangle. This is how Toby becomes mixed up with Mrs Wadman's other notions of household furniture, and how she comes to love him. But there may be a twist in the passage from outward to inward impressions; thus the beautiful fortifications of an enemy 'are esteem'd beautiful on account of their strength, tho' we cou'd wish that they were entirely destroy'd' (*T*, p. 637). Toby's and Trim's conflicting feelings as they contemplate the model of Dunkirk perfectly illustrate this.[13]

There are countless moments in Sterne's fiction where a touch, glance or gesture – prints of ideas as Tristram calls them – leave 'something more inexpressible upon the fancy, than words can either convey——or sometimes get rid of' (*TS*, 5.1.346; 5.7.361). Yorick is fond of reading his own feelings in the gestures of others, especially when physical proximity and a sense of kindred ('Tut! are we not all relations?' (*ASJ*, p. 191)) turn another person's countenance or heartbeat into a replica of one's own. Nor is the predominance of self effaced from the record of sentimental exchange: 'I thought I loved the man; but I fear I mistook the object – 'twas my own way of thinking' (*ASJ*, p. 181). In *Tristram Shandy* there is a particularly neat example of an idea acquiring the force of an impression by sympathy when Yorick starts at Walter's theory of the auxiliary verbs: 'He could not have looked more surprised.——I am surprised too, cried my father, observing it' (*TS*, 5.42.404).

Whenever the self can be located among ideas and impressions in this reciprocal play, belief as well as passion is assured. Because Trim finds his brother Tom in Yorick's sermon, he takes it for an authentic account; and

13 As far as I am aware, Alexander Gerard is the only associationist to apply the theory of the double relation to the reading of literature. He does so in two ways. First he maintains that works of genius set up an oscillation between each unfolding image or sentiment and the overall design (analogous to the relation of impressions to ideas), so that each succeeding perception acquires synecdochic force, rushing 'into the thoughts with double violence'. Secondly, he argues that the addition of the idea of passion to this double violence (he uses an example from *All's Well* where Bertram's departure is mourned as a figurative replay of his father's death), redoubles this effect: 'Those ideas which are not only associated with the present perception, but also suitable to the passion that introduced it, are dragged into the mind by a double force . . . A double relation belongs to them, and draws them into view by a double power.' In the course of this analysis Gerard shows how associationism is inevitably an aesthetics of reading, since the characters in a work of genius exhibit the same sequences of the double relation of ideas and impressions that their audience will experience. See *An Essay on Genius* (London, 1774; repr. New York: Garland, 1970), pp. 46, 162, 339.

because Yorick picks up the chestnut that has burned Phutatorius' groin, Phutatorius is convinced that the chestnut belonged to Yorick. The attachment of self to heterogeneous ideas, the claiming of a property in them, is responsible for the growth of Walter's systems, and of all hobbyhorses; and it is then that cool reason is enslaved by passion. The double relation of ideas and impressions is therefore implied in any scene where credulity and emotions are excited; but it is more than implicit in the conversation between Mr and Mrs Shandy that straddles the eighth and ninth volumes. He has accused her of being impelled by motives other than curiosity in wanting to look through the keyhole while Toby proposes to Mrs Wadman. Instantly he is struck with the idea of having said a wrong thing: 'His conscience smote him.' Then when his wife touches the back of his hand with her fingers in what he interprets as a tap of remonstrance, a sensation combines with an idea to produce the emotion of humility, or guilt: 'Conscience redoubled her blow.' This emotion becomes even more intense as her body follows the turn of his own, and he confronts an eye of 'blue, chill, pellucid chrystal' to which the motes of carnal longing have always been a stranger. In that eye he reads and believes the tale of his guilt: 'He saw a thousand reasons to wipe out the reproach, and as many to reproach himself' (*TS*, 9.1.599). The impression of the tap is related to an idea of self-reproach which blooms into a feeling of guilt when the object connected with the sensation declares its relation to the self by touch, marriage and reflection.

Language

Having suggested that Sterne's fiction utilises, or develops, versions of Hartley's vibrational system and Hume's psychology of belief, I will further suggest that it is Hartley's theory of the sign, not Locke's, which is appropriate to its scenes and narratives. For Locke, the accidental association of ideas constitutes one more example of the abuse of words in so far as it damages the conventional pairing of certain ideas with their arbitrary signs. The names of these ideas are not natural – Locke despised dreams of universal languages – but merely the knots by which they are tied together (*ECHU*, III, v, 10). This is the very metaphor turned on its head by Tristram during the episode of Slop's green baize bag. He unlooses the name *knot* among ideas of marriage knots, umbilical knots, knots as obstacles, nautical knots and hangmen's knots. Whether Tristram's wit is the tauter for knowing about those literal name-knots, the *quipos* of the Peruvians, mentioned by Warburton and by Mme de Graffigny in her *Lettres d'une Peruvienne* (1752),[14] he ensures his knot as name behaves the reverse of Locke's name as knot. He

---

14 William Warburton, *The Divine Legation of Moses*, 4 vols. (London, 1758), III, 83 n. g. Mme de Graffigny cited in Janet Gurkin Altman, *Epistolarity* (Columbus: Ohio State University Press, 1982), p. 15.

means to show that words are as subject to the attractive forces of association as ideas and impressions, and that under certain circumstances they can decay, expand, wound and suffer damage because they are altered by the situations in which they appear and which they partly constitute. So we hear of Toby's life being jeopardised by words, of the gallant word 'whiskers' trying to avoid ruin, of the noble names of Greece falling piecemeal to decay, and of the peculiar virtues attached by Walter to any word he writes in his pocket book.

Hartley's contribution to this way of thinking stems from the following proposition: 'Language is not only a Type of these associated Combinations, but one Part of the Thing typified' (*OM*, I, 320). The word is part of the associative process – part of what it names – not an arbitrary articulate sound attached by agreement to clusters of ideas of whose motions it is immune. Oblivious to Locke's joke about seeing by hearsay, Hartley maintains that words will easily reactivate optical vibrations in the brain, and that even the names of tastes will excite faint vestiges of the appropriate sensation. Words can raise ideas; contrariwise, ideas can 'call up the Ideas of Words, and Actions by which they are pronounced'. Associated with certain pleasurable or painful vibrations, words 'may transfer a Part of these Pleasures or Pains upon indifferent Things, by being at other times often associated with them' (*OM*, I, 212, 285). Finally,

Since Words thus collect Ideas from various quarters, unite them together, and transfer them both upon other Words, and upon foreign Objects, it is evident that the Use of Words adds much to the Number and Complexness of our Ideas, and is the principal Means by which we make intellectual and moral Improvements.

(*OM*, I, 286)

Hartley conceives of these improvements by means of two analogies. The less plausible is the analogy between ideas and words, for just as the former coalesce into complex ideas, and complex into decomplex, so syllables coalesce into words, words into sentences, and so on (*OM*, I, 75). More convincing is the analogy he implies between the development of language and the 'double Transmutation of Motions' which governs the alternation of voluntary and involuntary actions and the rhythmic contraction and relaxation of muscles (*OM*, I, 104). In language there is an endless reciprocation between the literal and figurative uses of words analogous to the see-saw of gestures we looked at before. At first names are few and literal, and can extend their range only by being associated with objects like or near to the ones they stand for. Thus the name of the human eye will be applied to the analogous organ in animals, to the hole in a needle, to the centre of a storm, until 'it would cease to be a Figure, and become an appellative Name'.

Many, or most common Figures, pass so far into literal Expressions by Use, i.e. by Association, that we do not attend at all to their figurative Nature. And thus by degrees figurative Senses become a Foundation for successive Figures, in the same Manner, as originally literal Senses.   (*OM*, I, 292)

The millenarian side of Hartley inclines him to interpret this process as an incremental case of higher rising, with figure piled on literalism, literalism on figure, and so on, until a climax is reached in the form of perfect happiness and a philosophical language with a proper name for everything (*OM*, I, 320). Hartley the aesthetician prefers to see it as a repetitive cycle in which figurative language mixes pain and pleasure, falsehood and truth, in just those proportions needed to arouse delight (*OM*, I, 429). Here it is important that the figure never be literalised, but retain that degree of friction between its vehicle and tenor without which pleasure would soon fade.

For when figurative Words have recurred so often as to excite the secondary Idea instantaneously, and without any previous Harshness to the Imagination, they lose their peculiar Beauty and Force; and, in order to recover this, and make ourselves sensible of it, we are obliged to recall the literal Sense, and to place the literal and figurative Senses close together, so that we may first be sensible of the Inconsistency, and then be more affected with the Union and Coalescence.   (*OM*, I, 429)

The rapid alternation of the two senses is not to blur into a continuous note. Like the double transmutation of motions which produces the pulsing of a muscle, one movement requires its opposite, and pleasure depends upon a degree of pain. In turn this is analogous to the double relation of ideas and impressions, and to the mutuality of originality and imitation. This pattern of analogies is broken if a millenarian literalisation takes place. In that event Hartley's names become no different from Walter's tabulated oaths or his structure of auxiliary verbs because they supplant experience (know the words and you will know the things – this is the promise of all universal languages) instead of entering into a dialogue with it. Tautological perfection once again is to be distinguished from the pleonastic superinduction of impulses, ideas of words in which no element is single or self-sufficient.

Hume's consideration of language is as cursory as Hartley's of the double relation. All he says is that 'We use words for ideas, because they are commonly so closely connected, that the mind easily mistakes them.' And he offers the figures of poets and orators as proof of the eccentric motion of the animal spirits down a trace (*T*, pp. 109–10). But Sterne demonstrates the adaptability of Hume's double relation to Hartley's theories of language whenever an idea gains the force of an impression, because a doubling or figuration of words always registers and constitutes the transition. Tristram likes nothing better than to refresh tired clichés such as 'He wouldn't hurt a fly' and 'Are we not here now, and gone in a moment?' Dead metaphors are equally suitable for restoration, and Obadiah's 'mix'd case' is one of my favourites:

In all distresses (except musical) where small cords are wanted,——nothing is so apt to

enter a man's head, as his hat-band;——the philosophy of this is so near the surface——
I scorn to enter into it. (*TS*, 9.1.165)

The dead metaphor is contained in the phrase 'to enter a man's head'. But transformed by the perspective of a superficial philosophy it describes the pressure of a hatband round the head which, in the appropriate emergency, conveys itself into the brain as an idea. Here the idea and the worn conceit that goes with it encounter an impression and its literal expression. Each pair gains vivacity in proportion as it adapts itself to the specific situation, reacting with but not losing itself among the circumstances and the words that comprise it. Figurative inconsistency is maintained at a level of maximum equivocation: a mixed case properly punned.

The reciprocal play of ideas and impressions always bears analogy to the reciprocal play of figurative and literal language. Mrs Wadman's attacks 'by plan' are carried out by means of an impression (the plan of Bouchain on the wall of the sentry-box) turning into an idea (or plan) for raising Toby's passions by using the plan as an excuse for touching his fingers and his thigh (*TS*, 8.23.575). The word reverberates with each alternation between the nerve-ends and the medullary substance, between the immediate tactile impression (the map still bears the print of Mrs Wadman's thumb) and the plot it suggests: 'If ever Plan, independent of all circumstances, deserved registering in letters of gold . . . it was certainly the PLAN of Mrs Wadman's attack of my uncle Toby in his sentry-box, BY PLAN' (*TS*, 8.23.575).

The word 'puff' resonates in the same way when Trim sets out to mimic the cannonade of Lille with two Turkish tobacco pipes fitted to a set of miniature brass cannon.

His first intention, as I said, was no more than giving the enemy a single puff or two;——but the pleasure of the *puffs*, as well as the *puffing*, had insensibly got hold of the corporal, and drawn him on from puff to puff. (*TS*, 6.27.454)

In these circumstances there is no such thing as a single puff, for each comprises an impression and an idea: the impression of literal smoking and the idea of figurative gunnery. The repetitive or incremental logic of the hobby-horse (the more you puff, the more you want to puff) yields a pun spanning the upper and lower reaches of the double relation. The ambiguity of 'puff to puff' survives Toby's entry on the scene because it excites impressions (his mouth waters for a pipe) that react with ideas of heroism. But once he retires to the sentry-box take the puff of puffs, the tautology of higher rising displaces the pleonasm of perpetual recurrency.

Doubles and reciprocals

Before looking at the narrative aspect of associationism, I want to review the double effects that it always seems to produce. In the reaction between ideas

and impressions a twin impulse lodges the copy of an impression in the brain
and empowers that copy to imitate its cause. Any attempt to render in
language the passage of such an impulse is bound to produce double forms
of speech: puns, metaphors and figures. Talking of what it means to be
intellectually sensible and sensibly intellectual, for example, Montaigne
declares, 'When I dance, I dance; when I sleep, I sleep.' This is how he enjoys
life 'double to what others do' (*Essays*, III, 542, 458). Such round assertions
may suggest that Montaigne's double dancing is an arrival at the very form
of dance, expressed as a tautology of higher rising, or higher stepping; but
I think it more likely to be a pleonasm of perpetual recurrency, a husbandry
of the twin impulse. Montaigne's coinages anticipate Addison's alignment of
equivokes and allegory with the double principle, and together they help open
up Sterne's associationism to Dryden's ideas about double-plotting and
Hogarth's about joint-sensation. The link between associationist scepticism
and the theorisation of double effects is strengthened by Hume in the *Treatise*.
He quotes from *The Spectator* No. 412, where Addison talks of the pleasure
afforded by the simultaneous appeal to the mind and the senses, to illustrate
'the association both of impressions and ideas' and to locate the 'double
impulse' behind 'the mutual assistance they lend each other' (*T*, p. 336).

The more complex the situation, the harder it is to track and formulate the
work of the double impulse. Hume talks of the confusing reverberations and
rebounds that occur in cases of sympathy, when you feel 'a pleasure in the
pleasure, and a pain in the pain of a partner' (*T*, p. 432). This can go as far
as the pleasure in the pleasure in the pleasure the owner of a fine estate may
take, both by beholding his possessions and by beholding the looks on the
faces of those beholding them (*T*, p. 414). Hartley talks of the 'mutual indefinite Implication' of vibration and association, 'the double Transmutation
of Motions' in the alternation of voluntary and involuntary actions, the
'perpetual reciprocal Effect' of rational and practical assent, the 'numerous
reciprocal Influences' exerted on one another by the passions, concluding,
'Thus all Things become comments on each other in an endless Reciprocation' (*OM*, I, 71, 104, 332, 369, 343). The endless reciprocation of associating
sensibilities, dependent on impulses that are double and sensations that are
joint, is particularly difficult to define and express. When Coleridge decided
that Hartley's philosophy was no longer plausible, he rejected it in terms particularly faithful to its primary insights: the will and reason are made 'causes
of their own cause . . . at once causes and effects'. The individual ('I myself
. . . poor worthless I') is reduced to no more than the medium of 'those
diminished copies of configurative motions . . . which form what we call notions, and notions of notions'. He is little better than 'the mere quick-silver
plating behind a looking-glass'.[15] The indignation with which Coleridge

15 Samuel Taylor Coleridge, *Biographia Literaria*, ed. J. Shawcross, 2 vols. (Oxford: Clarendon
   Press, 1907), I, 77, 82.

rejects the possibility of not being an original leads him to coin (like Montaigne) pleonasms of perpetual recurrency from the metalepsis, cause of cause.

'Notions of notions', 'causes of causes', 'pleasures of pleasures', and even 'associations of associations' are formulations merging into figures, and they are unavoidable in associationist thinking. Hobbes began by showing how heat might be both the cause and effect of anger. Without a faculty to mediate the double relation of impressions and ideas, or without what Hartley calls the 'Eye within the Eye' (*OM*, I, 379), the patterns of our thoughts and feelings are cyclical, and the propositions we utter are all reversible. And because there is no end to this process, there can likewise be no beginning to it. Hartley stuns himself with this discovery while considering the question of mutual indefinite implication.

> The Power of Association is founded upon, and necessarily requires, the previous Power of forming Ideas, and miniature Vibrations. For Ideas, and miniature Vibrations, must first be generated . . . before they can be associated. . . . But then (which is very remarkable) this Power of forming Ideas, and their corresponding miniature Vibrations, does equally presuppose the Power of Association. (*OM*, I, 70)

If an impression's reciprocal relation to an idea is both the condition and the effect of association, then the implications are fascinating. It is like Freud's discovery that repression has to exist before repression can take place.[16] Hartley concedes that without 'joint Impression', that is without the coalition of a sensation with an idea and a vibration with a vibratiuncle, no vestige of an impression would be left upon the medullary substance (*OM*, I, 71). This means there is no definite point of origin: always already, as modern scepticism has it, there is the trace, the cicatrice of an infinitely prior collision of two elements which leaves even the most primordial idea less than unitary, less than original. At the beginning of the second book of his *Treatise*, Hume concedes that 'the mind, in its perceptions, must begin somewhere . . . there must be some impressions, which without any introduction make their appearance in the soul' (*T*, p. 327); but the concession is made unnecessary by the confidence with which he states associationism's fundamental principle of causation: 'Any thing may produce any thing . . . therefore 'tis possible for all objects to become causes or effects to each other.' And again, 'Any thing may be the cause or effect of any thing' (*T*, pp. 223, 298). Wordsworth (a more faithful student than Coleridge) repeats it in *The Prelude*:

16 Sigmund Freud, *Repression* (1915), ed. Angela Richards, Pelican Freud Library (Harmondsworth, Penguin, 1984), XI, 147–8. There are a number of Freudian concepts and terms analogous to those of associationism. The charge that makes an idea especially vivid he calls 'hypercathexis'; his version of the double relation he calls 'supervalency'. Hartley's 'perpetual recurrency' has something in common with the compulsion to repeat, a parallel that will be explored in the next chapter but one. See J. Laplanche and J.-B. Pontalis, *The Language of Psychoanalysis*, trans. Donald Nicholson-Smith (New York: W. W. Norton, 1973).

Hard task to analyse a soul, in which,
Not only general habits and desires,
But each most obvious and particular thought,
Not in a mystical and idle sense
But in the words of Reason deeply weighed,
Hath no beginning.   (*The Prelude* (1805), II, 232–7)

Associationist narratives

The symptoms of endless reciprocation are evident not only in the casual
starts and indeterminate conclusions of Shandean stories, and of the stories
within those stories, but also in the incidents, gestures and phrases that compose them: 'Each Part, Faculty, Principle . . . seems to extend itself into the
Boundaries of the others, and, as it were, to enclose and comprehend them
all' (*OM*, I, 29). When characters *rotate* and discourses *roll*, when sermons are
composed on circuits and lovers go 'round, and round, and round the world',
it is fitting that the story itself should imitate the dual rotation of the earth
or the twin coiling motions of peristalsis (*TS*, 4.17.292; 3.34.224; 7.31.521).
Tristram is trying to 'make ends meet', to 'wind this round to where I set
out', by always 'going a little about' (*TS*, 8.6.545; 6.33.463; 5.7.362). The
signature of this boundless turning is always a doubling, whether of an impression and an idea, a literalism and a figure, or a beginning and an ending.
That is why pleonasms and pleonastic puns are so frequent: vexation upon
vexation, *Life* upon life, chance upon chance, chapter upon chapters, and so
on. *Tristram Shandy* is, after all, a 'book of books' (*TS*, 3.33.218) in which
originals and copies perpetually circle one another, and parallels accompany
each other to infinity. Everything encounters its double, so that even the
simplest proposition may look at itself: travellers have '*wrote and gallop'd*' and
'*gallop'd and wrote*', noses might fall off bodies and bodies off noses, you can
have '*an old hat cock'd*——*and a cock'd old hat*' (*TS*, 7.4.482; 4.258; 8.10.549),
and finally, in a combination of the pleonasm, the chiasmus and the
hypallage, you may suffer, or not suffer, from

> Zeal or Anger——or
> Anger or Zeal.   (*TS*, 8.2.541)

In an astute discussion of *Tristram Shandy*, Jina Politi argues that the ruling
figure of the book is syllepsis, the constant play between the levels of literal
and figurative meaning, and that it transcends its rhetorical function to
become 'the great principle of union and generation'.[17] Friedrich Nietzsche,
whose favourite figure in the undoing of 'the old error of original Cause' is
the hypallage, counted *Tristram Shandy* his favourite novel because it is a

---

17 Jina Politi, *The Novel and its Presuppositions* (Amsterdam: Adolf M. Hakkert, 1976), p. 144.

history of a birth and a rebirth.[18] The importance of both figures is undeniable. Syllepsis belongs with hendiadys as a branch of the pleonasm; hypallage, 'an interchange of two elements of a proposition, the natural relations of these being reversed' (*OED*), is the dominant figure within the narrative structure of the novel. The reversal it always accomplishes is that of cause and effect, as Walter explains to Toby in a conversation about love:

As my father told my uncle Toby upon the close of a long discussion——'You can scarce,' said he, 'combine two ideas together upon it, brother Toby, without an hypallage'——What's that? cried my uncle Toby. The cart before the horse, replied my father———And what has he to do there? cried my uncle——Nothing, quoth my father, but get in——or let it alone.   (*TS*, 8.13.552)

Walter goes on to give his brother an example of a hypallage when he tells him that love is 'not so much a SENTIMENT as a SITUATION' (*TS*, 8.34.589). In effect, he is saying that any narrative of love mistakes its upshot for its outset.

The love stories favoured by Tristram are all reversible. The 'shock' at the end of the Amours caused by the 'blow' at their 'first spring' is merely a repetition inside the metaphor of love-militancy of events in Flanders that renders cause and effect interchangeable. The cannon that caused the damage to Toby's groin is duplicated by Mrs Wadman's eye, whose carriage (compared with a gun's) gives it the power to cause alterations in the same place. Toby is equally patient under both accidents, until his sieges of citadels (including Mrs Wadman's) are thwarted by a woman's underhand diplomacy – Queen Anne's Treaty of Utrecht and the 'secret articles' in the widow's instrument of surrender. The metaphor keeps exact pace with the historical framework, just like an impression and an idea, until maximum excitement is reached with Mrs Wadman and Toby manoeuvring over the actual map of Namur, when it becomes hard to say which determines which.

The Strasburgers at the end of Slawkenbergius' Tale await a man with a big nose who doesn't arrive, repeating the beginning when Julia lingers days and nights at her lattice for the large-nosed man who fails to appear. The predestined ball that finds its billet in Trim's leg parallels the predestined hand that goes to the same spot, and his fall in the field of battle, like his fall in the field of dalliance, is owing to an explosion that 'burst upon me, an' please your honour, like a bomb' (*TS*, 8.22.573).

An intriguing short narrative in *A Sentimental Journey* – not of love but of dying – provides a fine example of narrative hypallage. In the episode entitled 'The Fragment. Paris' Yorick meets his specular double in the form of the notary who is about to transcribe from the last words of a moribund gentleman a story that will 'kill the humane, and touch the heart of cruelty herself with pity' (*ASJ*, p. 255). Inflamed with a desire to begin, the notary has

18 Cited in Paul de Man, *Allegories of Reading* (New Haven: Yale University Press, 1979), pp. 83, 108–9.

his loaded pen poised over a sheet of paper, awaiting the incidents of this remarkable tale of misery. When Yorick discovers that this is the only part of the story he possesses, the notary comes exactly to resemble him as he, no less inflamed with a desire to translate the transcription, sits with his pen hopelessly poised above a sheet of paper. Apart from the obvious parallels between unspent pens in this story and thwarted love in the others, there is a further reverse symmetry. The story which causes Yorick to resemble the notary could equally well be the story that a man confronting a blank sheet of paper might write down as a parable of his blockage, inventing a notary who resembles him.

It is worth treating the novel as a 'whole' – a history of a birth and a rebirth and a conception and a reconception – in the light of the narratives it contains, because its failure to evolve as a coherent story of origin and growth is a repetition of their hypallagic structures. Broadly speaking, the book begins and ends with the same elements of copulation, conception and impotence being put into agitation by an interruption. The earlier version of this scene is almost an associationist parable designed to show how causes and effects involve each other and how it can have no claim itself to originary status. In the animalculist account we are given of Tristram's conception, the homunculus is darted, or dribbled, from Walter's vasicles into his wife's womb. The miniature infant is printed first with the shock of Mrs Shandy's interruption, and subsequently with the frets and tumults of her arguments with her husband about how and where to give birth. This far Tristram's interpretations of the event would be Locke's too: the mother's unfortunate question, arriving at the very moment when the transfusion of animal spirits is taking place, twists the 'tracks and trains' of his ideas out of alignment and leaves them forever awry. But if this affliction is to be credible, the homunculus cannot be a *tabula rasa*; he must already possess a brain marked by the traces of association. The shock of the interruptive conception can distort associated ideas only if they are there to be distorted. Three chapters later it turns out that the shock itself was owing to the associated ideas of copulation and clockwinding in Mrs Shandy's brain, put there by Walter Shandy's habitual discharging of heterogeneous family duties on the same day of the month. By this time it isn't the misinscription of a blank slate that is being dramatised, but association as a cause of association. Here is comic proof of Hartley's hypothesis that association is self-empowering, and that the associative trace is always already there.[19]

Is Tristram saying simply that the homunculus bears the marks of paternal associations, and that the male blood-line determines his temperament as it

19 The Derridean implications have been studied in Lockean terms by Ralph Flores, *The Rhetoric of Doubtful Authority* (Ithaca: Cornell University Press, 1984), pp. 116–44. A wider-ranging and more authoritative discussion of the Shandean contribution to the history of thwarted conceptions is supplied by Michael Seidel, *The Satiric Inheritance: Rabelais to Sterne* (New Jersey: Princeton University Press, 1979), pp. 250–62.

does Toby's? I think such an explanation is suspiciously straightforward and, given the bend sinister on the Shandy arms, implies a greater power of origination on the part of the father than he is elsewhere seen to possess. It is more plausible to see the conception as an allegory of what is to become the standard pattern of hobbyhorsical shock. A collection of ideas is dispersed by pain, surprise or consternation, then the ideas are gradually recollected in a slightly different form. In the conception scene the collection is represented by the ideas dictating Walter's methodical conduct of his Sunday nights; the shock is supplied by Mrs Shandy's question; the recollection under a different form is Tristram. He is not so much *conceived*, as *combined*.

In these terms Tristram has survived because he functioned as an impression that was occasioned by, and could instantly locate, cognate associated ideas. In their primitive form these associations are linked pairs of ideas: conception/interruption and copulation/time. The suggestion in the second pair – that life begins to decay as soon as it has been created – is sharpened by the paradox implicit in the first – that the moment of generation is almost one of extinction. Just how closely notions of annihilation follow those of his own conception is evident in the train of ideas that leads Tristram from himself to Yorick, a man whose life is lost, narratively speaking, amidst the clutter of midwifery. A bit further on (and chronologically a bit further back) Mrs Shandy's wind and water pregnancy produces the nullity Tristram would have been had he not been combined with the very associations now linking pregnancy to annihilation. The perfect repetition in reverse of Tristram's conception, its hypallage, is the narrative of the arrival of the news of Bobby's death. Once again Walter is interrupted in the midst of a supposedly rational and repetitive exercise by a question from his wife; only this time he loses a child instead of acquiring one.

In these examples the death of a male is linked either to the intervention of a female or to ideas associated with human reproduction. These linkages are linked in turn to the stories of Cornelius Gallus and Trim's brother Tom, men who die, or who seem to have died, for the love of a woman. The hypallagic versions of these tales are those of Amandus and Amanda and of Mrs Le Fever, where the woman dies as well as the man, or instead of him. Still within the pattern of these associations is the account of Susannah's rising sexual interest in Trim as he talks of death; and so are the variations played on the theme of women and wounds: the Beguine and Trim's knee, Mrs Wadman and Toby's groin, Susannah and Tristram's penis. The wound given by La Fosseuse to the word 'whiskers' is the verbal equivalent. Tristram's lung haemorrhage in the middle of dalliance with Jenny is a restatement of the combined ideas of male vulnerability and female accessibility. It is what Jenny *says* then, by way of interrupting her lover's interruption, that Tristram, 'a man, proud, as he ought to be, of his manhood', confesses nearly sinks him to the centre (*TS*, 7.29.516). It tends to be the words of women

– statements of disbelief or curious questions – which throw into doubt the manhood Tristram is talking of.

Because Tristram's first impressions were instantly combined with ideas, he is unable to pursue his anti-feminist and anti-sexual biasses to a univocal extreme – although his parody of a Lear-like sexual disgust shows that he could manage if he did (*TS*, 8.11.550). By associating ideas of interrupting with ideas of sexuality he takes the sting out of both. To be interrupted in a sexual encounter is to be saved from the extinguishing sexual climax. To interrupt the account of Le Fever's death is to keep the Lieutenant in a perpetual alternation between opposite possibilities. In the stories of Diego and Julia, Trim and Beguine, Trim and Bridget, Tristram and Nanette and Tristram and Maria, the anxieties of sexuality are replaced by the delight of endless delay through an interruption that always prevents the conclusion, the consummation, the thing itself. As a child of interruption, then, Tristram bears the stigmata on his nose and penis: but to have had his beginning *and* his end cut off, as it were, are accidents rich in potential advantages. The tropes accompanying the hypallages of his narrative, for example, are calculated forms of self-interruption, the digression and the aposiopesis.

A Sentimental Journey is constructed in the same way. Yorick goes to France with nothing but ideas, most of which are irrelevant to his new circumstances as traveller. Out of his first impressions and the few ideas that are of use, he makes a set of metaphors that are endorsed or contradicted by his subsequent experiences. These impressions are derived from eating, drinking, parting with money, exchanging goods and holding hands. Of the ideas Yorick brings out of England, horror of absolutist government, a love of liberty and doubts about the sincerity of the French sublime are the most useful. Without doubt, the finest idea and the most perfect metaphor are evolved from the situation he finds himself in with Mme de L***, sustained (despite Yorick's crass commentary on such a remarkable chance) through nine exquisite scenes of lifted, proffered, withdrawn, regained and throbbing hands. Yorick ties his impressions and ideas into a metaphor announcing the prospects of his journey and even the literary form it will take:

What a large volume of adventures may be grasped within this little span of life by him who interests his heart in every thing, and who, having eyes to see, what time and chance are perpetually holding out to him as he journeyeth on his way, misses nothing he can *fairly* lay his hands on.   (*ASJ*, p. 114)

At some time during his journey all Yorick's metaphors will be realised. The metaphor (the effect of impressions received in accidental circumstances) will be reflected in a set of further circumstances, either as desire or satisfaction. A realisation is analogous to the double relation of ideas and impressions. It is also like a hypallage to the extent it reverses the development from impression into idea; and like a pleonasm because it superimposes a figurative arrangement on a literal one. Sentimental food and wine, for example, re-emerge in 'The Dead Ass' and 'The Supper'. The metaphor of sentimental trade is realised in 'The Sword' and 'Le Patisser', and that of equitable brokerage in 'The Gloves' and 'The Fille de Chambre'. In these two episodes Yorick gives money to women and they give him back the hand of his opening situation. The gloveseller offers her pulse, and the fille de chambre seals a bargain of honour with her hand. For his part, Yorick helps the fille de chambre dispose the two volumes of Crebillon's novel about her person and manages, what with hands and volumes, to realise perfectly the original metaphor of hand-travel in circumstances of mutual indefinite manipulation. In the sequel two hands, a lap, a neck and an ankle are traded and the result is a literalisation – the shock that always meets those who rise too high. After the tumble on the bed, Yorick's metaphor shatters into its literal elements. All figurative buoyancy is lost as cash becomes just cash, hands hands, volumes volumes, and women paid for giving pleasure to men, prostitutes.

For the next stage of his travels, Yorick develops two impressions first registered in the episode of The Monk. He replaces the trade metaphor with that of beggary; and having had the riddle of the Parisian beggar explained to him, he launches on his beggarly system of cheap eating. Disgusted with himself, he jettisons the begging for Lorenzo's higher rising, that glance 'at something beyond this world' (*ASJ*, p. 71), and this carries him to the pinnacle of Mt Taurira and the oscillations of the great 'SENSORIUM' itself. The book ends with a literalisation that retraces, in slightly modified form, the first impressions of travel. At the beginning Yorick moved from silence to food and wine, then from the false confidence they inspired to a hand, and from the hand to a woman to whom he makes an unsuccessful proposal about sharing a carriage. Here a woman again appears by chance, and stimulated by food and wine he makes a proposal about sharing a chamber; this results in a hand *unfairly* encountering a woman's body, followed by silence. Like *Tristram Shandy*, which ends with Walter once more interrupted by his wife while he is confounding the business of creation with that of destruction, *A Sentimental Journey* ends where it begins, interrupted *out* of a process it was interrupted *into*.

All parts of a Shandean narrative fall into patterns of indefinite mutual commentary, comparable to Hartley's world of endlessly involved analogies and Hume's of reversible sequences. The only constraint upon this widening gyre of associations is the core of combined ideas that constitutes the self. But then the possibilities of self-reproduction in mirror-circumstances and mirror-texts are *almost* limitless. The promotion of these self-reflections – one thing on top of another, one thing repeating or mocking another – is a peculiar form of narcissism because it never proclaims the unity or identity of the reflected object. The doubling is, like a hobbyhorsical pleonasm, a figuration of the fragmentary, one imperfection mirrored in another. Its virtue is the illusion that time and chance can never destroy things whose outlines shimmer into one another, and whose power of alternation and repetition seems endless. Because Tristram's identity is of uncertain origin and because there are at least two Yoricks, they are able to inhabit and be inhabited by other texts, while telling stories whose ends repeat their beginnings.

Certainly *their* texts were eagerly entered by Laurence Sterne, who first of all 'Shandied it away' until he adopted the sedater styles of Yoricking and Braminising. It was in fact *Tristram Shandy* that the Comte de Bissy was reading, not *Hamlet*, when the other Tristram paid him a visit at Versailles.[20] In the year before his death there were moments when Sterne felt his life had become part of the story of his first novel. He told Eliza Draper that every sleepless night he had suffered since her departure was a repetition of 'Corpl Trim's uneasy night when the fair Beguin ran his head'. A few days later he was subjected to a humiliating examination and diagnosis by his doctors, and thought it made a story 'as comically disastrous as ever befell one of our family – Shandy's Nose – his name – his Sash-Window are fools to it' (*Letters*, pp. 326, 329). The blurred line between fiction and biography, their reciprocal doubling, consoled Sterne because it suggested *perpetual* recurrency. In his last letter he tries to restage the scene of Le Fever's postponed demise, with Colonel James substituting for Toby, Lydia for Le Fever's boy, and himself, of course, for the Lieutenant whose death is never quite narrated.

20 See *Letters*, pp. 151, 157, 402–3.

4

Narratives and readings

Sterne's illusion that he was inhabiting his own text, or that his life had become a quotation or a continuation of it to the point where he could read himself in what he had already written, shows him exploiting (perhaps beyond reasonable bounds) two related associationist positions. If there is no point of origin at which the efficacy of a cause can be declared, then not only are causes interchangeable with effects, origins with ends, but authors are interchangeable with their texts, and readers with authors. This joint-sharing in the common fruit of literary labour is not possible, however, without a degree of *belief*, which arises from the intensification of an idea (analogous to an effect) to the degree where it may become indistinguishable from an impression (analogous to a cause). This intensification is in turn not possible without a prior structure of ideas forming either the inducement for the believer to believe or the frame of that belief. Sterne seems to be grasping all of these implications when he writes to Dr John Eustace: 'A true feeler always brings half the entertainment along with him. His own ideas are only call'd forth by what he reads, and the vibrations within, so entirely correspond with those excited, 'tis like reading *himself* and not the *book*' (*Letters*, p. 411). An examination of the development of this narrative intimacy will show how neatly Sterne was plaiting ideas and images from Hogarth into his imitations of Cervantes in order to foster opportunities for hypallagic rearrangements of writer, reader and text. It will also become evident that intimacy of this order is not achieved or maintained without risk.

Hogarthian outlines

While the first two volumes of *Tristram Shandy* were still in manuscript, Sterne was tackled by one of his readers for overdoing the description of Slop's arrival at Shandy Hall. He replied, 'I will reconsider Slops fall & my too Minute Account of it – but in general I am perswaded that the happiness of the Cervantic humour arises from this very thing – of describing silly and trifling Events, with the Circumstantial Pomp of Great Ones' (*Letters*, p. 77). Evidently the reconsideration produced little or no change, because the description we read of the collision between Obadiah's turbulent coach horse and Slop's

dainty pony is still filled with *minutiae*, particularly the sequence concluding
with the simultaneous loss of the doctor's seat and his presence of mind. It
is situated, however, at a point in the evolution of Tristram's narrative technique where the plan of being lavishly exact with the 'many circumstances
relating to myself' (*TS*, 1.6.10) is undergoing modification, reflected in the
adjustments made to the category of his work, which starts out as 'this
history', slips into 'a history book . . . of what passes in a man's own mind',
and is currently adrift as 'a book apocryphal' (*TS*, 1.10.17; 2.2.85; 2.8.104).
In this episode he settles the question of what to leave in and what to leave
out of his book by including all details up to Slop's arrival in the house, and
resorting to ellipses thereafter. The narrative paraleipomena make the spaces
the reader's imagination is called upon to fill: ' 'Tis his turn now;——I have
given an ample description of Dr Slop's sad overthrow, and of his sad appearance in the back parlour;——and his imagination must now go on with
it for a while' (*TS*, 2.11.109).

    In the beginning Tristram is untroubled by questions of what to include,
what to omit. He sees himself as an historian to whose work even the most
tangential facts are material. What with 'archives at every stage to be look'd
into, and rolls, records, documents, and endless genealogies' (*TS*, 1.14.37),
not to mention the anecdotes and hobbyhorses of the Shandy family, the story
itself is lost in the clutter of prefatory corroboration. Such devotion to the collection of facts and memorials allows Tristram to claim an impartiality which
distinguishes him in two respects from an historian like Tacitus: it is both all-
including and non-determining. 'My way is ever to point out to the curious,
different tracts of investigation, to come at the first springs of the events I
tell;——not with a pedantic *Fescue*,——or in the decisive Manner of Tacitus,
who outwits himself and his reader;——but with the officious humility of a
heart devoted to the assistance merely of the inquisitive' (*TS*, 1.21.66). Hence
the importance accorded to the dating of his conception, and the need to quote
documentary and oral evidence in support of his conjectures. The factuality
of his story is what makes it interesting, he seems to suggest, not the inferences that might be drawn from it; and the furthest reach of Tristram's
historical ambition is not to tell the truth, or to point a moral, but to recite
every circumstance connected with his life without danger of being thought
tedious or trifling (*TS*, 1.6.11).

    This, at least, is his ostensible design. In the story of Yorick's life and
death, told as part of the corroborative framework of his birth, he begins to
breach it. This isn't simply a collection of facts, but a moving tale of injustice
to which the reader is invited to respond, where appropriate, with indignation, pity and laughter. An index of the rhetorical momentum of the story is
the gradual disappearance of the phraseology of historical authentication,
such as 'the truth of the story', 'to prove the truth', 'to speak the truth', 'in
plain truth', and 'honest truth', and its replacement with allegory, dramatic

dialogue and the exploitation of the literary, rather than the genealogical connexions between Yorick and his Shakespearean ancestor. In this respect the
evolution of the narrative technique closely follows the disclosure of Yorick's
character. They both commence by being utterly straightforward, Yorick
translating his impressions 'into plain English without any periphrasis', and
his narrator transcribing his facts with equal fidelity from vellum manuscripts.
Yet the story has had to be told because Yorick has withheld 'the truth of the
story', assigning any reason but the real one for his odd choice of horse. The
story develops its own form of narrative reserve by having its final scenes or-
namented with metaphors, allusions and quotations, its narrator using other
words than the unparaphrased language of impartial history to draw 'the
moral of my story'. This shift from direct narrative methods to more oblique
ones, and from a commitment to purely historical truth to standards of
sententious probability, is taken a step further in the narrative at large when
Yorick's sermon subsequently drops into it so that it can be read out by Trim
to the company in the parlour of Shandy Hall, by way of extra commentary
on the story of his life and death.

    This shift is signalled by three references to Hogarth, as we partly saw in
the first chapter. The first is Toby's aposiopestic **** and the announcement
of the principle of the complemental *poco piu* and *poco meno*: 'Just heaven! how
does . . . the insensible MORE or LESS, determine the precise line of beauty
in the sentence, as well as in the statue!' (*TS*, 2.6.100). The second is the appeal to Hogarth's authority as justification for leaving the reader partly
dependent upon his or her own imagination: 'Such were the out-lines of Dr
Slop's figure, which,——if you have read Hogarth's analysis of beauty . . .
you must know, may as certainly be caracatur'd, and convey'd to the mind
by three strokes as three hundred' (*TS*, 2.9.104–5; Hogarth, *Analysis*, p. 135).
The third is the attitude struck by Trim for the sermon-reading, which falls
perfectly within 'the limits of the line of beauty' (*TS*, 2.17.122). These three
allusions form a quite subtle, if condensed, narrative manifesto. In terms of
immediate demands, centring on Slop, Hogarth is being used to answer
Sterne's Yorkshire critic. The happiness of the Cervantic humour, he is made
to point out, depends on a judicious mixture of the overdone (the *poco piu* or
three hundred strokes) and the underdone (the *poco meno* or three strokes). The
aim of implicating the reader by means of this dual appeal to curiosity and
imagination is going to have its ultimate application in the Amours, a story
both singular and 'Cervantick' from which Tristram will expect the maximum of narrative intimacy, since his reader's brain will receive 'the same
impressions . . . which the occurrences themselves excite in my own'
(*TS*, 4.32.337).

    The application of these Hogarthian references backward to Yorick's story
and forward into the reading of his sermon provides an intriguing commentary on the basic narrative position. It is clear, for example, that the gestures

of historical authenticity in the story of a parson who is explicitly compared with Don Quixote are meant to be weighed with the the three strokes, literally the three words – 'Alas, poor YORICK!' – which terminate it. Here the *poco piu* and the *poco meno* are typically in action before they are mentioned, practised before they are theorised. The inclusion of the reader in this alternation of minuteness and tact is likewise accomplished before it is formally demanded, since the momumental inscription of those three words is already 'read over' by everyone walking past Yorick's grave, and echoed 'with such a variety of plaintive tones' as suggests attempts to match the enigmatic 'Less' with an historical 'More' (*TS*, 1.12.32). As he prepares to read Yorick's sermon, Trim is just a more prominent reader of a lengthier inscription. The obsessive, almost parodic, detailing of the graceful, oratorical turn of his body forms a narrative flourish of three hundred strokes whose counterpart lies in the three words (' 'Tis my brother') which preface the breakdown of Trim's voluble self-confidence into mournful silence. The arrangement of excess and privation repeats the gestures of historical amplitude in Tristram's tale, whose counterpart is formed out of the three words inscribed on Yorick's monument and the wordless mourning of the black page. In both sequences the emptiness finally described by the elegant curve of the *poco piu*, whether represented by the details of Yorick's indirections or by the attention paid to the physical circumstances of Trim's speech, anticipates the hieroglyph of loss Tristram is to make out of the curl of Jenny's hair, where the swelling 'More' implicates itself in the exiguous 'Less'.

The sermon Trim more or less reads is both a restatement of the principles evolved from the narrative this far and a redramatisation of them specifically as a problem of reading. At the core of the sermon lies the question of belief, or *trust*, proposed by St Paul in the text from Hebrews. Do we believe something to be true or false, good or bad, on the basis of 'evidence and facts', and are the conclusions we reach matters of '*certainty* and fact' (*TS*, 2.17.126)? Or are our minds themselves obscured by motives and interests which 'rise up and perplex the faculties of our upper regions'? Yorick adopts the rhetorical ploy already twice used by Tristram (in his narratives of Yorick himself and of Slop) by asserting the primacy of evidence, of historical circumstances and facts: 'Surely if there is any thing in this life which a man may depend upon, and to the knowledge of which he is capable of arriving upon the most indisputable evidence, it must be this very thing,——whether he has a good conscience or no.' The proposition is no sooner made than it is overthrown by examples of the innumerable self-deceits and partial judgments blocking the road to this sort of certainty. These arise from misreadings, or rather from a false reliance on the texts of honour, law, morality, and so on, which distort or obliterate the testimony of conscience. The right way, Yorick argues in a legal parallel, is to have conscience read the history of an individual's actions against 'that law which he knows already written' (*TS*, 2.17.140).

While reading this doctrine of double reading, Trim manages both to obey and disobey it. When Yorick starts to illustrate the errors of a church that demands nothing but implicit belief from its adherents by going into the Inquisition for an allegory of persecution, Trim starts to read the history of his brother Tom against the written narrative in his hands; or, in associationist terms, the ideas already in his mind start to react with the strong impression of horror he is getting from the sermon. Instead of an oscillation of perpetually recurrent motions, however, his ideas rise quickly into an identity with the impressions because the feeling of anxiety long associated with the former, and newly excited by the latter, provokes that especially vivid interchange Hume calls the double relation of impressions and ideas. This causes the historical and imaginative elements of Trim's reading to collapse into each other, and with a belief as implicit as any Catholic's, Trim beholds his own brother Tom on the rack. 'Oh! 'tis my brother, cried poor Trim in a most passionate exclamation, dropping the sermon upon the ground, and clapping his hands together' (*TS*, 2.17.138). Walter intervenes impressively to re-establish the difference between the two texts:

I tell thee, Trim, again, quoth my father, 'tis not an historical account,——'tis a description.——'Tis only a description, honest man, quoth Slop, there's not a word of truth in it.——That's another story, replied my father. (*TS*, 2.17.139)

In his last three words he marks a point between the extremes of reading Slop represents, that is with total belief or total incredulity, by suggesting that there is a way of finding the truth in a probable fiction ('a description') that doesn't confound it with history. Very economically Walter establishes the common ground shared by good reading, by the sort of moral tale Tristram wanted to make out of Yorick's life, and by the ethics of *trust* Yorick was trying to recommend in her sermon. All three rely on an exemplary adjustment between more and less that controls the relations of history to fiction, and writing to reading.

The lesson Walter teaches Trim is already enshrined in Yorick's monumental inscription and the responses it attracts. It is set out in the familiar form of the pleonasm:

> Alas, poor YORICK!

This is the epitaph, mounted on top of its various readings, which forms the elegy,

Alas, poor YORICK!

The epitaph is Yorick's history contracted to three words; the elegy is a quotation from Shakespeare. Here we tread on the same treacherous ground of comparison as the Count de B**** in *A Sentimental Journey*. It is important not

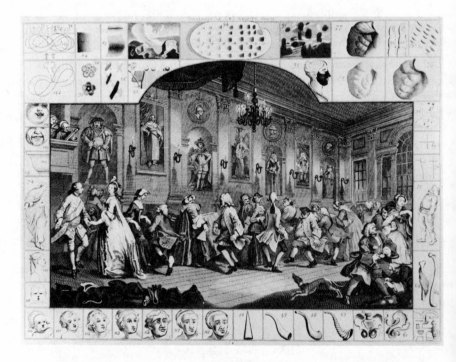

Plate 1

Hogarth's illustration 'The Country Dance' from his *Analysis of Beauty* (1753), with an enlargement (above) of two of his sketches which appear in the borders of the main illustration.

to say that the epitaph and the elegy are 'all one', otherwise we will be guilty of the confusion Trim is shortly to make between historical ideas and literary impressions. At the same time, the resemblance between them, like the resemblance between Yorick and Yorick, is close, and must govern the inflection of the repetition.

A similar lesson, also in the form of a pleonasm, is given by Hogarth on the border of *The Country Dance*, one of the two plates he used to illustrate his *Analysis of Beauty*. Figures 71 and 123 at the top left-hand border (enlarged on plate 1) form a double recapitulation of the scene below. The stenography on the top represents the attitudes of the dancers, from graceful curve to crude semicircle; the rococo flourishes underneath chart the movements of the same figures through the whole set of the country dance. That is to say, the lower box represents motion in time – the history of the dance – and the upper one a moment or a cross-section of that history. Plainly this is the iconic equivalent of Hogarth's remarks about joint-sensation, where our delight in movement, or in lines that suggest it, arises from the combined impressions of bulk and motion. To arrive at that delight in terms of this illustration requires the printing of the top upon the bottom, not to merge them into one, but to locate the point of exquisite coincidence and counterchange.

Although there is no exact analogy between the two pleonasms, it is possible to relate Hogarth's cross-sectional shorthand to the inscription of the momentary, the record of the impression of humanity in action, which is transferred intact to the reader's imagination; and to relate the pattern of the dance to ideal conceptions or memories of the whole, and therefore to the associations that form the background of reading. Thus the upper box corresponds to the elegiac exclamation, the immediate response to the passing of life represented by the bare inscription on a gravestone; and the lower matches the inscription-as-epitaph, the history of a life comprehended in a quotation. The relation is like that of *plan* to *whole*, whose mutuality and interdependence Tristram will later claim as the characteristic of his semi-spontaneous narrative (*TS*, 8.2.540), since it is a question of seeing the same words as manifestations of different impulses – one belonging to immediate circumstances and the other to their ordering through time.

Thus an impression of the moment, printed on the reader's sensorium by means of the *poco meno*, is fetched into a potentially idealising alliance with a set of ideas whose symmetry is suggested by a flourish – in the line itself or in the literary allusion the inscription includes – gesturing at the *poco piu*. Tristram's reading of Jenny's greying curl works like this: the real, immediate sign of age achieves pathos in the doubling over of the impression of the instant with the idea of passing time, which is then honoured in the paraphrase from Job. On the other hand, if the sermon-reading is squeezed together, it forms the very reverse of these relations. It begins with the flourish of Trim's oratorial attitude, struck while he quotes the text of scripture; but the ideal elements associated with this coincidence of rhetorical competence and textual authority are successively expelled until he is left reading then experiencing the present fact of his brother's torture and death.

The joint-sensation expected by Tristram is, like Hogarth's, a multifarious compound. The primary impulse in its formation is the play of resemblance and difference; this is heightened by the twin apprehension of the moment and of passage, which tilts the vertical axis of the pleonasm and the hendiadys into the horizontal line of the hypallage. It is like drawing out the structure of a pun into a narrative sequence. Almost inevitably, this will be accompanied by mixed feelings of sadness and merriment as the comic underplot (or overplot in Hogarth's case) crepitates against the tragic ideal. Yorick on Yorick, like stick-figure upon swirl, merely schematises the mixture that is represented at large in the narratives they border – of a parson who dies in a joke for telling jokes, and of a dance comprising the most elegant and the most unlovely of human gestures. Needless to say, the growth of joint-sensations is aborted by the failure of an idea to encounter an impression or by an impression so powerful it leaves no trace of the ideas it has combined with. Slop's incredulity during the sermon-reading is a specimen of the first; Trim's passionate exclamation an example of the second. Good writing and good reading, like the *trust* recommended by the sermon, depend on a binocular engagement with the facts and the texts that assist our response to them.

A sign of the risk of an imminent excess of belief, both in Yorick's story and his sermon, is allegory. The last scene of his tragedy is a tableau, with Cruelty and Cowardice, urged on by Malice, striking Yorick some fatal blows in the dark. In the Inquisition, Religion, Mercy and Justice precede the poor victim to the torture. These allegories are textualisations of history, nods by the narrator in the direction of the reader indicating a bookish symmetry that will enlarge quotation to the status of caption, and reduce representation to that of emblematic illustration. Allegory is a privileging of Hogarth's lower box or of the elegiac version of 'Alas, poor Yorick!' It generates incredulity among its audience because mere ideas supplant human agents and, as eighteenth-century critics often noted, verisimilitude becomes impossible.[1] But for the allegorist, the perfect shaping of the plot and its agents towards a moral point is what deserves belief, for nothing is imprecise, nothing can be otherwise than it is. When an allegory incorporates an historical character,

---

1 ALLEGORY . . . has this advantage over most other fables, that in it the Author is by no means restricted to such an exact probability, as is required in those fables that instruct us by a representation of actions, which, though not real, must always however be such as might have happened.' Duff, *An Essay on Original Genius*, p. 173. Horace Walpole praises Hogarth for disdaining the standard iconological conceits: 'Another instance of this author's genius is his not condescending to explain his moral lessons by the trite poverty of allegory. If he had an emblematic thought, he expressed it with wit, rather than by a symbol.' *The Works of Horatio Walpole*, 5 vols. (London, 1798), III, 456.

a Yorick or a Tom for example, as one more figure in the play of personifications, it is significant that the circumstantial surplus which nurtures the illusion of contingent and unprescriptive outcomes is pared away to leave the character and his fate in a perfect fit. In fact the allegorical tableau of Yorick's ambush is Eugenius' narrative of Yorick's future, and he is so convinced of its moral accuracy that he interprets Yorick's last joke not as a feat of redoubtable clowning but as the sign of his friend's broken heart. In personifying Yorick as something like Sacrificial Innocence, the victim of Malice and Cruelty, etc., Eugenius forgoes joint-sensations for a message whose clarity requires Yorick's sacrifice. His quotation from Archbishop Tenison on the subject of scapegoats forms the entry upon an elaborate but fatal literary artifice.

While Trim is incapable of this conscious transformation of actual circumstances into moral configurations, his belief combined with Yorick's allegorising strain reconstitutes Tom as a personification along the same lines. Walter is poised on the same sort of bad reading when, peering at the lacquered plate on Toby's coffin – the next best thing to an epitaph – he declares, echoing Tristram, the unparalleled excellence of the dead man. The most amiable impulses account for the need to call the dead unique, and to extract a moral from their departure; but in a literary economy where readers and writers can change places, a bad reading can be self-destructive, especially when it is committed near a grave. But all allegorising moves are dangerous. This accounts for Tristram's antagonism to his father's doctrine of the destiny of names, which translates *Nicholas* or *Tristram* into epithets decreeing (like Cowardice or Cruelty) everything one will accomplish in one's allegory of a life. It explains his warnings to the reader not to mistake his book for a satirical allegory, which would restrict each character to the public history of the person whom he is supposed to represent. Toby's misadventures with Galileo and Torricelli show how overzealous readings destroy more than a book, rebounding literally upon the health of the reader. When Sterne told Eustace he wanted an act of Parliament to cover his novels, 'that none but wise men should look into them', the hint is strong that the readers, not the books, need the protection.

Sterne's sense of this danger partly emerges from the battles being fought among his clerical brethren over the proper reading of the Book of Job, where of course the combative William Warburton headed the allegorising faction who would see the book in no other light than a parabolical representation of the history of the Jews after the escape from Babylonian captivity. It was Warburton's view of allegory as a code with a single clear meaning that encountered the resistance of readers such as Richard Grey and Laurence Sterne, who saw no need for a story to end with Warburtonian éclat, 'where the fable and the moral meet, and, as it were, concur to throw off the mask, and expose the true face of the Subject' (*Divine Legation of Moses*, IV, 277).

Impatient with Warburton's vituperative dismissal of his own reading of Job
as an unresolved dramatic dialogue concerning the question of the hero's integrity, Grey compared the bishop to Esdras Barnivelt, the author of Pope's
Key to the Lock, who interprets *The Rape of the Lock* as a point-by-point satirical
allegory of the Barrier Treaty. Sterne improves the hint in his own *Political
Romance*, where the members of the York political club become vehemently
attached to similar interpretations of the fable of the watchcoat; and we catch
Walter Shandy in the same Warburtonian posture when, with penknife in
hand, he tries to scratch an allegory out of Erasmus' story of Pamphagus and
Cocles.[2] If Sterne needed further evidence of the dangerous perversity of
allegorisers, he had the opportunity of witnessing Warburton, driven to ever
more desperate shifts in defence of his vulnerable reading of Job, allowing
John Towne to accuse Robert Lowth of Jacobitism – a capital offence for
which the Lords Kilmarnock and Balmerino had been beheaded only a few
years before – because he failed to agree either with his hypothesis or with
his dating of the Book of Job.[3]

Incredulity and belief may be occasioned by an overdose of history as well
as of allegory. Had Tristram pursued his early intention of piling up
memorials and genealogies, multiplying the little circumstances of his life
without enquiring into the purpose of the exercise, he would have lost the attention of a reader like Samuel Johnson who, discussing the realism of books
such as *Tom Jones* in his fourth *Rambler*, opined that one might as well look
through the window at what is passing in the street as read a narrative which
limits itself merely to 'a train of events . . . agreeable to observation and experience'. On the other hand, Tristram would have pleased a critic like
Thomas Blackwell, who read the memorials of the *Iliad* with growing fascina-
tion: 'When we sit down to HOMER, and hear him tell over the Number of
his *Ships*, recount his *Auxiliaries*, and produce as it were the *Muster-Roll* of the
two Armies, we can no longer defend ourselves; and in spite of all our Precau-
tion, an Opinion creeps upon us, *"That every Title of what he says is true"*.'[4]
For his part Hogarth was contemptuous of readers who could not see beyond
the accuracy of his representations, praising them solely because they yield
objects 'as they really exist in life . . . without heightening or enlarging them,
and without adding any imaginary circumstances'.[5] Trim's story of the
King of Bohemia and his Seven Castles is an example of the failure of
pointless realism: a haphazard accumulation of little circumstances (except for

2 See Richard Grey, *An Answer to Mr Warburton's Remarks on the Book of Job* (London, 1744), p.
    15; *A Political Romance* in *A Sentimental Journey*, ed. Ian Jack (Oxford: Oxford University Press,
    1972), pp. 214–22; and *TS*, 3.37.229–30.
3 John Towne, *Remarks on Dr Lowth's Letter to the Bishop of Gloucester* (London: L. Davies and C.
    Reymers, 1766), p. 21.
4 Thomas Blackwell, *An Enquiry into the Life and Writings of Homer* (London, 1735), p. 290).
5 Joseph Warton, *Essay on the Genius and Writings of Pope*, 2 vols. (London, 1782; repr. Farn-
    borough: Gregg International Publishers, 1969), II, 82.

the giants), whose petering out is just one more contingency to go with the contingent details it was aimlessly accumulating. As a narrative of chances it has much in common with the three hundred strokes of the Shandy marriage articles – a sort of story told by a lawyer and consisting of nothing but contingencies piled up in hypothetical form – which Tristram contemptuously reduces to three words.

The happiness of the Cervantic humour

In *Don Quixote* the focus for the coalitions and contests between dispersed historical minuteness on the one hand and the formal limitations of allegorical of poetic tableaux on the other is Cid Hamet Benengeli, the Arabian compiler of the knight's achievements. He is partly the result of Cervantes' interest in the possibility of comic prose epic, formally exhibited in the speech of the Canon of Toledo and more unevenly practised in books such as *Tirante lo Blanc*, where 'knights eat and drink, sleep and die natural deaths in their beds, nay, and make their last wills and testaments' (*DQ*, II, 193–4; I, 43). He is also an embodiment of the narrative implications of a story about two such contrasted characters as Don Quixote and Sancho Panza, one transported by dreams of selfless chivalry, the other given up to the practical pursuit of creature comforts. From his first introduction into the complicated narrative machinery of the book, Cid Hamet is praised as 'a very exact historian', one who 'takes care to give us an account of things that seem so inconsiderable and trivial' (*DQ*, I, 179). Thereafter he is regularly saluted as 'the most punctual inquirer into the minutest particles of this authentic history', a chronicler whom no circumstance escapes, not 'even the most minute and trifling' (*DQ*, III, 46). To complete the effect, Cid Hamet turns out to have the ambitions of a poet, despite his skill at chronicling little circumstances. He longs for 'the liberty of launching into episodes and digressions', and mourns the contraction of 'his fancy, his hand, and pen . . . to a single design' (*DQ*, IV, 68).

As a result, his work is the queerest compound of historical exactitude and poetical ornament. He takes several chapters to describe the friendship which developed between Sancho's ass Dapple and the Knight's horse Rozinante. With Don Quixote's arrival at Don Diego de Miranda's house he rises to the occasion and lists every item it contains. Neither of these valiant attempts at historiography survives, the first being suppressed by Cid Hamet himself, and the second being removed by the translator. Their aftermath or shadow is still there, however, in Benengeli's careful weighing of the evidence for five or six kettles of water as being the correct number used by Don Quixote to wash the curds out of his hair (*DQ*, III, 141). But when he indulges his creative bent, he does morning scenes in pastoral ('Scarce had the fair Aurora given place to the refulgent ruler of the day . . .'), he vents philosophical reflections on the shortness of life, and he breaks out into exclamations and apostrophes:

'What praises can be coined, and eulogies invented, that will not be outvied by thy superior merit, though hyperboles were piled on hyperboles!' (*DQ*, III, 106). In terms of Hogarth's double image of *The Country Dance*, Benengeli can manage separately the detailing of local circumstances – the stenography of the *poco meno* – and the larger flourishes of literary ornament which belong to the *poco piu* of formal romance and its interludes; but he has no talent for superimposing them.

By mirroring these alternations between historiographic duty and poetic inclination in the sub-narratives of the main story, Cervantes complicates the question of Benengeli's divided loyalties. His technique is to assign the appropriate narrative mode to the character – history for Sancho, romance for the knight – and then to let them air their disagreements not only with each other but also with Benengeli, of whose methods of telling their story they eventually gain an inkling.

Sancho's stories are composed almost entirely of trifling circumstances, and as long as these are used to corroborate an uncontentious point they are quite successful. Don Quixote reacts to them rather like Blackwell to the muster roll of the Greek ships in Homer: 'Thou producest so many witnesses, Sancho, and mentionest so many circumstances, that I must needs own, I believe what thou sayest to be true' (*DQ*, II, 200). But the more one of his stories multiplies its circumstances, the less likely it is that they will serve any purpose beyond their mere accumulation. When the gathering of detail for its own sake becomes a formal item in the litany of a folktale, all vestiges of narrative intention – plot or moral – are gone: 'I tell it to you', says Sancho of his story of Toralva and the goats, 'as all stories are told in our country, and I cannot for the blood of me tell it any other way' (*DQ*, I, 157). There is as little freedom in listening to this tale as in telling it. When Don Quixote fails to fulfil the preposterous narrative contract Sancho has imposed on him, requiring him to imagine the passage of three hundred goats over the river Guadiana, one by one, the story stops. Any inattention on the part of its audience or its narrator breaks the series of its 'events' and loses the story the medium through which it has immemorially told it itself. 'The story happened neither more nor less, but such as I tell you' (*DQ*, 159). If it is to go on telling itself, it requires the implicit belief Sancho always brings: 'She had a kind of beard on her upper lip; methinks I see her now standing before me.' Like the story of the King of Bohemia and his Seven Castles, which in all respects it resembles, the story of Toralva and the goats is unsustained by any faith on the part of its audience or any purpose on the part of its narrator beyond the enumeration of trifling details for the satisfaction of his own credulity.

Chivalric romance is not much different. It articulates a set of conventional images and encounters – lakes of pitch, gleaming towers, silent damsels and ferocious giants – altogether as arbitrary as the circumstances of this peasant anecdote. It is the habit of hearing and telling them alone that renders them credible. Cardenio's story of an unfaithful mistress and self-exile is typical. It is in fact a replay of Amadis' mad interlude in the wilderness which Don Quixote, prompted by Cardenio's antics, is shortly to imitate himself; but the narrative contract Cardenio insists on (that he must on no account be interrupted) at first reminds the knight of Sancho's story, which likewise demands obedience from the audience as total as the narrator's mesmerised absorption in the truth of what he tells. For Cardenio need merely recite the incidents of his suffering to experience it again: 'The very remembrance of my former misfortunes proves a new one to me' (*DQ*, I, 207). Without an audience that perfectly mimics in its listening the rapt involvement of the narrator in its telling, the tale cannot survive. Lacking all narrative reserve, with no interesting excess to interpret or speculate upon, the story's pretence that it *is* what it tells is destroyed by any symptom of its audience's autonomy – interruptions, questions, comments.

In these two examples Cervantes explores the extremes of narrative self-sufficiency corresponding to the moment-to-moment contingencies and the fatal literary symmetries Tristram associates with history and allegory respectively. The challenge Cervantes sets himself is to show how a story can successfully combine elements of both, agreeable to the Canon of Toledo's theory of comic epic. The adventure of the Cave of Montesinos is the most spectacular failure to meet it. A grotesque compound of *chanson de geste* and trifling circumstances (the exact weight of Durandarte's excised heart, the poor state of Belerma's teeth, and so on), this absurd reverie wins nobody's belief, much to the disappointment of its narrator, Don Quixote, who believes, or claims to believe, every tittle of it.

The puppet-show of *Gayferos and Melisandra* fails in a more instructive way. Here there is a collision between the narrator's taste for historical overproduction and the audience's anticipation of the marvellous economy of a chivalric romance. It produces an outcome very like Trim's response to Yorick's sermon. Master Peter's boy is so keen to establish the authenticity, as well as the heroic pathos, of the simple romance he is narrating, that he emphasises those 'useless and contingent details' which are 'the medium par excellence of the referential illusion'.[6] Despite the knight's impatience with what he takes to be the narrator's impertinence (he even quarrels with the accuracy of some of the details of local colour), the mixture of particularity and chivalric formula excites in him a peculiarly intense belief in the reality of what is being narrated and shown. So he draws his sword to defend the escaping lovers and demolishes the pasteboard figures of which the illusion consists.

6 Gerard Genette, *Narrative Discourse*, trans. Jane E. Lewin (Oxford: Basil Blackwell, 1980), p. 165. See also Edwin Williamson, *The Half-way House of Fiction* (Oxford: Clarendon Press, 1984), pp. 150–60; and for a valuable conspectus of Augustan theories of imitation, probability and narrative, see Douglas Lane Patey, *Probability and Literary Form* (Cambridge: Cambridge University Press, 1984), pp. 177–259.

A comparable mixture of allegory and history, as we have seen, excites in Trim a belief so potent that he drops the sermon he is reading and has to let Walter carry on. In both cases the critical mixture of shapeless fact and artistic form destroys the narrative, not simply because the party stricken with belief interrupts it, but because belief coincides with the fragmentation of the leading characters. Trim tells how Tom is being disjointed on the rack; in his efforts to match his account of her rescue with deeds, Don Quixote cuts off Melisandra's eye and nose. His excuse for this barbarity has the familiar tautologous ring: 'To me Melisandra appeared to be Melisandra, Don Gayferos was Don Gayferos, Marsilius Marsilius, and Charlemain was the real Charlemain' (*DQ*, III, 214).

Laddered stockings and the story of Le Fever

I want to extend the comparison between Benengeli's and Tristram's narrative techniques by analysing two stories where they are at the fullest stretch. Benengeli's best story about Don Quixote is told at an uncanny pause in his career. The knight is the increasingly unwilling guest of the Duke and the Duchess, both of whom have been such ardent and credulous readers of the first part of his history that they have decided to hijack the second part, and by means of an elaborate series of practical jokes to start writing what they have hitherto only read. Their entry into the narrative is like Quixote's intervention into the story of Gayferos and Melisandra and Trim's into Yorick's sermon, but on a vaster and more ambitious scale.

On first arriving at their castle, Quixote has basked in the tautologous glow of being himself twice over ('This was indeed the first day he knew and firmly believed himself to be a real knight-errant' (*DQ*, III, 244)), but his unease grows with each false adventure, not simply because each is more humiliating than the last, but because he cannot question its reality without questioning the groundwork of his own being. He exists because he is believed in, and if belief torments him then pain is his destiny. His adventures are predicated on this belief, which reappears in the creed of Shandeism: 'Were it not that I am positively sure that all these inconveniences are inseparable from the profession of chivalry, I would abandon myself to grief, and die of mere despair' (*DQ*, I, 110). In the castle he is close to that despair; in fact he is tasting the flavour of the death he will die after another reader ambitious to be a writer, Bachelor Samson Carrasco, has contrived for him a terminal humiliation. Like Melisandra he is finding out how the belief of one's audience can ruin one's life.

Dwelling in this twilight world of bad readings turned narrative, Don Quixote is intensely miserable in a way he cannot fully account for. However, he knows he is missing Sancho, who has been despatched to Barataria to be invested in his false island governorship; and he is mortified by the factitious passion of Altisidora, who has been induced to test his fidelity to Dulcinea with outrageous offers of her person. Feeling lonely and trapped, Don Quixote goes off to bed.

As he was straining to pull off his hose, there fell not sighs, or anything that might disgrace his decent cleanliness, but about four and twenty stitches of one of his stockings, which made it look like a lattice-window. The good Knight was extremely afflicted, and would have given then an ounce of silver for a drahm of green silk; green silk, I say, because his stockings were green.   (*DQ*, IV, 73)

After relating this trivial accident with meticulous care, Benengeli then breaks out in an exclamation:

O poverty! poverty! . . . why dost thou intrude upon gentlemen, and affect well-born souls more than other people? . . . Unhappy he, whose honour is in continual alarms, who thinks that at a mile's distance every one discovers the patch in his shoe, the sweat of his forehead soaked through his old rusty hat, the bareness of his clothes, and the very hunger of his famished stomach!   (*DQ*, IV, 73)

Here is a little circumstance, possibly the smallest in the whole book, accompanied by a pompous reflection apparently out of all proportion to the accident. Yet the laughter Benengeli works for in other scenes by means of this sort of contrast is not expected. Introducing us to the story he says it will not make us laugh outright, but 'it may chance to make you draw in your lips, and show your teeth like a monkey' (*DQ*, IV, 70).

Benengeli has an interest in Quixote's distress. He suffers too from the preemptive readings of the Duke and Duchess; for while the hero is stuck inside the structures of their belief, the narrator has nothing to do but merely to record the fantastic excesses which now constitute the story he used to manage. At the beginning of this chapter of the laddered stocking, he complains of the loss of his own freedom; and finally when all the practical jokes have been played, it will be he who avers that, 'Those who played these tricks were as mad as those they were imposed upon' (*DQ*, IV, 68). In the apostrophe to poverty he gives examples of the humiliation his hero feels, so that the gesture of sympathy ('Even I that am a Moor . . .') neither undercuts nor is undercut by the affirmation, 'All these melancholy reflections are renewed in Don Quixote's mind, by the rent in his stocking.'

Without this ridiculous and minute circumstance, Benengeli has nothing to hang his sympathy upon. The detail provides the impression with which his ideas about poverty and shame can react; at the same time, it allows him back into the story on his own narrative terms, dealing with a matter so insignificant that the Duke and Duchess can know nothing about it. And not only in its trifling and quotidian nature is this incident different from the elaborate mockeries of chivalric achievement being stage-managed through the day. They are all designed to begin in a flourish of knightly competence and to end in comic disaster. Benengeli begins with a tiny example of destruction and ends with a flourish that is a consolation disguised as a mockery. Like the consolations discussed earlier, this is one managed by representing defectiveness or limitation in such a way that it reflects, supererogatively and reconstitutively, the limitations of the consoler.

In Hogarthian terms, Benengeli cuts into the repetitive sequences of the usurped narrative to make a cross-section that relates the impression of an isolated, contingent circumstance to a different order of narrative possibilities. His is a sort of furtive underplot designed to retrieve the narrative flexibility that belonged to him in the first part of 'this most grave, high-sounding, minute, soft and humorous history' (*DQ*, I, 179), but which has now been ossified into the tedious indignities inflicted by the Duke and Duchess on their guest. So he cannot counterpoint his little circumstance against their parodic designs; he must resituate it in a structure their mockery cannot reach. The vertical relation of the laddered stocking to the reflection on poverty fosters a set of horizontal links backwards and forwards along the line of the narrative. These links are Benengeli's private flourish, the equivalent of Hogarth's map of the country dance, and they are made (like Don Quixote's desiderated darn) out of green silk. The reference to the thread the knight needs so badly for his laddered green stocking recalls the green ribbons he tied to his helmet before his very first adventure. It also reminds the reader of the sneers of the hidalgos who watched a yeoman farmer getting ideas beyond his station, one of 'your old-fashioned country squires that . . . darn their old black stockings themselves with a needleful of green silk' (*DQ*, I, 16; III, 25). It anticipates the nets of green thread belonging to the aristocratic Arcadians in which Don Quixote will become entangled as soon as he leaves the castle. Four separate scenes are linked to a ladder in a stocking – a trifling accident that nevertheless organises and represents the associated ideas of poverty, vulnerability and the arrogance of the wealthy. The effect is not unlike those discovered by Robert Lowth in Hebrew poetry, where 'embellishments of diction, derived from one low and trivial object, (as it may appear to some,) . . . add a lustre to the most sublime, and a force to the most important subjects' (Lowth, p. 81). At any rate, when we show our teeth like monkeys, we are experiencing a joint-sensation very close to the mixture of impressions and ideas forming Benengeli's sympathy for the knight. Its efficacy as consolation for a character damaged by the excessive belief of careless readers lies precisely in the government of the level of credulity by careful addition of the ridiculous. Here the minuteness of the little circumstance, just hovering on burlesque, is of great help in Benengeli's enterprise of communicating 'the same impressions to every other brain, which the occurrences themselves excite in his own'. It is a comic token of something serious. In short, Benengeli is demonstrating, inviting and even describing the symptoms of what Sterne calls 'trust'.

The story of Le Fever is like the episode of the laddered stocking because it manages to incorporate a remarkably subtle critique of reading into a narrative which provides an exemplary object, as well as a dramatisation, of the preferred response. This exemplarity is the result of a competition for a structure of maximum probability that takes place between different readers over the bare bones of Le Fever's short life and death. Like the Duke and Duchess, readers want to become writers, and this requires that they draw their own flourishes under the stick figure of the dying Lieutenant. In order to emphasise and stimulate this readerly competition Tristram sets the story off from the background of parlour discussions and bowling green campaigns by separately dedicating it to Lady Spencer and by giving it a running title.

The story of Le Fever is first of all Trim's story. He tells it to Susannah, Jonathan, Obadiah and the cook while, in the parlour, Walter is impersonating Socrates. Evidently it was intended as a further contribution to the array of funerary rhetoric caused by Bobby's death; but it is lost to the narrative at that point, and is finally squeezed in between Walter's theories of education and the beginning of the bowling green campaigns. Tristram can't remember what hindered him 'from letting the corporal tell it in his own words;——but the occasion is lost,——I must tell it now in my own' (*TS*, 6.6.416). A good third of the story is still in Trim's words, however, and he plays a prominent part in arranging and interpreting the facts that compose it. In undertaking to supplement the landlord's account of a sick soldier and his boy with 'a full account', Trim makes himself responsible for all those circumstances – names, dates, origins, destinations, and family histories – which are missing from his story of the King of Bohemia and his Seven Castles. Like a regular history this account goes 'straight forwards', following the same line in which it was acquired. What stops it from becoming a self-telling tale is Trim's desire to give it an ending and a narrative symmetry: 'But alas! said the corporal,——the lieutenant's last day's march is over.' He is partly influenced by the landlady, who has heard the deathwatch all night long and concludes, 'But alas! the poor gentleman will never get from hence.' He is also drawn to establish some sort of connexion between the circumstances of stories and the belief they attract, and he does this by means of a digression on prayer, which fills up the ten minutes between making Le Fever's toast and going up to his bedroom. The landlord explains what is happening above stairs: 'I believe he is going to say his prayers.' The curate remains incredulous, even after the landlady says she heard him say his prayers the night before, 'or I could not have believed it'. Trim gives the curate a briskly circumstantial account of the inconveniences of a soldier's life in order to affirm, 'I believe . . . I believe . . . that when a soldier gets time to pray,——he prays as heartily as a parson.' This leads Toby, Trim's audience at this point, to an affirmation of his belief, on the basis of no facts whatsoever, in the justice of the promotions and breakings that will occur when God conducts 'the great and general review' of his troops on the latter day.

More distinctly than in either Slawkenbergius' Tale or the Amours, the matter of belief – not simply how characters respond to characters but how they start to interpret evidence and signs as probable fictions – is being dramatised within the story itself. Trim's linkage of belief to data is very different from Toby's ample faith in providence. Their memorable disagreement about Le Fever's future, leading to Toby's sublime oath, is owing to Trim's reluctance to ignore the evidence, or to change his allegiance to the landlady's outline of the story, which then collides with Toby's commitment to the landlord's original position, 'I hope in God he will still mend.' 'He shall not die, by G—', is the happy ending of Toby's story, which includes the removal of Le Fever to his own house, the hiring of a doctor, attentive nursing, his recovery and his return to his regiment. This is the story Toby is trying to tell Le Fever when unfortunately he expires. Because Trim's full account contains not the slightest hint of this, Toby objects, 'Thou hast left this matter short.' He has left out the money to get the doctor, and the invitation to Le Fever to change his quarters.

In this conflict of stories, Le Fever's own story – the one about the unfortunate death of his wife by a musket shot – is left the shortest of all. Trim remembers it, and so does Toby, together 'with a circumstance his modesty omitted', although he is unable to recollect why it was, even prior to Mrs Le Fever's death, she and her husband were pitied by the whole regiment. The circumstances put into the reader's hands – that she was killed while being embraced by her husband in a tent at Breda – are startlingly incongruous and fit into no probable sequence of events. The hint of wild impropriety surrounding this misadventure with a firearm is not weakened by the reference to modesty.

The story of Le Fever, then, is formed out of three stories (five counting the landlord's and landlady's), four of which are told by the characters in the story as their preferred ending. As readers of their readings we are equipped (despite the isolation of the tale from its context) with Tristram's flourishes along the horizontal line of his narrative. His equivalent of green silk is two great fables of curiosity, Slawkenbergius' Tale and the Amours, which flank Le Fever's. All three are about the need to find out, about the torment of knowing only a portion of the whole. In words the drummer's wife and Mrs Wadman would readily echo, Toby complains, 'I wish I had not known so much of this affair,——or that I had known more of it' (*TS*, 6.6.418). The three stories deal solely with the methods taken to solve this problem. The parallels with the Amours are very close indeed because the first step taken by Toby and Mrs Wadman is to set their servants on the track of the mystery. Trim goes off to drink with Le Fever's servant, promising, 'I shall get it all out of him.' Bridget promises the same thing to Mrs Wadman of him: 'I'm confident Mr Trim will be for making love to me——and I'll let him as much as he will . . . to get it all out of him' (*TS*, 6.6.418; 8.28.582). After these surrogate investigations have yielded all they can, the parallels run even closer. Toby's six declarations about Le Fever's recovery are matched by the six declarations about looking at Toby's wound blushed by Mrs Wadman; and the five questions he puts to Le Fever are matched by the five Mrs Wadman puts to him (*TS*, 6.10.426; 9.20.623).

While these resemblances are intended to display the difference between interested and altruistic enquiries, between curiosity and what Tristram chooses to call inquisitiveness, they reveal structural similarities which bind all Shandean stories together. They all begin with an enigma whose attempted elucidation will form the body of the story, and whose resistance to elucidation will cause its ending. This means that readers and characters form alliances based on a common need to spell these puzzles into satisfactory meanings; and this means in turn that the story is largely taken up with hypotheses of its ending, often told as small stories within the main one.

The structural flourish beneath the little circumstances of Le Fever includes, of course, the two fables of reading we have already discussed: Eugenius' forecast of Yorick's death and Trim's mistake with Yorick's sermon. If Slawkenbergius' Tale and the Amours show how much damage can be caused by incredulity, they remind us (significantly in the reading of scenes of dying) that excessive belief can be ruinous too. Overcredulity in both is caused by a coalition of circumstantial detail and allegorical symmetry, very like the mixture of authenticity and romance convention that causes all the havoc in Cervantes' *Gayferos and Melisandra*. The allegorical elements in Le Fever comprise the personification of Death, who appears on the lieutenant's last morning with a hand 'press'd heavy upon his eye-lids', and in the semi-personification of the lieutenant himself as the cause – the fever – of his own demise. Once more, we find that it is Trim who bends verisimilitude into the service of a fatal allegory, reading forward to Death itself; and we see Toby basing his trust, as he will again in the Amours, on ignorance.

Each reading is determined by the reader's own story. When Toby thinks of wrapping himself up in his roquelaure and braving the cold and the rain to see Le Fever the night before he dies, Trim makes the connexion between two soldiers who, eight years apart, have had a brush with death: 'Your honour's roquelaure . . . has not once been had on, since the night before your honour received your wound.' Toby tries to read Le Fever's story as his own, where he *was* able to get back on his legs and join in marching of a sort. Trim's pessimistic estimate of the odds against rising owes a lot to his experience of the battle of Landen, where 'the number of wounded was prodigious', and where, as 'no one had time to think of any thing, but his own safety' (*TS*, 8.19.569), he lay for twenty-four hours before he was picked up.

At this point the story is taken up by Tristram in his own words. He contrives in the one short death scene to exploit he characteristics of the other stories. He is as historically punctual as Trim: the story goes straight forward

in minute detail, ending with the five failures and the four recoveries of Le
Fever's pulse. But it doesn't reach the fatal closure Trim and the landlady so
confidently predict because modesty, or something like it, leaves the matter
short. A saving silence reprieves Le Fever and gives the optimistic readings
of Toby and the landlord a temporary plausibility. The uncertainty of the outcome in Tristram's reading is matched by the careful pitching of its tone between sedulous pathos and mocking indeterminacy. If one were to read it like
Trim, looking for the death, then one would be inclined to emphasise the
mimesis of its asyndeta. The broken last sentence might represent a grief so
keen that it shuts itself up, or the moment of its ending might be taken to be
coincident with the ending of Le Fever's life. A Tobian reading would stress
the figurative transformation or postponement of the death by discovering in
the sentence's dashes and breaks a rhetorical strategy designed to shift attention from the referent to its own infinite rhetorical ingenuity ('Shall I go on?').
But the point is that neither reading can remain unaffected by the other.

Tristram is cutting his way back into a usurped narrative just like
Benengeli. He is given the opportunity by the extraneous and potentially
ribald circumstance of Mrs Le Fever's death which, like Quixote's laddered
stocking, provides an impression to which his own ideas can be attached.
When we ask what these are, the answer lies in the faltering rhythm that ends
in an interruption: it is the story of his own conception. The ambivalent silencing of a hopeless repetitive movement, reproduced in the stories of Maria
and the goat, of Walter and the Ox-moor, and, in *A Sentimental Journey*, of the
fille de chambre, is the pattern of his own beginning. It also seems to have
been the pattern of Mrs Le Fever's ending. As far as Tristram is concerned,
an aposiopesis in such a place is at least pregnant with possibilities. Without
moving into the sober inferences of Trim's interpretation or behind the
rhetorical screens of Toby's, he can figure the failure of Le Fever's pulse as
an accident equally associated with the start of things and the end of them.
It is a consolation that superimposes the narrator's privations on the circumstances of his stricken character and provokes, like Benengeli's tragicomic
account of twenty-four dropped stitches, joint-sensations which make us show
our teeth like monkeys.

Reader-reflecting narratives

Although reading a story is a reading of oneself, there is usually enough
resistance from other readers, combined with accidents incident to the warfare of literary production (Walter's metaphor applies to the deliberate feroci-
ty of readers such as Didius, Slop and Warburton), to prevent it from acquiring the symmetry we have seen associated with allegory. Occasionally this is
not the case, and the results are as dangerous as Trim's readings of Yorick's
sermon and Le Fever's story. At Le Fever's funeral, for example, Yorick

preaches a sermon which he subsequently reads over to himself with great approval, because underneath it he writes, 'Bravo!' 'It seems to have been his favourite composition', Tristram explains, 'It is upon mortality' (*TS*, 6.11.428). This level of self-approval suggests the sermon would be barren of the sort of consolation Tristram offers the dying man: that it would neither excite joint-sensations, nor deviate from the allegory that began with the hand of Death pressing down the soldier's eyelids, because it is such a perfect sermon on *mortality*. Yorick's part in narratives of death, not to mention his frequent appearances as a death's head on horseback, give a sinister turn to the narcissism he displays on this occasion; for if the pleasure a story affords is proportionate to its resemblance to the narrator's own biography, then Yorick's narrative has a clear and irresistible route to the grave. This is not to allegorise Yorick as Death, but merely to show that unresisted narcissism in reading is another cause or index of the danger of excessive belief: there is no story more credible than a repetition of one's own.

Tristram's great act of narrative hubris flows from a pun that masks higher rising as perpetual recurrency. When he discovers that one day of his life takes up two volumes of writing, and that to write two volumes takes up one year of his life, he fashions himself a paradox of infinity by playing on life as living (life) and life as writing (*Life*). 'I perceive I shall lead a fine life of it out of this self-same life of mine; or, in other words, shall lead a couple of fine lives together' (*TS*, 4.13.286). This will come about because the law of hobbyhorsical incrementality has started to apply: 'The more I write, the more I shall have to write.' The corollary, 'and consequently, the more your worships read, the more your worships will have to read', is finally unnecessary because Tristram later proposes himself as reader as well as writer of his endlessly expanding narrative: 'For my own part, I am resolved never to read any book but my own, as long as I live' (*TS*, 8.5.544). He threatens the same sort of conversion of reading into writing which traps and finally kills Don Quixote, as well as causing the deaths of Melisandra and Trim's brother Tom.

That he is actually running this risk seems to occur to him when he is making his life–writing pun, because he begins with the proviso, 'Was it not that my OPINIONS will be the death of me.' When Death duly pays a visit at the beginning of the seventh volume, Tristram ruefully recalls his calculations and the accidents he excluded from them: 'No——I think, I said, I would write two volumes every year, provided the vile cough which then tormented me, and which to this hour I dread worse than the devil, would but give me leave . . . I swore [my book] should be kept a going at that rate these forty years if it pleased the fountain of life to bless me so long with health and good spirits' (*TS*, 7.1.479). The rolling up of a narrative into its reading produces 'mortality' as inevitably as Yorick's sermon, and Tristram escapes it only by recovering the art of exciting joint-sensations. His strategic pun, whose purpose was ultimately the enshrinement of a single meaning, has briefly transformed him into a personification akin to the self-coincident heroes mentioned in the second chapter, and cognate with Quixote's tautologous recognition of Melisandra as Melisandra. By collapsing *Life* into life, Tristram reads himself not as Tristram on Tristram, a binocular self-consoling double narrative formed out of pleonastic arrangements of little circumstances and textual flourishes, but as Tristram indeed, a self-creating creature who, in common with other personifications, 'is self-consciously obsessed with the grounds of [his] own allegorical being . . . [with] the perfect symmetry of a pure self-recognition'.[7] This allegorising move inevitably introduces destruction and Death into the story. Sterne's growing weakness for reading himself into his fiction is the same equation back to front: it was a sign of how close he was getting to death and Death.

The lesson for the reader, you or me, comes unsettlingly close. A story like Le Fever's presents us with a number of readerly options, one of which is the narrative of our own death.

---

7 Stephen Knapp, *Personification and the Sublime: Milton to Coleridge* (Cambridge, Mass.: Harvard University Press, 1985), pp. 3, 21. In terms of Knapp's Kantian distinction, Tristram's higher rising is a symptom of fanaticism, while his perpetual recurrences are symptoms of enthusiasm.

5

The Shandean sublime

The double principle has been seen operating in the imitative singularities of hobbyhorse riders, in the double relation of impressions and ideas, and in the hypallages and mirrorings of Shandean narrative. The reciprocal play of accident and design common to all these examples has its icon in Hogarth's joint-figure of the country dance, where the cross-section or outline stands in the same relation to the map of the whole set as the hobbyhorsical trifle to its history, as the single impression to the associative structure with which it acts and reacts, and as the minute circumstance of a narrative to the structure that accommodates a specular self-reading. In these analogous pairings, the cross-sectional element is incomplete, contingent, unpredictable and trivial, while the map represents the possibility of order and symmetry. The more this possibility is explored, the more the loose accidents of the upper box are turned into narrative, articulated into a series of necessary connexions that begins to read like a story. As well as reflecting the biography of its reader, this story is likely to cross the frontier of literature proper, either as quotation or as figure. The double principle is always most cleverly and effectively manifest in literary form when the natural incompleteness of the cross-section is reflected in a fragment of a text or in a defective archetype. Real imperfections are then matched with splinters of the written – the figures of a consoling rhetoric – rather than being formally completed by literary supplements. In this sense Hogarth's unfinished oilpainting of *The Country Dance* is more faithful to the schema of his diagrams than the copperplate they actually border.

In the last chapter it became apparent that it was perilous to make a single perfecting principle out the double: that Death is prompt visitor when the twin reading of accidental cross-sections and literary maps is deserted for a single, self-sufficient reading, whether in the form of a self-telling history or a specious allegory. If Tristram Shandy's greatest lapse in this respect is his confounding of life with *Life*, then one of his more remarkable successes is the figurative arrangement of the accidental circumstances of his life vis-à-vis that peculiar document, the *Tristrapaedia*. Joint-product of his father's prescriptive sexuality and his mother's chance associations, Tristram finds the reflection of his accidental reproduction in the ruins of the paternal text. He and his

father dance in and out of the figure of 'general wreck' (*TS*, 4.19.297),
retrieving bits and pieces for remedial purposes. Walter aims to recover his
son, Tristram to give an account of himself; and these desires culminate in
mirror-texts which share the same hero, the same theme and the same accident of a pen that goes slower than the life it chronicles. The more Walter's
book droops under the strain, the more it resembles Tristram's primal scene,
for now as then the father lies 'under an impuissance' which prevents him
from collecting 'his own scattered thoughts' (*TS*, 5.16.372, 374). It is this very
impuissance and scattering that Tristram is able to transform in his own
writing into a pleasant serendipity ('I shall never overtake myself') and then
into the dangerous paradox of recessive accumulation ('The more I write, the
more I shall have to write' (*TS*, 4.13.286)).

The complex relation of literal accidents to figurative wreck-retrieval is illustrated by the missing chapter of the *Tristrapaedia*, the one on sash-windows
and chamber-pots already glanced at under the heading of originality.
Tristram decides 'to render the *Tristrapaedia* complete' (*TS*, 5.26.384) by supplying it with a chapter summarising and moralising the circumstances of his
own seventeenth and twenty-sixth chapters, all about the accidental loss of his
foreskin. In a double move he first of all links the physical damage sustained
by his infant self to the defective pediatric text by way of cause and effect:
what was missing from it is responsible for what is missing from him; then
he links them by resemblance, for the book is curtailed at the same point, narratively speaking, as its hero. But this mutilation in the book gives the child
the opportunity of reconstituting himself by supplying the missing fragment;
a fragment, however, representing his own fragmentation beneath the sash-
window. The father is supplanted not by the act of filial virility pen-borrowing
normally implies: the son gets the right to figure in his father's text by telling
a story of penile reduction that re-establishes the associations between sexual
and autobiographical impuissance.

After Tristram has paid the price of mistaking the limitations of literary
self-production for the boundless liberty of self-origination, being forced to
flee the length of France to get away from Death, he re-founds his literary ambitions on a sounder basis of sexual imperfection. In his Invocation to Cervantes, Tristram mentions his patron's 'wither'd stump', which puts him in
mind of the pistol tinder box he lost in Italy, together with a bad bargain involving 'two hard eggs'. These equivocal accidents recall the injury to his
breeches caused by the ass in Lyons: a combination of rent fabric and a long-
eared animal repeated in the scene with Nanette, where the slit in her petticoat prompts Tristram to find a match for his impotence astride a mule. The
eighth volume begins with a hymn to physical infirmity, 'stranguries,
sciaticas, swellings, and sore-eyes', coinciding with Tristram's resumption of
his *Life*.

To begin a chapter on the sublime by discussing the damaged

hereditaments passing down the blocked passages of Shandean patrilinearity is to mark out the very modest limits of Oedipal resolution governing the Shandean version of it. Although it is impossible to think of the sublime, after the work of Harold Bloom and Thomas Weiskel, without an Oedipal dimension, any consideration of the obscurities, repetitions, digressions and infinities of Shandean texts and prospects (it needs to be said) has less to do with the projection of the father as a god-term, than with the figurative improvement of the general wreck by means of limited collaboration between the pseudo-creator and the quasi-creature. Bearing this in mind will cast some useful light on the texts besides the *Tristrapaedia* that are quoted, imitated and translated in Tristram's and Yorick's autobiographies. In analysing the figurative reconstitutions encouraged by the fragmentation of texts, I shall be indebted heavily to Neil Hertz's work on the sublime, particularly his remarkable essay, 'A Reading of Longinus'.[1]

I'd like briefly to postpone my setting off with one more Shandean Oedipal scenario whose relevance to the latter part of this chapter will, I hope, become clear. We have seen how Yorick's epitaph and elegy form the hinge of a complicated experiment in narrative technique. They fold no less significantly over an event of 1751 in Sterne's own life, which was the incarceration of his mother in the York debtors' prison at the instigation of his uncle, Jacques Sterne. In the letter of expostulation Sterne wrote to his uncle, it is plain he regarded this imprisonment as collusion between the two of them, designed, as he said, to 'do me (as Clergyman) the most real Disservice' (*Letters*, p. 33). The 'Singular Stroke of Ill-Design' aimed against 'a Defenceless Man Who Lives retired in the Country' too closely resembles the confederacy that levels a tale of dishonour at Yorick, ruining his name and ending his life, for the parallel to be accidental.

When the asterisks representing the leaders of this plot, ***** and *****, are made to read Agnes and Jacques Sterne, an odd double allusion to *Hamlet* begins to emerge. Sterne himself is in the position of the prince, his noble father dead ('you remember he died in the Kings Service' (*Letters*, p. 35)) and in his place a wicked uncle who enters into an unholy alliance with the widowed and unnatural mother ('she had forgot she was a *Mother*' (*Letters*, p. 36)) against the son. Like Hamlet, Sterne is tormented by his inability to make known the injustices he is suffering under: 'I own I should have set about immediately by telling my Story publickly to the World, – But for the following Inconvenience, That I could not do myself Justice this Way, without doing myself an Injury at the same time by laying Open the Nakedness of my

---

1 It appears in his collection of essays, *The End of the Line*, pp. 1–20. All the pieces revolve around some aspect of the sublime and add exciting, sometimes provocative, insights into the general theory of it. Figurative reconstitution (especially by means of quotation), the encounter with a specular double, and what Hertz calls the turn at the end of the line or, after Flaubert, *redoublements d'obscurité*, are of special relevance to the following argument.

Circumstances' (*Letters*, p. 33). In the fictional replay, the victim who resembles Sterne in the difficulties he faces in making the truth of potentially damaging stories known to the world, who nevertheless by precept and example recommends 'the naked temper' of a merry, undesigning heart (*TS*, p. 26), and whose root is smitten by the same sort of singular stroke, is called Yorick, not Hamlet. He is named after and likened to the silent skull Hamlet apostrophises in the graveyard scene. Why does Sterne displace his sense of injustice from the prince to the jester?

Apart from his strong preference for the tragicomical, the answer must lie in Sterne's residual fear of ventilating private grievances in public, still strong enough to restrain him from making even the literary parallels too direct. So he inserts two surrogates between himself and Yorick: Eugenius who predicts the jester's death, and Tristram who chronicles it. This leaves Tristram in Hamlet's role vis-à-vis the skull. He tells a tale about the gradual silencing of a man incautiously liberal of tongue – a narrative of a contracting public voice that arrives, via the obliquities of a becoming modesty and three short words on a gravestone, at the total silence of the black page. Yorick suffers in its final form the muteness that constitutes and favours the injustices suffered by Hamlet, Sterne and even Tristram ('I need not tell your worship, that all this is spoke in confidence', he says, still throttled by the need for reticence despite his decision to publish (*TS*, 1.13.36)). As Hamlet ventriloquises with Yorick's skull, using the defaced remnant of the dead jester to satirise the vanities of the living, so Tristram uses Yorick's death as permission to speak more at large; firstly about the very injustice neither Sterne nor Yorick could air in public.

Tristram's and Yorick's is not entirely a common cause of *ekphrasis*, the one causing the other's head to speak. They sit on a see-saw whose fulcrum is the gravestone, rocking backwards and forwards between lively garrulity and mortal stillness through the course of two novels. Apart from the breaks and gaps in his text, Tristram is carried close to silence by the hoarseness he acquired in Flanders, which becomes extreme when Death catches him by the throat so tightly that 'Eugenius could scarce hear me speak across the table' (*TS*, 7.1.480). After his early burial, Yorick pops up to have many a last word in his conversations with the Shandy family, including the very last ones of the book. In *A Sentimental Journey*, where Tristram is reduced to less than an epitaph – a mere monogram on a handkerchief (*ASJ*, p. 272) – Yorick twice loses his voice to end up as he begins, in the silence of embarrassment. That alternation works its way into the *Journal* too, as we saw in the third chapter, where Sterne as Yorick is interrupted by bits of Tristram's narrative at the crises of the very disease that reduces its victims to a whisper.[2]

---

2 The game of mutual substitution played by the living and dead through the medium of a bare name on a gravestone is definitively treated by Paul de Man, 'Autobiography as Defacement', *MLN*, 94 (1979), 919–30.

This competition between Sterne's two Hamlet surrogates for the right to speak in public of their injuries illuminates yet another aspect of the relation of the *poco piu* to the *poco meno*, the three hundred words and the bare three words, that suggested itself first to Tristram as a narrative device while he was trying to solve the problems of narrating Yorick's history. That this alternation between 'More' and 'Less' should keep on surfacing as unfinished business between the narrators-cum-narratees of Sterne's fiction, indicates that the secret narrative of the mother and the uncle they were invented to disclose is more intractable than Sterne, with all his caution, allowed. It is striking how little of that story is echoed in Tristram's family romance, for example, where the uncle is utterly amiable, the soul of benevolence, between whom and the mother there subsists a kind of rueful companionship in the face of the father's oppressions. Possibly this is owing to a displacement from the father to the uncle, so that Toby absorbs the military character of Roger Sterne and thrives; and another from the uncle to the father, so that Walter's beds of justice with Elizabeth represent an acceptable coalition of the uncle and the mother, cleansed of conspiracy and incest. But even if displacement is part of the solution, Sterne's guilt about his mother persists in spite of the elaborate preparations he took for doing himself justice, and it takes the form of Mrs Shandy, a mother who is still a mother (rather than an aunt) and who finds it harder than any other character to get a hearing, despite her injuries.

If the sublime depends, as Freudian critics suggest, on a reconciliation between the father and the son, we can already see something like this occurring between Walter and Tristram by means of figurative play on each other's genital imperfections. However, the uplift and magnanimity associated with the sublime is largely missing from this scenario of shared castration, no matter how cleverly conceived. For that we have to look to Toby, the hidden father and pseudo-soldier. But the stream of energy that flows from the acknowledgment and expiation of real guilt has to be sought in Tristram's case in the figures bordering the silence of the injured mother. We can return to these three levels or sectors of the sublime in a less enigmatic fashion by tracing Sterne's conceptions of sublimity from their 'first springs' to their fullest application in the scenes surrounding the arrival of the news of brother Bobby's death.

Figures of the scriptural sublime

Sterne's interest in Longinus grew out of his concern with preaching. Unlike many commentators and practitioners in the eighteenth century, he turned to the sublime first of all because it was the stamp of good oratory. In his efforts to 'direct five words point blank' to the hearts of his congregation he incorporated Longinian figures into his sermons because he found Longinus recommending the warm irregularities he admired, and mocking the frigid bombast he most detested. When he started writing fiction instead of sermons, Sterne discovered all sorts of new applications of this rhetoric that complicated and to some extent demolished the simpler distinctions of his preaching days. These alterations came about when he began accommodating the sublime to his insights about the functioning of the double principle.

In his sermon 'Search the Scriptures' Sterne arranges a contrast, already very popular, between the Bible and classical poetry. Starting with the Mosaic account of the creation, he introduces samples of both to prove the superiority of scripture over the whole corpus of Greek and Roman literature. His authority is Longinus, 'the best critic the eastern world ever produced', and the only one with the status of an ancient to have read and appreciated the septuagint.[3] Sterne concludes, 'In the classical authors, the expression, the sweetness of the numbers, occasioned by the musical placing of words, constitute the great part of their beauties; – whereas, in the Sacred Writings, they consist more in the greatness of the things themselves, than in the words and expressions.' This contrast is defended with a number of principles drawn from *On the Sublime*.

The first is the importance of the heart as source and object of all good language. Without the faculty of raising passions in himself and his audience, a preacher produces 'laboured and polished periods, an over-curious and artificial arrangement of figures, tinsel'd over with gaudy embellishment of words, with glitter, but convey little or no light'. Those who can be charmed by such frippery while condemning the noble simplicities of the bible as 'barbarism and solecism' have blocked up the channels of feeling (*Sermons*, II, 226–9). The clergy, whose duty is to warm their congregations with sermons that catch fire from fragments of scripture, have failed in their office if false refinement and self-love teach them to 'impose their own trumpery, and foist in whatever may best serve to aggrandise themselves, or enslave the wretches committed to their trust' (*Sermons*, II, 234). For Sterne's part, the cultivation of a gentlemanly, classical polish comprehends all the faults Longinus lists under the heading of pusillanimity – bombast, insipidity, meanness and frigidity – and deserves the contempt in which Longinus holds the servilities and impostures of enslaved minds (*OS*, pp. 102–8). All variations in style and all additions of ornament not vouchsafed by the warmth of emotion imparted to the soul by great things are empty embellishments, 'superficial Pomp and

3 See *Sermons*, II, 230. It is generally thought that Longinus, sometimes called Cassius and sometimes Dionysius, was a Greek writing in Syria in the third century AD. Although his work was rediscovered in the fifteenth century, it wasn't until Boileau's translation and commentary (1674) that he was fully acknowledged in Europe. His reputation in Britain was established by Dryden (*Apology for Heroic Poetry and Poetic Licence*, 1677), Dennis (*The Advancement and Reformation of Poetry*, 1701), and Pope (*An Essay on Criticism*, 1711). In the following discussion my references will be to the most popular eighteenth-century translation, and one Sterne was evidently familiar with: *Dionysius Longinus on the Sublime*, trans. William Smith (London, 1739; repr. Scholars' Facsimiles and Reprints, 1975). Hereafter cited as *OS*.

Garnish' (*OS*, p. 14). Longinus' test for the sublime is to separate those ideas conveyed by 'the mere Sound of the Words' from those ineffaceable 'Impressions on the Mind' made by what is intrinsically grand and lofty; and he suggests that any alteration in the order of the words will quickly expose deficiencies of sentiment (*OS*, pp. 15, 96). Sterne's test is translation. Whatever can be translated and 'yet break forth with as much force and vehemence as in the original' is magnificent and lofty in itself, and will appear so even in the most artless dress (*Sermons*, II, 230). To illustrate Longinus' claim that a naked thought, stripped of all clothing, can challenge admiration, Sterne turns to Joseph instead of Ajax for a silence 'truly eloquent and natural'. The primitive simplicity of the Hebrew sublime, here conveyed by a bare gesture and frequently by language entirely unadorned, ensures its susceptibility to 'simple and literal translations'.

The feeling heart and the powerful originality of its sentiments converse about objects 'grand and lofty, which the more we consider, the greater Ideas we conceive of [them]' (*OS*, p. 15): in Sterne's paraphrase 'the greatness of the things themselves', between whose splendour and the magnanimity of sublime expressions there exists a natural and unbreakable alliance. The sermon summarises a distinct set of preferences and assumptions which will form a powerful orthodoxy among critics of the sublime; so powerful it is often mistaken for a full and complete account of Longinus himself. A sign of this orthodoxy in operation is the equivalence frequently detected between the singularity of the sublime phenomenon and the unambiguous impression it makes, between (as Wordsworth puts it) 'the image of intense unity' and a force which 'suspends the comparing power of the mind'. 'Vast Objects', John Baillie declares simply, 'occasion vast Sensations.' Burke characterises such sensations as astonishment, when 'the mind is so entirely filled with its object, that it cannot entertain any other'. The figures poets are constrained to use on such an occasion induce the illusion that 'the very Objects are set as it were before us', Dennis argues. Dryden reckons that this illusion accounts for the peculiar intensity of Shakespeare's imagery: 'You more than see it, you feel it too.'[4]

When he praises the war-horse in Job (*Sermons*, II, 230), Sterne adopts a commonplace of scriptural criticism belonging to this orthodoxy. It dates back to at least 1712 when 'John Lizard' devotes a *Guardian* (No. 86) to considering

---

4 *The Prose Works of William Wordsworth*, ed. W. J. B. Owen and Jane Worthington Smyser, 3 vols. (Oxford: Clarendon Press, 1974), II, 353. John Baillie, *An Essay on the Sublime* (London, 1747; repr. University of California Press: Augustan Reprint Society, 1953), p. 7. Edmund Burke, *A Philosophical Enquiry into the Origin of our Ideas of the Sublime and Beautiful*, ed. J. T. Boulton (London: Routledge and Kegan Paul, 1958), p. 57. Hereafter cited as Burke. John Dennis, 'The Grounds of Criticism in Poetry' (1704) in *The Critical Works of John Dennis*, ed. Edward Niles Hooker, 2 vols. (Baltimore: Johns Hopkins University Press, 1939), I, 363. John Dryden, 'Of Dramatic Poesy: An Essay' (1668) in *Essays of John Dryden*, ed. W. P. Ker, 3 vols. (Oxford: Clarendon Press, 1900), p. 80.

the difference between classical and scriptural horses, and concludes, 'The classical poets chiefly endeavour to paint the outward figure, lineaments, and motions; the sacred poet makes all the beauties to flow from an inward principle in the creature he describes.' From the beginning of the century to its end, the distinction enforced by this commonplace in favour of the unity of scriptural objects and expressions is tirelessly repeated. In the notes to his translation of *On the Sublime*, William Smith substitutes a scriptural illustration for every classical example cited by Longinus. Hugh Blair authenticates the sublimities of Ossian on the grounds of their resemblance to scriptural figures.[5] More polemically, Dennis dares 'produce a hundred Passages . . . out of Sacred Writ, which are infinitely superior to any Thing that can be brought upon the same Subject, from the Grecian and Roman Poets'.[6] The reformed Jack Belford in *Clarissa* is ashamed to recall 'how greatly I have admired less noble and less natural beauties in pagan authors; while I have known nothing of this all-excelling collection of beauties, the Bible'.[7] The heartlessness of the Reverend Brand, in the same novel, is seen in his 'throwing about, to a Christian and country audience, scraps of Latin and Greek from the pagan classics' (*Clarissa*, IV, 66). Wordsworth's Note to *The Thorn*, where he praises the repetitions and tautologies of the Song of Deborah, forms, along with the Preface to the *Lyrical Ballads*, one of the last but most authoritative defences of scriptural sublimity along these lines.

Addison's contribution to the formation of this orthodoxy is enormous. Not only does he stimulate a new interest in the primitivisms of the Bible and old British ballads, he links the irregularities of ancient poetry to those of the British temperament and tongue (see *The Spectator*, Nos. 135 and 350), prompting a nationalism among English Longinians that makes orthodoxy a political as well as a religious and critical matter, hard to evade except by Europeanised infidels such as Gibbon and Hume.[8] Nevertheless if the

5 Hugh Blair, 'A Critical Dissertation on the Poems of Ossian', in *The Poems of Ossian*, trans.
James Macpherson, 3 vols. (London, 1805), I, 120.
6 'The Advancement and Reformation of Poetry' (1701), *The Critical Works of John Dennis*, I,
271.
7 *Clarissa*, IV, 8.
8 Although Gibbon read Longinus with great enthusiasm in 1762, significantly the period of his
exertions as captain in the South Hampshire militia, he recorded only his most cruel insight
in his great work. Of the effects of loss of liberty upon the sublime mentioned in the treatise,
Gibbon says, 'Here, too, we may say of Longinus, "His own example strengthens all his
laws." Instead of proposing his sentiments with a manly boldness, he insinuates them with
the most guarded caution, puts them into the mouth of a friend, and, as far as we can collect
from a corrupted text, makes a show of refuting them himself.' *The Decline and Fall of the Roman
Empire* (London: Chatto and Windus, 1875), p. 24, n.t. In his essay 'Of Civil Liberty' Hume
takes Longinus' equation between thriving arts and free government and shows how it doesn't
work because of the astounding advances made by the French in all the arts. *Essays Moral,
Political and Literary* (London: The World's Classics, 1903), pp. 91–2. In the same essay he
mentions Addison as a domesticator of Longinus' opinions. For Sterne one of the most plausible examples of this would have been *The Spectator* No. 350 – in fact written by Steele –
where Captain Sentry tells a story of French brutality and English patience and proceeds

double principle, which has exerted such an influence on Shandean characters
and narratives, is to include the sublime, Addison and Sterne are going to
have to be heterodox, and divagate in some way from the sublime triad of the
thing itself, the vast sensation and the original expression all so succinctly
outlined in 'Search the Scriptures'. Addison has been seen already to abate
his enthusiasm considerably for objects which exceed the capacity of the
imagination, because 'the Object [which] presses too close upon our Senses
. . . does not give us Time or Leisure to reflect on our selves' (*The Spectator*
No. 418). The need for this marginal turning room and free moment of reflection, without which the double principle cannot function, results in Addison's
sidelining the founding propositions of the two sublimes that are to dominate
the orthodoxy of the latter part of the century. The first is the immeasurable
vastness of 'the thing itself' that Burke will elaborate; the second is the germ
of the Kantian sublime of the supersensible intuition which Addison defines
but refuses to exploit when he writes: 'The Understanding, indeed, opens an
infinite Space on every side of us, but the Imagination, after a few faint
Efforts, is immediately at a stand, and finds her self swallowed up in the
Immensity of the Void that surrounds it: Our Reason can pursue a Particle
of Matter through an infinite Variety of Divisions, but the Fancy soon loses
sight of it, and feels in it self a kind of Chasm' (No. 420). He has already
defined the conditions of this rational liberty as oppressive to the senses and
inimical to the associative faculties of the mind.

To follow Sterne's parallel movement away from the sublime of identity
and self-comparability, where nothing is unlike itself and which naturally
enough I'd like to call the tautological sublime, we have to look at how he
practises Longinian standards in his sermons. Clearly his predominant wish
is to make his sermons 'dramatic', and to generate the illusion among his audience that they are beholding spontaneous ebullitions of feelings and words.
The figures appropriate to this aim are called by Longinus visions or images,
'when the Imagination is so warm'd and affected, that you seem to behold
yourself the very things you are describing' (*OS*, p. 39–40). The confrontation
of the unitary self with the plenary object is abetted also by the other two
figures of excited address, apostrophe and prosopopeia (*OS*, pp. 47, 66). The
finest 'vision' is undoubtedly of the last agonies of the Inquisition's victim in
'The Abuses of Conscience Considered' – the very sermon read out by Trim
with such tragic results – where each spasm and groan is represented in the
pathetic ejaculations extorted from the preacher by the warmth of his imagination. At this pitch it is easy to transfer one's own reflections to an actor
in the scene, to make the sordid and unmerciful wretch who appears earlier in

to draw a parallel: 'I believe what you Scholars call just and sublime, in opposition to turgid
and bombast Expression, may give you an Idea of what I mean when I say Modesty is the
certain Indication of a great Spirit, and Impudence the Affectation of it.' Here are the
rudiments of Captain Shandy's sublime modesty.

the sermon (for example) condemn himself out of his own mouth. In turn, the preacher cannot refrain from calling out to his characters when cruelty has made them especially distinct, either in a bitter sarcasm – 'Haste, Shimei! – haste; or thou wilt be undone for ever!' – or in the full form of the Longinian apostrophe – 'O Shimei! would to heaven when thou wast slain, that all thy family had been slain with thee' (*Sermons*, I, 187). Sterne can even run three figures together, combining a prosopopeia with an apostrophe in the figure Longinus calls *interrogation*: 'O *Popery*! What hast thou to answer for?' (*Sermons*, II, 72).

As Dryden affirms, no Longinian figures more powerfully convey the agitations of the heart than hyperbaton and asyndeton.[9] Sterne provides this specimen:

Is a cloud upon thy affairs? – see – it hangs over Shimei's brows——hast thou been spoken for to the king or to the captain of the host without success?——look not into the court-kalendar——the vacancy is fill'd up in Shimei's face——art thou in debt?— —tho' not to Shimei——no matter——the worst officer of the law shall not be more insolent.

Here interrogation is made to reinforce the effect of hyperbaton, creating those antithetical rhythms which force 'a transposing of Words or Thoughts out of their natural grammatical Order' (*OS*, p. 57), leaving the sentence grammatically loose but very dramatic. In the preceding paragraph of the same sermon there is a fine example of the jettisoned conjunctions of asyndeton.

'Tis a character we shall never want. O! it infests the court——the camp——the cabinet——it infests the church——go where you will——in every quarter, you see a Shimei.

The origin of Sterne's dash is clearly here, in the sentimental punctuation of the preacherly sublime.[10]

Less spectacular but still exceedingly useful in setting the scene for symptoms of passion is amplification, defined by Longinus as 'such a full and complete Connexion of all the particular Circumstances inherent in the things themselves, as gives them additional strength, by dwelling some time upon, and progressively heightening a particular Point' (*OS*, p. 33). Sermons such as 'The Levite and the Concubine' and 'The Character of Shimei' depend

---

9 'The poet must put on the passion he endeavours to represent: a man on such occasion is not cool enough, either to reason rightly, or to talk calmly. Aggravations are then in their proper places; interrogations, exclamations, hyperbata, or a disordered connexion of discourse, are graceful there because they are natural . . .' *Apology for Heroic Poetry and Poetic Licence* (1677), *Essays*, I, 186.

10 For an alternative account, see Ian Watt, 'The Comic Syntax of *Tristram Shandy*', in *Studies in Criticism and Aesthetics 1660–1800*, ed. Howard Anderson and John S. Shea (Minneapolis: University of Minnesota Press, 1967), pp. 315–31; also Michael Vande Berg ' "Pictures of Pronunciation": Typographical Travels through *Tristram Shandy* and *Jacques le fataliste*', *ECS*, 21:1 (1987), 21–47.

almost entirely for their effect upon the vignettes spun out of the bare hints of the text.

> Here then let us stop a moment, and give the story of the Levite and his Concubine a second hearing; like all others much of it depends upon the telling; and as the Scripture has left us no kind of comment upon it, 'tis a story on which the heart cannot be at a loss for what to say, or the imagination for what to suppose – the danger is, humanity may say too much. (*Sermons*, I, 205–6)

So Sterne spends time fleshing out the details of the Levite's feelings, just as, in the sermon on conscience, he turns hypotheses into scenes in order to awaken the passions and the belief of his audience.

He was helped in these experiments by someone he refers to in 'Search the Scriptures' as 'an able hand', one who has 'baffled and exposed' the bloodless precisians who follow the laws of syntax instead of their own hearts. Likely names for this hand would be either Richardson's favourite, Anthony Blackwall, whose *The Sacred Classics Defended* (1727) helps Belford to his change of taste; or Robert Lowth, the impact of whose *Lectures on the Sacred Poetry of the Hebrews* (published in Latin in 1753, and in translation in 1787) has already been mentioned. Their arguments anticipate the main heads of Sterne's, and are as follows: that the apparent solecisms of sacred poetry are really the signatures of powerful feeling; that ornament for ornament's sake is contemptible; that the force of Hebrew poetry survives translation; that the Book of Job is pre-eminent among the books of the Old Testament; and that scriptural verse derives its power from the vastness of the objects the poet confronts – 'the infinite greatness and dignity of the thing', as Blackwall terms it; and Lowth, 'the contemplation of the object itself, and of its inherent magnitude and importance'.[11]

But they carry the discussion (and Sterne) further than this. Not content simply to quote the majestic simplicities of the Bible, they want to analyse the effect of this language in specifically Longinian terms. Longinus teaches Blackwall that 'the idiotical phrase is sometimes far more expressive and significant than artificial dress' (Blackwall, p. 289), and he informs Lowth that sublimity need not necessarily be the exhibition of 'great objects with a magnificent display of imagery and diction' (Lowth, p. 155). The images of sacred poetry are drawn from the poet's immediate situation – the barn, the threshing floor, the vineyard, the river – and these are likely to be incorporated into expressions that are plain, inelegant or redundant. Tracing the sublimity of an 'idiotical phrase' that refers to low circumstances, Blackwall and Lowth come to appreciate the importance of figurative language to the Jewish poets. When God is compared to a dishwasher or a drunken sleeper,

---

11 See Anthony Blackwall, *The Sacred Classics Defended* (London, 1727; repr. New York: Garland, 1970), pp. 13, 120, 251, 324, 332; and Robert Lowth, *Lectures on the Sacred Poetry of the Hebrews*, trans. G. Gregory (London: S. Chadwick, 1847), pp. 50, 155, 47, 182, and chs. 32–4. Hereafter references will be cited as Blackwall and Lowth.

we should strive, suggests Lowth, 'to discover, if possible, the connexion between the literal and the figurative meaning . . . frequently depending upon
some very delicate and nice relation' (Lowth, p. 84). The wider the gap between the two, the greater the incitement to find the connexion. Lowth
outlines a kind of inverted burlesque, comprising images 'which in a literal
sense would seem most remote from the object, and most unworthy of the
Divine Majesty, [becoming] nevertheless, when used metaphorically . . . by
far the most sublime' (p. 181). Blackwall lays an equal stress on 'the language
of figurative construction' as inseparable from 'strong and bright notions of
things' and from the occasional appearance of impropriety (Blackwall, pp.
61–2). He gives the phrase 'girding up the loins of your mind' as an example
of the 'daring application and transferring of the qualities of the body to the
mind, or a communication of idioms, as the divines call it' (Blackwall,
p. 185). They both identify the shock of impropriety – of attaching a trifling
circumstance to a noble idea – as a valuable source of rhetorical energy.'

Lowth's and Blackwall's use of Longinus in scriptural criticism yields
variations and refinements of sublime figures that Sterne adapts not for his
sermons, but his novels. To his three basic figures (*ellipsis, pleonasmus* and
hyperbaton), Blackwall adds another, called by Longinus *changes*. This figure is
used by the Hebrew poets when they 'express a thing both affirmatively and
negatively, when they would say it with great certainty and emphasis . . . to
express a thing both ways' (Blackwall, p. 75). Lowth defines it as 'a description . . . carried on by a kind of continued negation' (Lowth, p. 180). In one
of his apparently most spontaneous apostrophes to Toby, Tristram exploits
this figure of continued negation by listing what Toby never did: 'Thou en-
vied'st no man's comforts,——insulted'st no man's opinions.——Thou
blackened'st no man's character,——and devoured'st no man's bread' (*TS*,
3.34.224). In his extensive canvassing of the causes *not* responsible for the confusion in his uncle's head (*TS*, 2.2.86), Tristram experiments with the same
figure. Closer to Blackwall's idea is the 'dialectick induction' of his Preface,
where an alternation of positive and negative hypotheses allows him to affirm,
'with great certainty and emphasis', the value of ambiguity. Rather more
obliquely, his affirmative opinions of speed in the seventh volume, and of love
in the eighth, are mingled with intensely negative ones.[12] Gazing at the mole
of Dunkirk, Trim likewise expresses a powerful feeling both ways ('It was a
thousand pities . . . to destroy these works——and a thousand pities to have
let them stood' (*TS*, 8.19.558)), and shows at the same time how smoothly
the figures of the sublime fit the traces of an associating brain.

Of the innumerable variations run by Tristram on hyperbaton and
asyndeton, among which aposiopesis and digression are the most prominent,

---

12 Gibbon finds Longinus using this figure in the opening chapters of *On the Sublime*. 'I approve
   very much of this inverted method of shewing first what a thing is not, and then what it is.'
   Journal to January 28, 1763 (London: Chatto and Windus, 1929), p. 155.

there is included that confusion of tenses Lowth notices in the Bible. There a past event is sometimes rendered as still to come (Lowth, p. 169), as it is when Tristram remarks that 'a cow broke in (tomorrow morning) to my uncle Toby's fortifications' (*TS*, 4.28.325). Here is the seed of the hypallage. Whatever Tristram contrives in the way of breaks, expressive silences and sudden shifts of thought and feeling, he freely supplies to his characters. Walter's falling on the bed, Trim's dropping of the hat, and Toby's *Lillabullero* are figures assimilable to what Blackwall terms ellipsis, 'a want of a word or words' (Blackwall, p. 65). He gives an example from Luke (13.9) where the vineyard dresser says of the fig tree, 'And if it shall bear fruit – but if not, cut it down.' This is very like Toby's musings to young Le Fever: 'But Fortune . . . Fortune may – And if she does . . . we will shape thee another course' (*TS*, 6.12.431).

Pleonasm, defined by Blackwall as 'the using more words than are strictly necessary' (p. 65), is partly exemplified by the symptoms of Toby's aroused feelings, when he starts to repeat himself. To the fly he intones, 'Go . . . I'll not hurt thee . . . I'll not hurt a hair of thy head:——Go . . . go poor devil, get thee gone, why should I hurt thee' (*TS*, 2.12.113). Here is the incipient parallelism that arises, says Lowth, when the Hebrew poets set a simple phrase resonating in their minds, and 'they repeat, they vary, they amplify the same sentiment' (Lowth, p. 59). The same effect is produced in Toby's by Trim's glorious, ever more detailed plan for laying sieges up in Yorkshire: 'Thou hast said enough . . . say no more . . . say no more . . . Thou hast said enough . . . say no more' (*TS*, 2.5.97). These refrains are antiphonal responses to heavily circumstanced, almost repetitive narratives, themselves a variation of Blackwall's pleonasm.[13] Longinus' name for these is '*collections*' (*OS*, pp. 60–2, 160, n.2), and Toby again provides a fine specimen in his impassioned retracing of the Duke of Marlborough's advance through the north German plain: 'From Kalsaken to Newdorf; from Newdorf to Landenbourg; from Landenbourg to Mildenheim; from Mildenheim to Elchingen; from Elchingen to Gingen; from Gingen to Balmerschoffen; from Balmerschoffen to Skellenberg . . .' (*TS*, 9.19.564).

Given the prominence already accorded the figure of pleonasm in this discussion, it is necessary to distinguish between the figure of repetition

---

13 Sterne's genius for Hebraising English is evident later when Tristram apostrophises Trim. The rhythm of parallelised sentiments is clearly heard framing each 'verse':

Weed his grave clean / For he was your brother;
Oh Corporal! had I thee / How would I cherish thee.

For a splendid discussion of the history of parallelism, and of Lowth's contribution to it, see James L. Kugel, *The Idea of Biblical Poetry* (New Haven: Yale University Press, 1981). See also Thomas R. Preston, 'Biblical Criticism, Literature, and the Eighteenth-Century Reader', in *Books and their Readers in Eighteenth Century England*, ed. Isabel Rivers (Leicester: Leicester University Press, 1982), pp. 97–126.

(which is how Blackwall, Lowth and others define it)[14] and what might be termed repetition itself. In the figure, it is an effort towards ampler expression, so that each iteration of a word marks the advent of a new idea or the intensification of a feeling. Either this can simply be implied, as in Toby's litany of the march, where the soritic coupling ('to . . . from') represents an emotional rung upwards as well as a geographical step eastwards; or it is supplied by the context. Trim's words apportion a fresh package of ideas to each of Toby's pleas for silence. Tristram's puns and metaphors always exploit the situation, every repetition complicating the 'very delicate and nice relation' between the literal and figurative meanings mentioned by Lowth. The relations between puff and 'puff', plan and PLAN, life and *Life*, knot and 'knot', fiddlestick and *fiddlestick* are revealed in the various inflections caused by the specific circumstances in which the word is used. The more the word has to adapt to unfamiliar ground, the more figurative it becomes. But the uninflected repetitions of an unmodifiable idea or feeling, like the sheer anxiety of Tristram's 'Sick! sick! sick! sick!' in the seventh volume (*TS*, 7.2.481), bears the same relation to situational punning as Sancho's story of Toralva to Toby's march:

In a country town in Estremadura, there lived a certain . . . goatherd . . . which goatherd, as the story has it, was called Lope Ruiz; and this Lope Ruiz was in love with a shepherdess, whose name was Toralva, the which shepherdess whose name was Toralva, was the daughter of a wealthy grazier, and this wealthy grazier——

The overlap of the clauses is a crude mnemonic, unrelated to stress of feelings or ideas, and it is rejected by Don Quixote as 'needless repetitions' (*DQ*, I, 157).

When words attain the power of a spell or conjuration, like the curse Sterne casts on Shimei's house, they have arrived at the force of the apostrophe, which Longinus calls 'this figurative manner of Swearing' (*OS*, p. 47). Toby concludes his march with a vision of King William at the Neerspeeken bridge so vivid that is transformed into a self-affirming oath. 'I see him with the knot of his scarfe just shot off, infusing fresh spirits into poor Galway's regiment ——riding along the line——then wheeling about and charging Conti at the head of it——Brave! brave by heaven! cried my uncle Toby' (*TS*,

---

14 Warburton takes a significantly different view from Lowth, arguing that the Hebrew poets repeat their words because they are short of them: 'The *Pleonasm* evidently arose from the narrowness of a simple language: the Hebrew, in which this figure abounds, is the scantiest of all the learned languages of the east . . . When the speaker's phrase comes not up to his ideas (as in a scanty language it often will not) he endeavours of course to explain himself by a repetition of the thought in other words; as he whose body is straiten'd in room is always dissatisfied with his present posture . . . The most scanty language therefore will be always fullest of repetitions.' *Divine Legation of Moses*, III, 156. Lowth responds, 'If you reduce the Psalmist to a single term or two, you strike him dumb, be he never so fond of Pleonasm . . . The Pleonastic character of Hebrew poetry must arise from the abundance of parallel terms and phrases in the language', *A Letter to the Author of the Divine Legation of Moses Demonstrated* (Oxford, 1765), p. 86.

8.19.568). Oaths are usually uttered on the edge of silence. They can either lead up to it as in this example, where strength of feeling takes the tongue to its limit, or they can be the means of emerging from it, as in the case of Dr Slop, who proceeds from mute astonishment ('——') to inarticulate cries ('pugh!——psha!'), and from there to an oath ('Lord! . . . curse the fellow' (*TS*, 3.10.168)). Oaths belong to the branch of the sublime Sterne defines in 'Job's Account of Life' as 'the words of that being, who first inspired man with language . . . opened the lips of the dumb, and made the infant eloquent' (*Sermons*, I, 112). The greatest effort made with an oath is once again Toby's, when, barren of all other consolations, he swears that Le Fever will not die. He is trying to bring his language to that degree of efficacy where 'what a man endeavours to do, or commands to be done by this strong and comprehensive way of expression, he is said to do; what he dissuades or advises against, he is said not to suffer to be done; what he offers, to give; and what he promises, to perform' (Blackwall, p. 120).

No account of Sterne's use of sublime figures would be complete without mentioning digression, so highly esteemed by Longinus when he meets it in Demosthenes: 'At length after a long Ramble, he very pertinently but unexpectedly returns to his Subject, and raises the Surprize and Admiration of all' (*OS*, p. 60). The mediators between Longinus and Sterne on digression are not Lowth and Blackwall, of course, but Montaigne and Dryden; especially Montaigne, whose praise of Plutarch coincides remarkably with Longinus' of Demosthenes: 'Good God, how Beautiful are his variations and digressions, and then most of all, when they seems to be fortuitous, and introduc'd for want of heed' (*Essays*, III, 295; *OS*, p. 60).

By this point it is evident that Sterne's mediated and unmediated use of Longinus is not an alternative to the double principle, but an important contribution to it. Demosthenes earns Longinus' highest praises not because he is a man agitated by powerful feelings, with his mind fixed upon some prodigious object or conception to the exclusion of all ancillary reflections, but because he is a skilful orator who uses art to conceal art, who proves in his apostrophe to the Greeks vanquished at Chaeronea that 'a Figure is then most dextrously applied, when it cannot be discerned that it is a Figure' (*OS*, p. 51). It is a matter of hiding the effrontery of artifice in its setting, overshadowing 'the Artifices of Rhetoric . . . by the superior Splendour of sublime Thoughts'. Tristram shows how well he can apply this rule when, after his first apostrophe to Toby, he instances the rule of *ut pictura poesis* to justify the subsequent break in his narrative:

——Writers of my stamp have one principle in common with painters.——Where an exact copying makes our pictures less striking, we choose the less evil; deeming it even more pardonable to trespass against truth, than beauty.——This is to be understood *cum grano salis*; but be it as it will,——as the parallel is made more for the sake of letting the apostrophe cool, than any thing else,——'tis not very material whether upon any other score the reader approves of it or not.   (*TS*, 2.4.91)

The effrontery of introducing a rule on such frivolous grounds conceals the fact that it has just been successfully practised.

The transition from sermons to novel is not made, then, because Sterne wishes for a closer encounter between vast objects and vast sensations, but because he develops an interest in the structure and application of sublime figures. His attention is caught by two aspects of their use. The first is the way they collaborate in their impropriety, anticipating their own burlesque either by the stark incongruity of their combined ideas or by the disorder or vulgarity of their language – sometimes a mere twelve-penny oath. The second, related to the first, is the remarkable feat of linking the crudest forms of thought and speech to the dexterity of art, and converting what ought to have been a blemish into an ornament. Figures multiply in the breakdown of intense unity, exploiting the division between the proper and the improper (God and a dishwasher for example) in order to generate a mixed response – a joint-sensation – which includes the double sense of design in accident, and of the aleatory element in intention.

Addison's and Sterne's fondness for these ornamental solecisms is exhibited, rather paradoxically, in the zeal with which they fly to protect them from mockery. In *The Spectator*, No. 160 Addison paraphrases the Song of Songs, where Solomon compares the nose of his beloved to 'the Tower of Libanon which looketh toward Damascus', and he alludes scornfully to the 'Field of Raillerie' this sort of writing opens up 'to the little Wits, who can laugh at an Indecency but not relish the Sublime'. In 'Search the Scriptures', where he is about to applaud the war-horse of Job 'who saith among the trumpets, Ha, ha', Sterne issues the same reprimand to those who 'make merry with the sacred Scripture, and turn every thing they meet with therein into banter and burlesque' (*Sermons*, II, 228). To attack the mockers of majestic simplicity is to project one's own sense of the incongruous on to a guilty substitute in order to cherish the illusion of the innocence of one's own response. But there is no doubt that a taste for the primitive is highly refined, and partly depends on the repressed urge to snigger (often unrepressed in Sterne's letters to Hall Stevenson). The 'very delicate and nice relation' discovered by Lowth between the coarse metaphiers and divine metaphrands of biblical poetry is available to him only on condition he finds their union shocking in the first instance.

In these terms no-one better exemplifies than Sterne the truth of his proposition that the translation of the sublime preserves the force of the original; for always he renews the sense of comic incongruity, whether translating from scriptural text into sermon, or from sermon into fiction. His signature as a preacher is the introductory flirt at the text: 'That I deny!' ('The House of Feasting') or 'Trust!——Trust we have a good conscience!' The plangent entreaty of 'The House of Feasting' – 'Turn in hither, I beseech you, for a moment. Behold a dead man,' – is translated in *Tristram Shandy* like this:

'Turn in hither, I beseech thee!——behold these breeches' (*Sermons*, I, 23; *TS*, 9.24.628). In the *Peri Bathos* he found innumerable examples of this kind of translation, either accidentally achieved by Blackmore or deliberately touched up by Pope, which revealed the absence of any safe criterion in the pursuit of the sublime or the mock sublime:

> When Job says in short, *He wash'd his Feet in Butter*, (a
> Circumstance some Poets would have soften'd, or past over)
> hear how it is spread out by the Great Genius:
> With Teats distended with their milky Store,
> Such num'rous lowing Herds, before my Door,
> Their painful Burden to unload did meet,
> That we with Butter might have wash'd our Feet.
>
> (*Art of Sinking*, p. 34)

Is it intrinsically more absurd to mention that a war-horse says 'Ha, ha', than to add, as Pope does in a burlesque of Blackmore's translation, that 'knots of scarlet ribbon deck his mane' (*Art of Sinking*, p. 35)? The fact that it is impossible to discover bathos in the translation without locating it in the original 'idiotical phrase', and that in some ways the worst translation is the best, possibly accounts for Sterne's desertion of the sublime of satirical indignation which he had pursued in 'The Character of Shimei' and 'The Abuses of Conscience', where outrage requires a certain homogeneous rhetoric, in favour of a comic sublime whose variety of figures is unmortgaged to standards of moral or rhetorical propriety.

When the sermon on conscience reappears in *Tristram Shandy* every attempt is made to complicate the reader's response by showing how variously and comically the sermon is received in the Shandy parlour, all with the intention of keeping us to one side of Trim's unreflective pathos. Although the anti-Catholic satire is partly promoted in the comic by-play between Slop and the rest of the audience, its effect is to distract attention from the Inquisition scene and considerably to lessen its impact. Tristram wants our sensations to be joint ones, so the scene of terror is blended with the account of its reception, which serves not only to make it funny but also to impede the flow of rhetoric and alert us to the art that might otherwise have been hidden in it.

The question of translation, particularly this translation of Yorick's translation of St Paul, invites further speculation about Yorick's place in the novel, for he still maintains the standards of 'Search the Scriptures'. He even paraphrases the sermon during the visitation dinner when he tells Didius that 'To preach, to shew the extent of our reading, or the subtleties of our wit—— to parade it in the eyes of the vulgar with the beggarly accounts of a little learning, tinseled over with a few words which glitter, but convey little light and less warmth——is a dishonest use of the poor single half hour in a week which is put in our hands . . . I had rather direct five words point blank to the heart' (*TS*, 4.26.317). The impossibility of his project in this context is instantly evident when the very phrase he chooses to convey his sense of the transparency of important ideas prompts Toby to think not of language but projectiles. Later in the scene Yorick proves himself once again oblivious to equivocal responses when he fails to note that Phutatorius' smile is for the company, his threat for him. Besides, Yorick frequently shows the extent of his reading. When he says to Eugenius, 'If I was you, I would drink more water', and Eugenius responds, 'And, if I was you, Yorick, so would I', Tristram adds that this 'shews they had both read Longinus' (*TS*, 8.5.544; *OS*, p. 19). Assuming (as I have done in the first section of this chapter) that Tristram and Yorick are in competition for a public voice, these examples show Tristram convicting Yorick of naivety about the rhetoric of the sublime – a naivety evinced by Sterne himself before he started to write fiction.

It is not possible to make or appreciate the joke of translating Longinus' transcription of Alexander's joke without reading, a point Tristram is concerned to make at some length in a previous joke. After one of the more boisterous declarations of his spontaneity and originality ('A sudden impulse comes across me——drop the curtain, Shandy——I drop it——Strike a line here across the paper, Tristam——I strike it' (TS, 4.10.281)), he goes on, 'O! but to understand this, which is a puff at the fire of Diana's temple——you must read Longinus——read away——if you are not a jot the wiser by reading him the first time over——never fear—— read him again.' The paradoxical connexion between impulsiveness and reading is emphasised here with a practical joke. Tristram is really referring his reader to Longinus' analysis of the figures of asyndeton and repetition in Demosthenes, where, like Tristram's carefully advertised line-striking, 'Order seems always disordered, and Disorder carries with it a surprizing Regularity' (*OS*, p. 56); but the 'puff at Diana's temple' is an allusion hidden in Smith's notes (*OS*, p. 113, n. 6), where a first reading might not reach. Hence the need for a double effort, an over-reading and an under-reading as it were, that gives the reader room to reflect on the controlled use of impulsiveness and disorder – room that Yorick fails to occupy because, owing allegiance to the myth of the point-blank utterance, he doesn't want to be known as a reader.

Sterne synthesises his opinions about the shift from scriptural to comic sublimity in his version of the *Art of Sinking*, a sort of anti-'Search the Scriptures' known as the 'Fragment in the Manner of Rabelais'. This tells the story of a clerical hero called Longinus Rabelaicus, 'one of the greatest Critick's in the western World, and as Rabelaic a Fellow as ever piss'd', who is trying to compose a 'KERUKOPAEDIA', an institute or grammar of sermon-writing and sermon-preaching. He pursues this task in one room, while in another the clerical villain Homenas is frantically plagiarising bits from Samuel Clarke's sermons.[15] Apart from the Rabelaisian aim of setting the scriptural

15 Melvyn New, 'Sterne's Rabelaisian Fragment: A Text from the Holograph Manuscript', *PMLA*, 87 (1972), 1088–90. Further references will be cited as 'Fragment'.

sublime in a context of jokes about non-naturals, such as turds, tears, piss and farts, Sterne's piece is intended to set standards for the reading and translation of sublime sentiments. Longinus Rabelaicus is rather like Ernulphus in wanting to list and tabulate the language of passion, but at least he is aware that the imitation of originals requires the active cooperation of the borrower's sensibility. Mixing his metaphors, he argues that with text properly absorbed, 'the Whole *cleanly* digested', a 'skillful Body' will catch the 'tune' of exotic discourses, and preach with becoming harmony. Presumably those sermons of Yorick's marked with musical terms, such as 'adagio' and 'lentamente', are digested and melodious in the way Longinus Rabelaicus recommends, although other pieces of his work are significantly less well arranged ('For this sermon I shall be hanged,——for I have stolen the greatest part of it' (*TS*, 6.11.427)). It is Trim, the instinctive orator, who best exemplifies the lessons of the 'Fragment': he adapts his skilful body (he is not called 'corporal' for nothing) first to the rhetoric of Yorick's sermon and then to his own discourse on mortality. Above all, he knows how vital it is to preserve 'the sportable key' of voice which gives 'sense and spirit' to preaching and storytelling (*TS*, 9.6.607).

Homenas knows nothing of this. Descended from Rabelais' distracted hermeneut, who spends his days praising the virtues of the decretals, or papal glosses, and soon to reappear in *Tristram Shandy* as the dwarfish imitator whose compositions suffer from such rapid change of key that the thefts cannot be concealed, he is a glutton of text, gobbling up 'Five whole Pages, nine round Paragraphs, and a Dozen and a half of good Thoughts all of a Row' ('Fragment', p. 1089). Here there is none of that clever shaping of material 'into one body' which, says Longinus, 'must necessarily produce the Sublime' (*OS*, p. 27). Homenas is a dwarf on a giant's back; he is the imitator who tells 'the tale of a roasted horse' – Tristram's and Panurge's (of the 'Fragment') phrase for frigid bombast of bad impersonation – and when caught out, is so horribly affrighted that his cold tears play 'the Devil and all, with the Sublimity'. Homenas – a double dwarf because he brings along the stick that will measure him (*TS*, 4.25.316) – stands as intermediary between Longinus' image for the human spirit denied its liberty and Yorick's meditations on the numbers of dwarfs in Paris. Longinus compares tyranny, or 'the Prison of the Soul', to the 'Cases in which Dwarfs are kept' to prevent their growth (*OS*, p. 104). In Paris the cramped apartments of the inhabitants do the job of the cases, accounting for the numbers of dwarfs in the city, at least in Walter's opinion (*ASJ*, p. 177). That Yorick bothers to quote it, however, underlines a connexion in his own mind between the tyranny of the French monarchy, physical insignificance and the suspect tone of the French sublime which (like Homenas') 'Is *more* in the *word*; and *less* in the *thing*' (*ASJ*, p. 159).[16]

16 Robert K. Merton has done such a magnificent job of mapping the journeys of this image, or aphorism, of the dwarf on the giant's back, that I was sure he would run it down to this Shandean branchline. By means of some remarkable detective work he traces it backwards from Burton

Despite its clumsiness, the piece offers an intriguing commentary on Rabelais and the sublime. The two Homenasses are false idealists: Rabelais calls his secondary texts *uranopet*, 'angelically written', and he treats them with all the reverence due to a divine original ('those in your country are only transcripts of ours' (*GP*, IV, 279)). This devaluation of transcription, translations and copies attends a mystical belief in the virtue of these papal decrees: 'If you read but one demy canon, short paragraph, or single observation of these sacrosanct decretals, how wonderfully I say, do you not perceive to kindle in your hearts, a furnace of divine love . . . bold contempt of all sublunary things . . . and extatic elevation of soul even to the third heaven' (*GP*, IV, 288). Sterne's Homenas is working on Clarke with the same belief, but Longinus Rabelaicus understands that the business in hand is no more than translation, or what Longinus himself calls imitation; that is, when you read a text so well – so musically – that 'those, who naturally are not of a tow'ring Genius, [are filled] with the lofty Ideas and Fire of others' (*OS*, p. 37). All are agreed that transport is the aim; but they are divided over what provides it, a pseudo-original or a well translated copy.

In opting for the latter, Sterne deliberately places the kerukopaedic plan amidst the crude physicalities into which Homenas' enterprise will accidentally disintegrate. The cooperation of the sublime with bodies, coarse language and copies in Longinus Rabelaicus' section of the 'Fragment' establishes a link between imitated sublimity and the Lowthian transactions of low metaphiers and high metaphrands, already hypothesised by Rabelais in the Prologue to his first book as follows: 'Put the case that in the literal sense you meet with matters that are light and ludicrous . . . yet you must not stop there . . . but endeavour to interpret that in a sublimer sense, which possibly you might think was spoken in jollity of heart' (*GP*, I, cxxv). Sterne improves the link in his novels. In a Preface that owes much to Pantagruel's

---

(*Anatomy*, I, 25) to Didacus Stella, otherwise Diego d'Estella who makes his appearance in Tristram's fragment on Whiskers complaining about the equivocations overtaking words such as trouse, spigots and chamber-pots (*TS*, p. 347). This is another Shandean junction missed by Merton. But it is cavilling to point at the missing links in this cornucopian account of an image so central to arguments and theories about imitation. It is significant that people bad at borrowing, or worried about it, end up committed to literalisms like Rabelais' Homenas, or to clear definitions of words, like d'Estella. Merton quotes a symptomatically truncated and tautologised version of the aphorism from the doughty defender of originality, Edward Young:

> Pygmies are pygmies still, though perched on Alps,
> And pyramids are pyramids in vales.   (*Night-Thoughts*, VI, ll. 9–10)

For my purposes the dwarf on the giant's back (provided he doesn't fall off like Tristram's Homenas) presents the ideal of Longinian imitation in the shape of a pleonasm, specifically a pleonasm of imperfection since it represents one imperfect creature on top of another. For all this and more, see Merton, the full title of whose book is *On the Shoulders of Giants: A Shandean Postscript* (New York: Harcourt Brace Jovanovich; 1985), especially pp. 239–58.

speeches on practical wisdom, Tristram is able to locate the image he needs for the high reach of his argument in the chair he is sitting on, by trusting to his arse more than his head. Yorick's doubts about the sublime of a Parisian barber, who grandly declares that his wig will survive immersion in the ocean itself, arise from the same instinctive taste for expressions and conceptions that have a practical or figurative bearing on real circumstances – a bucket, in this case, being better than the ocean (*ASJ*, p. 159). Blindness to the figurative possibilities of low images, improper words and imperfect bodies is always disastrous. When Tristram removes the figurative ballast from the process of his *Life*, he has to start shouting 'sick! sick! sick!' When Yorick forgets, at the end of his journey, that sentiments which have gone up have to come down, he has to shut up. After his dishonest bid for sublimity Homenas falls off his pulpit and breaks his neck and his head.

Whether as circumstantial wit or as violent disappointment, Sterne's sublime scenarios operate between an upper and a lower level. The sharp vertical movements incident to pure sublimity and sheer bathos probe the extremes of this topography; but when they are softened into a more delicate and mutual relation of physical impressions and literary ideas, they form a line of comic sublimity that can be drawn out into an undulation, a waving line of incipient impropriety. Before the sermon-reading the curve of Trim's body advertises this line as well as constituting it. The time spent on the advertisement shows how much importance Sterne attaches to the 'incorporate' element of a sublime impropriety. He wants it neither to sink into bathos nor to be a springboard into unequivocal altitudes. When Homenas weeps away the sublimity of his stolen fragments, 'The aforesaid Tears, do you mind, did . . . temper the Wind that was rising upon the aforesaid Discourse' ('Fragment', p. 1090). Clearly to be heard is the phrase Maria of *A Sentimental Journey* will use in describing the goodness of God, who '*tempers the wind* . . . to the shorn lamb' (*ASJ*, p. 272). For some years Sterne's readers consulted their Bibles and concordances to find the source of a sentiment so evidently scriptural, but they looked in the wrong places. The words and the image derive from Rabelais' fourth book, where Panurge illustrates the proverb 'A small rain lays a very high wind' with the story of Jenin Toss-pot, who stopped his wife farting in bed by pissing on her backside (*GP*, II, 191). Urine and the tears of compassion; flatulence and the gusts of sublimity: these are volatile ingredients and very likely to cause an explosion upwards or downwards; but the risk had to be run, or Sterne would have got stuck either in the schoolboy blasphemies he shared with Hall Stevenson or in the disembodied 'Scripture Language' he wrote to Eliza Draper.

Little circumstances and the sublime

In common with Lowth's scriptural sublime and Pope's mock-sublime, Sterne's comic sublime requires careful numbering of the streaks on the tulip. Without the addition of silly and trifling circumstances, or of images that heighten the sense of incongruity, the variety of possible figures is severely curtailed; and the energy derived from daring associations – God and a drunkard, integrity and butter, grief and a pair of ruined trousers – is lost. Sterne's branch of the sublime is preoccupied with figures – even the *Art of Sinking* provides an extremely interesting collection, especially of figures of repetition, such as macrology, pleonasm, periphrasis and anadiplosis – and figures demand techniques very similar to the cross-sectionalising of narrative discussed in the last chapter. A low circumstance excites an impression that reacts with a larger, nobler or more complete idea, and out of this reaction a figurative relation emerges. As this is the crux of disagreement between Sterne's school and the orthodoxy of 'the thing itself', it deserves closer examination.

Johnson is speaking for the orthodoxy when he asserts that 'sublimity is produced by aggregation', and that 'great thoughts are always general, and consist . . . in descriptions not descending into minuteness'.[17] John Baillie had already argued that 'the Sublime rather composes, than agitates the Mind; which being filled with one large, simple, and uniform Idea, becomes . . . one simple, grand Sensation'.[18] Burke affirms that astonishment is the greatest effect of the sublime, occurring when 'the mind is so filled with its object, that it cannot entertain any other'.[19] When Coleridge tackles the 'matter-of-factness' of Wordsworth's poetry – 'a laborious minuteness . . . the insertion of accidental circumstances' – he rejects it along with Wordsworth's other translations of natural passion as 'incompatible with the steady fervour of a mind possessed and filled with the grandeur of its subject'.[20] This line of critics from Johnson to Coleridge shares with Kant an estimate of the sublime object as the '*absolutely great* . . . a greatness comparable to itself alone'. It is a phenomenon that outstrips the senses, outrages the imagination and can be recovered only by an effort of the reason that carries the soul infinitely beyond 'the height of vulgar commonplace'.[21] In such an encounter the self is dwarfed, or even cancelled, by a force which assimilates everything to itself, and which may be intuitively understood only on condition that the understanding makes the self-annihilating gesture upwards. It is in this state of mind, induced by the torrents, chasms and overhangs of a sublime landscape,

---

17 'Cowley', *Works*, IX, 21.
18 *An Essay on the Sublime*, p. 11.
19 Burke, p. 57.
20 *Biographia Literaria*, II, 68, 101.
21 Immanuel Kant, *Critique of Judgement*, trans. James Creed Meredith (Oxford: Clarendon Press, 1952; repr. 1973), pp. 94, 97, 111.

that Mrs Radcliffe's heroines are prone to 'sublime reflections, which soften, while they elevate the heart, and fill it with certainty of a present God'.[22]

Sterne's heterodox company of critics entertains much more empirical notions of the thing itself. Although Blake is not altogether consistent in his views, he powerfully opposes Johnson with the maxim, 'Singular & Particular Detail is the Foundation of the Sublime.'[23] An unlikely ally is Pope who, reflecting on Longinus' poor opinion of the *Odyssey*, wonders 'how far a Poet, in pursuing the description or image of an action, can attach himself to *little circumstances*, without vulgarity or trifling'.[24] Pope gives countenance to a number of classical critics who resolve not to be disgusted by the details in Homer's poetry. When Joseph Warton deserts his rather narrow views of modern realism, he speaks for Thomas Blackwell, Henry Fielding, Edward Gibbon, Joseph Priestley and even William Hogarth in applauding 'the number of *natural, little* circumstances . . . which make [the *Iliad*] so *lively*, so *dramatic*, and so *interesting*'.[25] Pope's hint begins to improved by Blackwall (pp. 61-2) and then it becomes the linchpin of Lowth's researches, which are based on the belief that every scriptural figure has a local origin. 'It would be a tedious task to instance particularly with what embellishments of diction, derived from one low and trivial object . . . the sacred writers have contrived to add a lustre to the most sublime, and a force to the most important subjects' (Lowth, p. 81). Lowth is joining hands with Thomas Sherlock, who likewise opposed Warburton in the Job debate by supposing an historical, rather than an allegorical, reason for scriptural figures: 'Metaphors', Sherlock declared, 'do not arise out of nothing.'[26] It is no less important a principle of Tristram's narrative that the greatness or littleness of things, together with the rhetorical power of the words employed about them, is determined by the circumstances which gird them (*TS*, 3.2.158).

The plainest difference between the two lines of critics is that the second does not allow for a disappearance into the immensity of the thing itself. Burke's astonishment, Kant's supersensible intuition, and Baillie's vast sensation cease to have dialogue with the impressions that caused them – these are dismissed by Baillie as the 'Cockle-shells, and the Butterflies' of the

22 *The Mysteries of Udolpho* in *The Novels of Ann Radcliffe* (London: Hurst, Robinson & Co., 1824), p. 235. For a catalogue of Ann Radcliffe's debts to Burke, see Malcolm Ware, *Sublimity in the Novels of Ann Radcliffe. Essays and Studies*, XXV (Copenhagan, 1961).

23 Cited in Thomas Weiskel, *The Romantic Sublime* (Baltimore: Johns Hopkins University Press, 1976), p. 67.

24 Postscript to The Odyssey of *Homer* in *The Works of Alexander Pope*, ed. Maynard Mack (London: Methuen, 1967), X, 387.

25 Warton, *Essay on the Genius and Writings of Pope*, II, 166. See T. Blackwell, *Enquiry into the Life and Writings of Homer*, p. 24; Fielding, *The History of Tom Jones*, p. 880 (XVII, ii); Edward Gibbon, *An Essay on the Study of Literature* (London, 1764; repr. New York: Garland Publishing Co., 1970), p. 25; Joseph Priestley, *A Course of Lectures on Oratory and Criticism* (London, 1777; repr. Menston: Scolar Press, 1968), p. 84.

26 'Four Dissertations', in *The Works of Bishop Sherlock*, 5 vols. (London, 1830), IV, 163.

sublime (*An Essay on the Sublime*, p. 13). It is with precisely these trivia that the minds of Tristram's characters act and react, 'their cockle-shells, their drums and their trumpets . . . their maggots and their butterflies' (*TS*, 1.7.13). By these additions the hobbyhorse acquires the sublimely burlesque potential of Job's war-horse. As the critic's task, defined by Blackwall and Lowth, is to study the incongruous but potentially figurative relation between these trifles and ideas and feelings connected with nobler things, there is never an opportunity to enjoy the transcendent composedness of mind Johnson talks of, or Coleridge's 'steady fervour', or Mrs Radcliffe's softened certainty. The rapid oscillation of the mind between repulsion and attraction which, Kant argues, procedes the reason's calm apprehension of the boundless self-comparability of the sublime idea, is what Blackwall, Lowth and Sterne take to be its constitutive character: its cause and effect, its beginning and its end.

The difference may be further illustrated by considering how landscape plays a part in these discussions, not just as the most popular location of sublime experiences but as a metaphor of strongly oscillating feelings. Although Mrs Radcliffe is naturally drawn to the steepest, most twilit and murmurous Alpine scenery, she occasionally plays with mixtures of the rugged and the pastoral because, as she confesses of descriptions of the former, 'A repetition of the same images of rock, wood and water, and the same epithets of grand, vast and sublime, which necessarily occur, must appear tautologous, on paper, though their archetypes in nature . . . exhibit new visions to the eye, and produce new shades of effect upon the mind.' So variation is sometimes offered in the form of 'a perfect picture of the lovely and sublime – of beauty sleeping in the lap of horror'.[27]

In order to illustrate how 'those seeming embarrassments and harshnesses' of the idiotical phrase strike more forcibly on the fancy than smoother diction, Blackwall goes to the same picture of beauty in the lap of horror, with comfortable lowlands ('flowery meadows, open champains stretcht out into a large extent, clear gently flowing rivers') backed by terrifying steeps ('falls of water . . . that murmur loud, that toss loose stones, and dash against broken rocks; threatening precipices and rugged mountains'), to show how the combination of opposites 'entertains the mind and imagination with a most grateful variety of sensations and reflections' (Blackwall, p. 86). Lowth interrogates every sublimely awkward or unaccountable phrase for the contours of real landscapes and the history of human activity upon them. He explains, for example, how the flooding of the Jordan comes to be associated with the symptoms of grief, so that 'this image . . . may be accounted peculiarly familiar, local, in a manner, to the Hebrews' (Lowth, p. 74). When he talks of figurative and mythic wheels in his seventh volume, Tristram is being archly Lowthian in

---

27 Mrs Radcliffe, *A Journey made in the Summer of 1794* (London, 1795), p. 419; *The Mysteries of Udolpho*, p. 248.

his discrimination between the wheel of Ixion and the wheel of David's curse, judging the latter to be a large cart-wheel suitable for the hilly country of Palestine (*TS*, 7.13.493); but no-one is readier than he to mine the rich seam of figures embedded at the meeting point of physical and mental terrains. The landscape most productive of figures and least liable to provoke repetitive exclamations of wonder, is, as Mrs Radcliffe and Blackwall agree, the one that comprehends extremes of rough and smooth.

When David Hartley considers the impact of landscapes and figurative language upon the imagination, he decides that both require a degreeof harshness, and of inconsistency bordering on pain, if they are to sustain the vibrations of pleasurable surprise; and he introduces the analogy with a scene of beauty in the lap of horror 'Fruits and Flowers, the Melody of Birds, and the grateful Warmth or Coolness of the Air' coexisting with 'a Precipice, a Cataract, a Mountain of Snow, etc.' (*OM*, I, 419, 422, 429–30). It is not simply that the terrain produces figurative expressions, as Lowth argues. Beauty in the lap of horror is a metaphor of the figurativity of all inconsistent and improper mixtures. It is the antithesis, both compositionally and rhetorically, of the scene of uniform grandeur which, Mrs Radcliffe reluctantly observes, yields nothing but the figure that expels all others, the tautology.

As Mrs Radcliffe's thinking about the sublime is greatly indebted to Burke's, and as Burke's is marginalised by Kant as contributing much to 'empirical anthropology' and nothing to 'transcendental philosophy' (*Critique of Judgement*, pp. 117, 131), it might be supposed that her mentor is as close to the sublime of 'vulgar commonplace' as Sterne and his associates. But it is not so. Burke discusses joint-sensations and obscurity of language as signatures of the encounter with an essentially unitary phenomenon whose equivocality is merely technical, or prefatory. Despite his emphasis on delight and sympathy as compound responses 'which cannot exist without a relation, and that too a relation to pain' (Burke, p. 36), it is only in the lesser branches of art, where the imagination has the liberty to play between its response to the object and its response to its representation, that this compound has a place. An oscillation is possible there, Burke suggests (closely paraphrasing *The Spectator* No. 418), because the object is too trivial to arrest the attention – 'a cottage, a dunghill, the meanest and most ordinary utensils of the kitchen' (Burke, p. 49). Undetained by any strong feeling, the mind can alternate freely between the two points of image and object. The next step in the Addisonian scale, towards a landscape where the simultaneous appeal to different senses encourages what Hume calls the 'double impulse' (No. 412; I, p. 336), is not followed by Burke. 'The sublime', he says, 'always dwells on great objects, and terrible' (p. 113), whose pressure on the sensorium mounts to the single point of astonishment, attained when the motions of the soul are suspended and 'the mind is hurried out of itself' (pp. 57, 62). The sliding scale or relational responses is calibrated to the status of the thing, reaching a maximum when we are entirely unconcerned by it, and moving towards the minimum when 'the power of the poem or picture is more owing to the nature of the thing itself' (pp. 49–50). If the thing itself is a prospect of sublime scenery, where no art mediates between the power of the object and the unreflecting passivity of the viewer, the relational quality of the latter's response – the delight that arises from feelings of horror mitigated by a minimal sense of security – is an aesthetic fiction.

As astonishment is produced by 'great and confused images' (p. 62), the language of astonishment is appropriately obscure, being symptomatic of the transported mind rather than accurately descriptive of what caused it. Indeed any attempt to give a clear account of experiences which 'make some sort of approach to infinity' risks the ludicrous, and Burke is as convinced as Kant of the incompatibility of the sublime and the ridiculous (Burke, p. 63; Kant, *Critique of Judgement*, p. 128). Nowhere does Burke suggest, like Lowth, Blackwall and Hartley, that the force of an obscure expression depends upon an inconsistency – potentially risible – developing between ideas, feelings and an 'idiotical phrase', or that its force is renewed only as often as the sense of that inconsistency. Obscurity itself is what imparts force to expression, because Burke cannot admit figurativity into his account of the sublime. Having sacrificed Addison's margin of reflection to the infinite excess of the thing itself, the only figure he can accommodate to a symptomatology of that excess is repetition, the endless refrain of the madman whose 'every repetition reinforces it with new strength' (Burke, p. 73). It is the same sort of repetition that Mrs Radcliffe is forced upon in her descriptions of Burke's natural sublime, involving the same cuckoo-figure of infinite iteration, the tautology.

Reading Burke after Longinus, Gibbon wrote:

> It is surprising how much Longinus and Mr Bourke differ as to their idea of the operations of the sublime in our minds. The one considers it as exalting us with a conscious pride and courage, and the other as astonishing every faculty, and depressing the soul itself with terror and amazement. If it should be found that the sublime produces this double, and seeming contrary effect; we must look out for some more general principles which may account for it.[28]

He was not being quite fair to Addison, who had not only introduced the double principle into the vocabulary of critical terms, but also succinctly marked the limits of its operation. Natural and represented scenes alike must be able to return to the perceiver an image of the mind's own choices, otherwise the reciprocal flux of impressions and ideas will be halted; as they are when we confront a real scene of torture and execution. Burke's opinion is the very opposite. The finest tragedy at its most affecting moment would be deserted instantly, he maintains, if the audience were promised a real

---

28 *Journal*, pp. 180–1.

execution, conflagration, or earthquake nearby which might be witnessed without danger (Burke, pp. 47–8) – not because they are bloody-minded, but because the thing itself holds out ampler and more astonishing opportunities for sympathy.[29]

Sterne's representations of death are always coloured with the ludicrous, his efforts always being directed at a full implementation of the double principle so that the ghostly intensity of the 'catastrophe itself' may be dissipated and to some degree controlled. We have already seen with what finesse he manages Le Fever's, so that it is complicated by little circumstances and doubled up in narrative and counter-narrative. It has also been evident that Trim's response to the scene of death by torture in the Inquisition, which he takes for the thing itself, is erroneous, a failure to reflect on the difference between an *historical account* and a *description*. The portion of his novel Sterne was content should be called sublime, the allegory of heaven's Chancery, is written with the same attention to the cockle-shells and butterflies which keep the sublime within the ambit of the vulgar commonplace.

Marching on the spot with one shoe on and the other off, Toby troops himself into such desperate optimism about Le Fever's prospects that he swears an oath, and the oath is carried up by the 'ACCUSING SPIRIT' to the 'RECORDING ANGEL' for entry against Toby's name. The first part of the scene combines figurative language with gestures of specifically burlesque provenance. In a series of statements that perform a chiasmus, Toby moves from caution ('He might march') to confidence ('He shall march') back to the glorious minimalism of his last position: 'He shall not die, by G—.' Here Toby's mind, fixed upon its object, repeats, varies and amplifies the same sentiment (as it has done before with the fly and the prospects of siege warfare) in a series of parallelisms formed out of his repetitions and Trim's chiming contradictions. At the same time he strikes an attitude recalling that of Prince Volscius in *The Rehearsal*, whose half-shod condition expresses his divided allegiance to love and honour.[30] Toby's search for an accommodation between the positive law of Trim's evidence and the natural law of his own feelings is announced both in the grand irregularities of his speech and in the comic disorder of his footwear. This duplicates the opposition between honour

---

29 An extended, and not very plausible, commentary on this portion of Burke's *Enquiry* is run by James Beattie, 'Illustrations on Sublimity', in *Dissertations Moral and Critical* (London, 1783; repr. Stuttgart: Friedrich Fromman, 1970), pp. 607–15. The problem arises not so much from the altruism Burke supposes in such an example of curiosity, as from the scant likelihood of self-reflective opportunities in a scene whose attraction must lie in its power to remove the mind's ability to make comparisons.

30   How has my passion Made me Cupid's scoff!
        This hasty Boot is on, the other off,
        And sullen lies, with amorous design
        To quit loud fame, and make that Beauty mine.
  Burlesque Plays of the Eighteenth Century, ed. Simon Trussler (Oxford: Oxford University Press, 1969), p. 33.

and compassion at the beginning of the chapter, when Toby faced a conflict between a natural and a positive law and knew intuitively which way to turn himself; and the oath causes the same conflict to be renewed in heaven. There the accusing spirit stands for the positive law against swearing, and the recording angel stands for the natural law of sympathy; so that when a tear from the latter blots out an entry demanded by the former, heaven not only acquiesces in but also *imitates* Toby's two instinctive reactions to the crisis. The spiritual, allegorical realm is revalued in terms of a human criterion, measured by what it was supposed to measure, and a common oath is endowed with the passion of one of Demosthenes' apostrophes. In this arrangement, going up is just another way of coming down. The burlesque circumstances at the foot of it are the source, emblem and object of higher thoughts. Like Maria and the goat, or the death of Le Fever, the sublimity depends on the continued oscillation of odd, mixed and tragicomical impulses, not their transcendence.

Figuration and fragmentation

When Sterne defends his reading of Longinus by developing a Rabelaisian view of how things and words of low degree thrust themselves into books of high rhetoric, he hints at an even subtler synthesis obtainable by reading Longinus as if he were Rabelais. After Homenas' failed attempt at the sublime, he tumbles off Clarke's back and out of the pulpit, and the spectators cry, '*He has broken his Neck, and fractured his Skull and beshit himself into the Bargain* . . . Alass poor Homenas!' ('Fragment', p. 1089). His accident serves as a reminder to all higher risers that overreaching ends in physical damage. (Once again, with the three words of condolence, Homenas' story seems to cast a perverse glance in the direction of Yorick's.) Friar Tickletoby, who insults the carnival with his whey-faced pieties and is paid out by being dragged by a bolting horse until there is nothing left of him but his right foot, is a more extreme example of the ruinous consequences of ignoring human needs in favour of idle schemes of transcendence. Of all the texts he mentions, Tristram particularly urges his readers to peruse this story of Tickletoby and *On the Sublime* (*TS*, 3.36.226; 4.10.282).

Rabelais' and Longinus' books contain a good deal of violence: storms, beatings, battles, dismemberments and deaths of various sorts; but it is intriguing that Longinus gets closest to Rabelais in this respect when he mentions little circumstances and the 'idiotical phrase'. Longinus' recommendation that circumstances be formed skilfully into 'one body' is illustrated by a poem about the disintegration of Sappho's body, 'She is at a loss for her Soul, her Body, her Ears, her Tongue, her Eyes, her Colour' (*OS*, p. 28). As an instance of the happiness of vulgar terms, he quotes Herodotus' description of the madman Cleomenes, who, 'with a little Knife that he had, cut his Flesh into small Pieces, till, having intirely mangled his Body, he expired' (*OS*, p. 72). This forms part of the thirty-first section, dealing with burlesque, itself a badly mutilated portion of precisely that part of his treatise that helped Blackwall and Lowth to their idea of the scriptural sublime: a sublime they associate with images or events of violence, such as shouting, scattering, breaking, flooding. The agricultural metaphors praised by Lowth – reaping, pruning, threshing and winnowing – are generally used to express the vengeance God is denouncing against His chosen people. The Song of Deborah, which claims Lowth's (and later Wordsworth's) special attention, culminates in the nailing of Sisera's head to the floor of his tent. Rabelais' carnivalesque scenes likewise involve physical destruction: bodies broken, jointed, and reduced to the parlous condition, for example, of Picrochole's troops after Friar John has finished with them: 'Never was corn so thick and threefold thresh'd upon by plowmens flails, as were the pitifully disjointed members of their mangled bodies, under the merciless baton of the cross' (*GP*, I, 268–9).

The difference between this violence and that of Burke's hypothesised execution, which would empty all the theatres, is that it always remains within the purview of representational art. Without that parallax, as Addison points out, the sight of 'Torments, Wounds, Deaths, and the like dismal Accidents' afford us neither 'Time nor Leisure to reflect on our selves' (*The Spectator*, No. 418). Violence left to its own devices, *unfigured* ruin, will never produce a joint-sensation or a double impulse. But the violence disclosed by the addition of little circumstances is inseparable from the figures in which it makes its appearance – collections, visions, amplifications, apostrophes. These figures of repetition or enumeration always exploit difference – basically the difference between nature and art – and never, like the repetitions of Burke's madman, or Tristram's 'sick! sick! sick!', or the cries of some wretch on the scaffold, do they manifest the bare symptoms of untranslated agony. The nailing of Sisera's head is the occasion of a silence and an apostrophe more forcible, says Lowth, than 'all the powers of language' (Lowth, p. 149). Like the circumstances of Sappho's disintegrating body, the wounds inflicted on Picrochole's men are *collections*, as medically faithful to the successive breaching of skin, muscle, ligament, flange and bone as Toby's to the unfolding geography of the Duke of Marlborough's march. Penologist and literary man, Henry Fielding declares himself of Montaigne's school (and therefore of Rabelais' and Tristram's too) when he says that the aesthetic effects of physical destruction are produced not by 'the Essence of the Thing itself' but by 'the Dress and Apparatus of it'.[31]

---

31 Henry Fielding, *An Enquiry into the Causes of the late Increase of Robbers*, ed. Malvin R. Zirker (Oxford: Clarendon Press, 1988), p. 170. Fielding is speculating about the ceremony of execution in order to identify the elements that make it terrible. He refers to Montaigne's fear (shared by Tristram) that the ceremony of the deathbed will be more fatal than any disease. In the same

Here it is right to reintroduce Neil Hertz's idea of the reconstitutive function of Longinian figures. If a threat, a wound or a death is replicated in a
figure that causes or results from analogous damage to the ordonnance of a
text – the anxiety caused by the danger of losing oneself in a digression (*OS*,
p. 60), the quotation or cutting up of another work (Hertz, *The End of the Line*,
p. 14), anatomy by little circumstances (Sappho's Ode), the loss of words that
mimics the loss of life (the death of Le Fever), and so on – then damage suggests the mode of its most eloquent representation, and the orator and poet
look for their best effects among the most ruinous subjects. Successful
representation of damage is not a matter then, as Burke argues, of pursuing
ruin for its own sublime sake, and of finally deserting the copy for the original,
but of reproducing it most aptly in figurative form. That involves identifying
certain symptomatic obscurities in the language of pain – repetition, say –
and nursing them to the stage where they can function like formal devices
while still appearing natural. Their most ingenious arrangement is specular,
with the figure deployed simultaneously with the set of circumstances in which
it first appeared as a natural obscurity – a digression on the very theme of
anxiety caused by digressions, for example, or a quotation on the topic of cutting things up.

If the match fails, as it does with Homenas' attempt to incorporate Clarke's
bits and pieces, unfigured damage rebounds from the text upon its
mishandler; and in this case the 'Joynt' intended for Clarke's sermon appears
instead in Homenas' neck. But if it works, the specularity or mimicry of 'ruin'
upon ruin ameliorates the literal fact with a figurative double. Addison's portrait of a lady, where defect and disappointment are translated into alluring
melancholy; the mimic structure of consolation, where a fourth kind of
mockery finds a way to ease the heart; the genealogy of hobbyhorses, where
accidental pain is transformed into customary pleasure; and the hypallages
and palindromes of associationism, where shocks are absorbed into the alternating and reciprocal cycles of perpetual recurrency: these are all branches of
the same double principle, and all need a defect in the object, whether natural
or acquired, to get started.

In the case of the sublime, it is very easy to mistake the pleonastic super-
imposition of words on things and of figurative upon literal language for a
tautology of self-comparability; and this is owing to the reflexive pattern tradi-
tionally adopted for the praise of Longinus. 'En parlant du Sublime, il est lui
mesme tres-sublime.' 'His very Rules are shining Examples of what they

essay, however, Montaigne recommends the cultivation of those 'Circumstances [which]
amuse, divert, and turn our thoughts from the thing in it self' ('Of Diversion', *Essays*, III,
61, 65). But there is a closer parallel in 'Of Physiognomy' where he talks of public execution
as a species of tragedy: 'My Curiosity makes me in some sort please my self with seeing with
my own Eyes this notable Spectacle of our publick Death, its Form and Symptoms . . . Thus
do we manifestly covet to see, tho' but in Shadow, and the Fables of Theatres, the Pomp of
Tragick Representations of Human Fortune' (*Essays*, III, 365).

inculcate.' His '*own Example* strengthens all his Laws'. He has 'exemplified several of his Precepts in the very Precepts themselves'.[32] Dennis and Pope are at least in agreement about Longinus: 'His Sense is every where the very thing he would express', and he '*Is himself* that great *Sublime* he draws'.[33] This criticism-by-enactment didn't appeal to everyone. Warton comments irritably, 'He is ever intent on producing something SUBLIME himself',[34] and Gibbon, as we have seen, remarks on the shiftiness which makes Longinus slavish on the theme of slavery, or dwarfish on dwarfs: 'Here, too, we may say of Longinus, "His own example strengthens all his laws." '[35] But there seems to have been complete unanimity about Longinus' skill at accomplishing the very thing he is mentioning. 'Skill' would be too poor a word for those who take the sublime on the sublime to be the creative charge that converts the word 'light' into the thing itself, or that transfuses the violence of a storm into Homer's description of it, so 'the Danger is discerned in the very Hurry and Confusion of the Words', or that imparts to Demosthenes' oration against Midias the violence of the assault it describes (*OS*, pp. 23, 30, 56). In this interpretation Longinus enacts his precept of imitation, becoming so 'ravished and transported by a Spirit not his own' (*OS*, p. 36) that it is impossible to tell criticism and inspiration apart, or the representation from the thing itself.

There is a cooler estimate of his achievements which pays attention to his self-conscious deployment of the figures he is enumerating. Smith notes that he uses a hyperbaton about hyperbata (*OS*, p. 157), Gibbon that he addresses Terentianus in the second person while discussing that very ornament – the buttonholing of the audience or reader – in Herodotus (*OS*, p. 64; *Journal*, p. 164). He begins the section on interrogations with a question, and on digressions he disgresses. These figures on figures or figures to the second power, are structurally homologous with 'ruin' on ruin: the referent is mimicked in the text as figure, and because the referent is a figure in the first place, the shimmer of specularity is peculiarly intense. Critics of the sublime are extraordinarily alert to this sort of performative doubling. Considering how Addison quotes an attack on criticism instead of mounting one himself, Dennis tells him, 'You have oblig'd the World with the thing it self, with Criticism upon Criticism.'[36] Maurice Morgann quotes the lines from Macbeth, 'I would *applaud* thee to the very Eccho / Which should *applaud* again', as a perfect marriage of sound and sense because the lines echo the

---

32 Nicolas Boileau-Despreaux, *Le Traité du sublime* (Paris, 1674; repr. New York: Scholars' Facsimiles & Reprints, 1975), p. ii; p. xxvi; Pope, *Essay on Criticism*, l. 679; *The Spectator*, No. 253.
33 Dennis, *Advancement and Reformation of Poetry*, p. 223; *OS*, p. 115; Pope, *Essay on Criticism*, l. 680.
34 *Essay on the Genius and Writings of Pope*, I, 179.
35 Gibbon, *The Decline and Fall of the Roman Empire*, p. 24, n.t.
36 'To the Spectator on Criticism and Plagiarism', *Critical Works of John Dennis*, ed. Edward Niles Hooker, 2 vols. (Baltimore: Johns Hopkins University Press, 1943), II, 24.
   about the poignancy of the fragmentation of utterance when it is rebounded', p. 61.

echo to which the applause promises to ring: 'This', says Morgann, 'is the
Thing itself.'[37] In Tristram's 'book of books' (*TS*, 3.31.218) a chapter on
chapters and a plagiarised attack on plagiarism belong to this line of wit; so
does the uncanny punctuality of Yorick's double apology for the digression
and the material of the Bevoriskius episode: 'I twice – twice beg pardon for
it', he says, talking twice of twice (*ASJ*, p. 229). Montaigne's dreams of
dreaming, and his determination to excuse himself for nothing but his excuses
(*Essays*, III, 125, 142) give further weight to R. A. Sayce's opinion that he
and Longinus present their eighteenth-century readers with closely parallel
experiments in cultivated disorder.[38]

The rhetorical impact of a self-realising or self-performing statement is proportionate not to the plenitude but the imperfection of what is realised or performed. The shift from the root pleonasm – let us say quoting on cutting,
since Longinus in fact quotes Herodotus on Cleomenes' self-slicing madness
(*OS*, p. 72) – to the figure on the figure, aptly summed up in this case by
Swift, who observes that Longinus' disciples read him 'translated from
Boileau's translation' and then use him to 'quote *Quotation* on *Quotation*',[39] is
always supplementary, never self-affirming. Although it seems directed
towards transforming something that is not itself – madness or quotation –
into the thing itself, and is assumed by Dennis and Morgann to have suc-
ceeded, the scar of the cut can never be erased by the quotation no matter
how many times the figure is doubled over itself. Like quotations, criticisms
and echoes are no more than secondary effects, fragments of some prior voice
whose power they cannot recover unless the original is as defective as their
mimicry, which then gains the supererogatory edge. Longinus' book of
criticism – the flotsam of a literary shipwreck as Boileau calls it – is the
exemplary antithesis of Homenas' decretalist idolatry because instead of wor-
shipping a factitious unity he figures and refigures the ruin of his originals.
To employ these figures of ruin upon themselves, to digress on the topic of
digressions, is his recompense and consolation; it is to experience the strange
omnicompetence got from an engagement with what is, in Pierre Macherey's
suitably parodic phrase, 'incomplete *in itself*'.[40]

37 *Shakespearian Criticism*, ed. Daniel A. Fineman (Oxford: Clarendon Press, 1972), p. 258.
38 R. A. Sayce, *The Essays of Montaigne: A Critical Exploration* (London: Weidenfeld and Nicolson,
   1972), pp. 45 n. 3, 46, 312.
39 *On Poetry: A Rhapsody* in *The Poems of Jonathan Swift*, ed. Harold Williams, 3 vols. (Oxford:
   Clarendon Press, 1958), II, 643, 649. Also important to this discussion is David Quint, *Origin
   and Originality in Renaissance Literature* (New Haven: Yale University Press, 1983). Christopher
   Ricks considers the relation between pleonastic wit and the political split of civil war in *The
   Force of Poetry* (Oxford: Clarendon Press, 1984), pp. 34–59. John Hollander gives a fine account of echo games in *The Figure of the Echo* (Berkeley: University of California Press, 1981),
   where he shows how echoes of echoes echo best: 'Sandys "echoes" Jonson, *in* an echo device,
   about the poignancy of the fragmentation of utterance when it is rebounded', p. 61.
40 Pierre Macherey, *A Theory of Literary Production*, trans. Geoffrey Wall (London: Routledge and
   Kegan Paul, 1978), p. 79.

Burke's sublime cannot exploit this fragmentation because it is predicated on an excess associated with transcendent order rather than ruin; yet the difference between his examples and Longinus' is sometimes hard to find. An execution, a conflagration or an earthquake may be more impressive than represented ruin, but they can scarcely be called the things themselves; each is, strictly speaking, a process in which a thing – a malefactor, a building or a city – comes to be less than itself. A landscape so vast and irregular that it exceeds the bounds of the imagination might as well be ruin. And if ruin is left unfigured in deference to a notional identity to which its terrible force is ultimately owing, then the mind of the observer is vulnerable to that rebounded violence which breaks Homenas' neck. The wound to the psyche will produce precisely the opposite of what was supposed in the object, for it will make itself heard as repetition – the sound of someone beside himself. Witnesses of an event or scene who resort to repetition because of its terrible uniqueness signal therefore one of two unintended destructive effects. The first takes place in the mind of the beholder as the compulsion to repeat. The second is the more collected effort to reproduce as tautology the self-comparability of the absolutely great (Kant, *Critique of Judgement*, p. 94), in which case repetition is transferred to the figure ('Nothing but itself may be its parallel' or 'We call plums, plums') and makes mockery of the wholeness it alleges by cutting it in two, so that the *thing* might be measured against *itself*, affirmed of itself.

Tristram's privative sublime, which makes no concessions to the unitary qualities of any thing or person, abounds with figures upon figures of the incomplete. His chapter upon chapters – the chapter that discusses the formal fragmenting of a text of which it is itself a semi-spontaneous specimen – claims Longinus as the inspiration for this type of performed pleonasm. (*TS*, 4.10.281). The use of the very rule of self-interruption he is frivolously expounding, his disappearance into one the very gaps he is writing about, the writing of a digression upon digressions, are examples of figures upon figures with the same Longinian pedigree (*TS*, pp. 2.4.91; 6.33.462; 9.15.618), and all derive from an imperfection of body or mind (brains like an unsaleable piece of cambric, for instance) which guarantees the figure its safe recurrency to ruin ultimately in the form of a pleonasm. The difference which makes something less than itself, or not quite like itself, provides the opportunity for its multiplication into itself, but only on condition that the difference is never obscured. Tristram's sublime occasions are always accompanied by loss, or take their rise from it: a death, a wound or some reduction of the self. When Toby replays the siege of Namur with Mrs Wadman as his guardian nurse, his sublime transport – 'Heaven! Earth! Sea!——all was lifted up' – coincides with her leading him 'all bleeding by the hand out of the trench' (*TS*, 9.26.637). Ideas of shaving are associated with sublimity for the same reason, the 'highest pitch of sublimity' being reached with the flourish of an instrument that removes the upper insignia of masculinity as easily as it could despatch the lower. Like Longinus' treatise, accidentally but happily prevented from being 'toute entière', Tristram's text nurses those 'good cursed, bouncing losses' that are as good as a pension to him (*TS*, 7.29.518).

After his great work of fissiparous wit, the plagiarism upon plagiarism, Tristram makes a bridge to the 'Fragment' on Whiskers with some mock-scathing remarks about imitators and plagiaries in general.

If there is no catachresis in the wish, and no sin in it, I wish from my soul, that every imitator in Great Britain, France, and Ireland, had the farcy for his pains; and that there was a good farcical house, large enough to hold——aye——and sublimate them, *shag-rag and bob-tail*, male and female, all together: and this leads me to the affair of Whiskers.   (*TS*, 5.1.343)

The catachresis lies in the pun on 'farcy', which confounds the meanings of disease and stuffing. The swelling of inflamed glands leads, in Tristram's chain of ideas, to a swelling caused by exotic material; and from there to a kind of collegiate swelling as the stuffed become the stuffing in the infarction of the farcical house. At that point he combines the ideas of laughter, sublimation and fragments. The farcical house isn't a punishment so much as a kind of refuge for folk whose coats are torn (shag-rag) and whose tails are docked (bob-tailed), a place where the painful literalisms of disease, privation, impuissance·and plagiarism (listed once again as 'stranguries, sciaticas, swellings and sore-eyes' in the eighth volume) are troped into a joint expansion which, though not one of those 'pompous and magnificent Swellings' that are supposed to accompany sublime imitations (*OS*, p. 6), reconstitutes imperfection in a tolerable form. Shandean sublimity, in fact, is misery making sport to mock itself, a pleonastic mock-mockery.[41]

It was suggested in the first chapter that the Book of Job supplies the privative material of such a sublime. Job talks of the boundlessness of his misery in a pleonasm, 'He breaketh me with breach upon breach', and compares his insignificance to a dwarf's, 'He runneth upon me like a giant' (16:14). A good deal of the Shandean sublime is to be found in comic readjustments of the figure and the image. Let us take the figure first, which is echoed and punned upon throughout *Tristram Shandy*. It is reproduced most exactly in Toby's sieges, where the paralleling of parallels requires that a breach ('a practicable breach . . . made by the duke of Marlborough') be

41 The phrase crops up earlier in a letter written from Paris to Hall Stevenson: 'We have lived (shag-rag and bob-tail), all of us, a most jolly and nonsensical life of it.' But he describes a passage of thwarted love anticipating both the sexual disaster Tristram alludes to in his apostrophe to Jenny in the seventh volume, and the terrible haemorrhage he was to suffer when Eliza Draper left for Bombay: 'Now she is gone to the South of France, and to finish the comedie, I fell ill, and broke a vessel in my lungs and half bled to death' (*Letters*, pp. 213–14). As a saving figure of fragmentation and imperfection, it bears comparison with the pleonastic misbehaviour his French critics accused him of: 'bouffoneries sur bouffoneries, saletés sur saletés'. *Journal Encyclopédique* (May, 1761), pp. 131–2; cited in Arthur Cash, *Laurence Sterne*, 2 vols. (London: Methuen, 1986), II, 140.

represented by a 'breach': 'What intense pleasure swimming in his eye as he stood over the corporal, reading the paragraph ten times over to him . . . lest, peradventure, he should make the breach an inch too wide,——or leave it an inch too narrow' (*TS*, 6.22.445). The same exclamation used when Mrs Wadman escorts her bleeding lover from the Namur trenches is made hère in a vain effort to express the sublimity of his delight in being able to recreate the very effects of bombardment that damaged him: 'Heaven! Earth! Sea!—— but what avails apostrophes?' Apostrophes certainly avail less than the pleonasm in showing how a disaster doubled can become scarcely disaster at all. Not until Toby confronts the model of Dunkirk, a thing built for no other purpose than to be destroyed, does the paradox of breach upon breach disturb him.

Tristram is much more alive to the hypallages and equivokes that this single pleonasm breeds. Mrs Wadman enters into the economy of breach upon breach because she fears a breach within breeches, a version of the ruin suffered by Phutatorius and Tristram where breaches in the fabric of breeches provoke ideas of breached masculinity. The hypallagic pun is made out of cannon whose raised or lowered ornamental breeches caused the breach Mrs Wadman fears is hidden by Toby's red plush breeches, which in turn would impede that raising or lowering of breeches (in Trim's metaphor) that allows aim to be taken at 'the thing itself' (*TS*, 9.8.609). Worse than cannon for making breaches, however, are the breeches or buttocks of Trim and Bridget when they fall on Toby's drawbridge and crush it to pieces. 'No bridge', mocks Walter, 'that ever was constructed in this world, can hold out against such artillery' (*TS*, 3.24.211), extending the pun on breach and breech to bridge. The pun rebounds upon him when Slop tries to repair the breach he has made in Tristram's countenance with a *bridge*. The remedy for that accident mimics the disaster of Tristram's conception, where the breach of Walter's rhythm occurs in the vicinity of his wife's ****, ass, arse or breech.

Except as pun-fodder, these variations played on Toby's basic figure are all unsuccessful because they are not undertaken in the true spirit of imitation, which demands a resemblance between the original breach and its copy sufficiently supererogatory to cause the imitator's mind to 'swell in Transport and an inward Pride' at what seems to be its own invention (*OS*, p. 14). Merely to make good by restoring a damaged thing to its supposed former entirety is to overvalue the skill of the repairer and to undervalue the figurative possibilities of privation. When Tristram discovers the breach or 'Joynt' in Homenas' sermon, and calls him a double dwarf for not borrowing material that matched his limited capacities, he is identifying the same fault. Homenas' thefts run upon him like a giant. 'It was', says Tristram quoting Montaigne at Homenas' plagiarism, 'so perpendicular a precipice——so wholly cut off from the rest of the work, that . . . I found myself flying into the other world, and from thence discovered the vale from whence I came, so deep, so low, and dismal, that I shall never have the heart to descend into it again' (*TS*, 4.25.316; Montaigne, *Essays*, I, 193). By borrowing in such examplary fashion on borrowing, and matching the fragments in his own work with those in Montaigne's (just as Toby does with the Duke of Marlborough's), Tristram gains a stature that may not be equal to a giant's but is at least twice that of Homenas.

Something finally ought to be said of the excitement of breach on breach, for there is no doubt that Tristram is pleasantly agitated by the witty efficacy of figure on figure that lets him do and say the same thing at the same time, like Longinus being sublime on the sublime. His imitations of Burton, whose fragments are liberally strewn through both of Sterne's novels, show this excitement most clearly because Burton's fault is to get carried away by his own fragments and quotations. He calls this overshooting. Transcribing from Castro and Mercatus on the topic of melancholy in young women, Burton suddenly calls out, 'But where am I? Into what subject have I rushed? . . . I am a bachelor myself' (*Anatomy*, I, 417). Tristram quotes Burton's cry of alarm when he catches himself fancying a revival of the cult of Priapus: 'But where am I? and into what a delicious riot of things am I rushing? I——I who must be cut short in the midst of my days' (*TS*, 7.14.495). In both cases there is an advance into an imagined state of wholeness, followed by a retreat into the customary state of incompleteness: Burton's monastic existence, Tristram's abbreviated life (hieroglyphically rendered in the slicing of 'I—— I'). But the swell of successful imitation compounds for the bob-tailed vision it discloses and for the quotations (cuts on cuts) by which it has had to be reached. In fact Tristram finds in Burton's weakness for borrowing then running with textual crutches the most dramatic examples of the imitative transport recommended by Longinus; so, supererogatively, he imitates these imitations, never failing to recur to the privation that makes them both possible.[42]

Parents and stones

It ought to be a simple matter now to set out the analogy between an imitator who reproduces the imperfections of his original text and a son who recovers the deficiencies of his father as art. Divided into 'I——I' since the moment of his conception, Tristram repeats the damage in all the figures of cutting, shaving, shag-ragging and interruption he is so fond of, until the stage is reached where he can supplement his father's impuissance with the chapter of the *Tristrapaedia* that deals with his own bob-tailing. This is where we came in. The difficulty in completing the analogy seems to lie in the intractable

---

42 For an interpretation almost exactly the opposite of this one, see Elizabeth W. Harries, 'Sterne's Novels: Gathering up the Fragments', *ELH*, 49 (1982), 35–49.

paradox of blocked patrilinearity, for if the badge of true succession is at the same time the vile mark of illegitimacy (how can you *inherit* impuissance?), the relations between father and son are stuck in a simple opposition: Either the son does inherit from the father, and the question of impotence does not arise; or he doesn't and he must be filiated elsewhere. This stark alternative obliterates the supererogatory resemblance characteristic of other incorporations of defective originals, unless one chooses to resituate Tristram's relation to his father inside a species of reproductive hypallage where sons can beget fathers as well as fathers sons.[43] Being by conviction at least a Filmerian patriarch, Walter cannot be a willing confederate in this sort of mutuality. For his part, Tristram seems to regard his father, as he does Yorick, as someone with whom he alternates, and even competes, for the right of speech. That is to say, their defects may dovetail with one another, but never reach the intense specularity of Tristram's reading of Burton (say) or Yorick's of Yorick.

The scene that tests most fully the relation of father to son, and charts most decisively its unfigurable imperfections, is that formed out of the Shandy household's various responses to the news of Bobby's death. Unlike the death at the end of Yorick's sermon, this one is a true account, not a description; and as an account of a death, it has not yet attained the narrative density of the story of Le Fever. Raw and unimproved, it is sheer loss awaiting the words that will soothe it. These come first from Walter, a steady stream of quotations of consolatory sentences gathered from the 'fragments of antiquity'. The quotation of *bits* at *loss* ought to constitute a notable pleonasm of imperfection; yet it is clear from the reactions of Toby and Mrs Shandy that these words come nowhere near the problem of grief.

The relish with which Walter recites them shows that they are designed to defer and obscure the pain, rather than to palliate it. His quotations therefore cannot enter into a figurative relation with the loss of Bobby; instead they form one with the geography of the country where they were first invented – a place where everything, even the names of great cities, 'are falling by piecemeals to decay', and where 'the proudest pyramid of them all . . . has lost its apex, and stands obtruncated in the traveller's horizon' (*TS*, 5.3.353–4). These images of ruin taken from incomplete texts make a screen of fragments on fragments (fragments-as-quotation devoted to fragments-as-debris) commemorating no loss but their own: they mourn the condition of having been reduced from wholes to parts. They are self-consoling consolations. Walter's lips haven't been touched by the gracious powers 'which erst have opened the lips of the dumb in his distress'. They have been opened by the desire to sentimentalise a fragmented but once perfect world at the expense of confronting the wreckage in his own family. This is characteristic. He quotes Spencer at Tristram's damaged penis, and paraphrases Locke during the destruction of

---

43 Again I direct the reader's attention to the chapter on Sterne in Seidel, *The Satiric Inheritance*, where I first found these ideas formulated.

his nose. His faith is relentless in the power of books to recall or invent alternatives to the havoc he would otherwise have to acknowledge, and it makes him (at least in the deliberative part of his fatherhood) resemble Homenas rather than Burton or Tristram. He is after all 'very short'.

The most puzzling part of the scene concerns Mrs Shandy's transformation into a ruined statue while she listens at the keyhole to her husband making his transition from the death of Cornelius Gallus to that of Socrates. When she first stoops down, her son is moved (possibly by Walter's allusions to ruin and the image of the obtruncated pyramid) to associate her with stone: 'the listening slave, with the Goddess of Silence at his back, could not have given a finer thought for an intaglio' (*TS*, 5.5.357). And no doubt a perverse loyalty to these images of stone-work – Mrs Shandy as statue and as intaglio – leads him to exclaim, when he remembers how long he has left her bent in this posture while pursuing the underplot in the kitchen, 'Your most obedient servant, Madam——I've cost you a great deal of trouble', and to imagine her reply: 'I wish it may answer;——but you have left a crack in my back——and here's a great piece fallen off here before,——and what might I do with this foot?——I shall never reach England with it' (*TS*, 5.11.367). The conceit of turning his mother into a talking and nearly walking piece of the ancient ruins his father began by mentioning is almost as awkward and opaque as that of the fiddle-playing which ends the scene.

It is a maxim of associationism that all ideas, even the most enigmatic, can be analysed into their constituent parts, so it ought to be possible to explain why this strange image of a crumbling mother is necessary to the account of how the news of his brother's death was received, and to decide whether it supplements or subverts the fragments of pseudo-consolation arranged by her husband. It is best to begin by outlining parallel associations in Montaigne's *Essays* and Job, for the one book tells Tristram a great deal about the impediments to a simple connexion between the son and the father, and the other is his digest of the problems of consolation, drawn on throughout this scene.

Montaigne explores his genetic relation to his father and its literary analogues in three essays: 'Upon Some Verses of Virgil', 'Of the Resemblance of Children to their Fathers' and 'Of Experience'. In the first Montaigne performs his own version of the self-consolation performed by Tristram under the heading 'shag-rag and bob-tail'. Ruined by old age ('one poor Inch of pitiful Vigour') he turns first to memories of his sexually active years and then, more profitably, to the love poetry of Ovid and Virgil. Cashing in on his discovery that the most exciting verse is the most oblique, he makes it more so by cutting it into quotations. Then he finds a satisfaction which mimics and eases his wretched condition: After quoting from Ovid a line about the twining of two naked bodies, he exclaims, 'Methinks I am *eunuch'd* with the Expression' (*Essays*, III, 130). In the second essay he establishes a link between himself and his father that he will develop in the third. 'What a wonderful thing it is, that the drop of Seed from which we are produc'd, should carry in it self the Impression not only of the bodily Form, but even of the Thoughts and Inclinations of our Fathers' (*Essays*, II, 642–3). It isn't quite so wonderful that the disease of the 'great *Stone in his Bladder*' has also been passed from the father (whose name appropriately was Pierre) to the son.[44] He now passes stones in turn, in an involuntary travesty of the act and agency of his begetting, when the father called 'stone' passed on the kidney-stone to his son. It is a sign of how well inured he is to the double principle, that Montaigne is able to study the oscillation of literalism and figure in this exigent: to pass stones when he passes stones:

Years have evidently help'd me to drain certain Rheums; and why not these Excrements which furnish matter for Gravel? but is there any thing sweet in comparison of this sudden Change, when from an excessive Pain, I come, by the voiding of a Stone, to recover, as from a flash of Lightning, the beautiful Light of Health? . . . 'Tis some great Stone that wastes and consumes the Substance of our Kidneys, and of my Life, which I by little and little evacuate, not without some natural Pleasure, as an Excrement henceforward superfluous and troublesome.   (*Essays*, III, 431, 434)

Supplementing the consolation he takes from the alternation of pain and pleasure in the voiding of stones and from the conceit of viewing his life as one large stone that is gradually chipping itself away to nothing, is a collection of writings Montaigne calls his 'Sibyl's Leaves'. These are the notes of previous attacks which he reads at the onset of a fresh one: 'I never fail of finding matter of Consolation from some favourable Prognostick in my past Experience' (*Essays*, III, 431).

The analogy between 'Upon Some Verses of Virgil' and the other two essays turns on a message from the past, a father's or a poet's, which damages (literally or figuratively) the sexual organs of its receiver; yet this damage, whether reproduced in tropes or on paper, will establish an intimate and satisfying resemblance between the poet and his reader and the father and his son. The image quoted, or cut, from Ovid is not only erotic: its twining bodies encompass the critical conjunction of father and child, when the message of the seed is transfused from one to the other and life takes place as a promise of disease and death. The effect of this disease ('some sharp and craggy Stone, that cruelly pricks and tears the neck of the Bladder' (*Essays*, III, 429)) is mimicked in the castrating effect of the poem. Yet the poem, like the Sibyl's leaves, consoles the sufferer for the images of pain its reading provokes; so does the play on the name of the father. By means of this reconstitutive figuration, cause and consequence are bound into a kind of hypallage that makes patient and agent alternate with one another. In dying, for example,

---

44 A thorough exploration of this pun and its implications for the *Essays* generally has been conducted by Antoine Compagnon, *Nous, Michel de Montaigne* (Paris: Seuil, 1980).

Montaigne as it were reconceives his father in a process of fortunate death, expelling the residue of the first, paternal seed as pieces of the great stone which created, and now wastes, his life. When the stone is fully passed he will have accomplished his conception in reverse, consummating his ruin in one last ejaculation of 'stone'. In his reading of Ovid he takes the same two-sided delight in a ruinous sexuality that leaves him de-stoned but wearing the lineaments of satisfied desire.

Montaigne quadrates four distinct elements to produce these ambiguities and reversals: stone, flesh, text and father. Each is linked to the other by interlocking puns. For example, the written leaves record the cut made on the neck of Montaigne's bladder by the cruel stone that was implanted in him by his father, and so inscribe at large the message hidden in the seed. Ovid's poem is a text cut (quoted) to yield an especially vivid image of copulation whose effect on Montaigne's stones reproduces figuratively the damage caused by the paternal stone – a stone that was inherited, what is more, at a moment of carnal ecstasy just like this one which eunuchs him. That damage is run in reverse as Montaigne pisses out his life piecemeal in stones, a process inseparable from Montaigne's fragmented issue of himself in written form, whether in his Sybil's leaves or in the larger fragments of his *Essays*. The play between the four elements is as rapid and as interinvolved as Tristram's on breach, achieving the same equivocal solace out of figuring want and pain as pleasant supplements.

To compare Montaigne's complex readings of the paternal text with Walter's self-consolation for the loss of a child, we need first to recall that Bobby's death, Tristram's conception and Mrs Shandy's imagined pregnancy make a laminate of related ideas and images. Prominent among them is the father's refusal to accept responsibility for the disappearance or mutilation of his offspring. He excludes 'weakness of the body' (*TS*, 1.16.42) from his calculations, being convinced that the message from his loins is sound and clear enough and that it has been distorted (like the imprint of Dolly's thimble upon the hot wax) by extraneous factors, principally his wife's feebleness of mind. Hence the mirror-pattern of the conception of Tristram and the loss of Bobby, both marked and as it were occasioned by an interruption from Mrs Shandy. Walter turns to texts therefore as a means of re-transmitting the message in its original form, clear and full, not as a way of matching textual cuts to physical limitations. So the four elements of stone, flesh, father and text fail to quadrate. Stones – obtruncated pyramids – stand in the same relation to 'cut off' sons as quoted texts: that is, as signs of desiderated perfection that never really impugn the paternal stones, from which he derives the power to stamp a comprehensive destiny on the life of his son. As the very temporary medium of this power, flesh and physical proximity have only a mechanical importance – like the real Tristram to the *Tristapaedia* or the real father to the literay substitutes who sail for Aegina towards Megara and who ask the Athenian bench to consider the plight of three desolate children. Neither his own genitals nor his son's corpse enters into Walter's economy of fragments. The whole point of his eloquence seems to be to divide the animate from the inanimate so that the latter can speak freely. Tristram, on the other hand, can read his father only by insisting on the textual-fleshly impuissance that marks all his productions, particularly the *Tristrapaedia*.

Job's contribution to this quadrature is fully apparent only from the perspective of the commentaries generated by the Warburtonian controversy, which turned on these critical verses: 'Oh that my words were now written! oh that they were printed in a book! That they were graven with an iron pen and lead in the rock for ever! For I know that my redeemer liveth, and that he shall stand at the latter day upon the earth: And though after my skin worms destroy this body, yet in my flesh shall I see God' (19: 23–6). For the sake of his allegory, Warburton had to read this powerful condensation of the elements of text, stone, father and flesh as a promise of temporal deliverance, in which the afflicted Job (standing for the Jews as a whole and the tribulations they suffered in their efforts to re-establish Jerusalem) looks forward to a vindication before he dies. He therefore takes the rock to be God, and Job's allusion to it as a parabolical statement of is entire reliance upon providence (*Divine Legation of Moses*, IV, 301, n. x). Warburton's opponents, reading it as a prophecy of Christ and the day of judgment, unite in seeing the rock as a gravestone, and the desiderated words as an epitaph.[45] The most fluent and interesting of these speculations is Richard Grey's who, it will be recalled, reads Job as a dialogue on integrity:

So far from being an Intimation that he expected a temporal Deliverance, [these] are the Words of one, who look'd upon himself as a dying Man; and was, as it were, ordering his own Epitaph, which he wishes might be engraved in the Rock for ever . . . as a standing Monument of his Appeal to God, for the Truth of that Innocence which had been so barbarously traduced, and which his extraordinary Sufferings might give Posterity . . . a Handle to suspect. (*An Answer*, p. 88)

Grey establishes the ground of a comparison between Yorick and Job that is worth exploring; but neither he nor his anti-Warburtonian colleagues are able to exploit the quadrature fully. In their interpretation the inscribed stone replaces injured innocence in order to be read and vindicated by God at a time when the suffering party will no longer be of flesh, but of spirit. Warburton's reading keeps flesh as flesh, but loses stone to a periphrasis of the father, the rock of rocks (*Divine Legation of Moses*, IV, 301, n. x). Since Job's rhetorical question – 'Is my strength the strength of stones? or is my flesh of brass?' (6:12) – resists the first interpretation to the extent that the substitution it supposes is reckoned impossible by Job while he is still Job; and since his

45 See Charles Peters, *A Critical Dissertation on the Book of Job* (London, 1757), p. 240; Thomas Sherlock, *Works*, IV, 172; William Hawkins, *Tracts in Divinity*, 3 vols. (Oxford, 1758), I, 338.

frequent mention of the dwindled and breached condition of his flesh makes
the optimism of the second implausible, it becomes tempting to wonder if Job
is not offering his own commentary on 'breach upon breach'. Is he pointing
to a text cut in stone not as a future vindication of his innocence nor as a
metaphor of his enduring confidence in providence, but as the sole means of
finding a link between his physical torments and the Father who has ordained
them? In which case, what Job wants to write in the rock (let us say the Book
of Job) is much closer to Montaigne's Sybilline leaves, in being a representation of breach that founds a continuity – or even an equality – between creator
and creature *in cut stone*, than to Walter's perfect textual alternatives to present
wreckage. The consolation of such writing is based, like Tristram's supplementary chapter of the *Tristraphaedia*, on parallel defects of the father and the son
disclosed and mediated, like Montaigne's three essays, by writing and stone.

Mrs Shandy's interruption of Tristram's father follows Toby's in demanding some fleshly referent, such as details of times and places, to justify her
husband's stones and texts. Her statuesque disintegration is Tristram's
attempt roughly to solve this problem by recombining stone fragment and
flesh – first linked of course in Toby's wound at Namur – in the person of
his mother as she bends herself towards the chink made by the parlour door.
When bits begin to fall off her, the quadrature is technically complete, her
body supplying the specular moiety of the *bits* on *pieces* uttered by her husband. Despite the lurch of this readjusted combination, the prosing of the
inanimate is silenced in favour of more fleshly discourse, of which Trim's con-
current speech in the kitchen is the best example, since it is harkened to by
characters of the flesh, like the scullion and Susannah, and is delivered with
such gestural aplomb that Tristram explicates it under the Jobian heading,
'We are not stocks and stones.'

Is Mrs Shandy merely the excuse Tristram needs to sideline his father's
rhetoric and to reintroduce what it leaves out, or is her cracked appearance
part of a broader association of stone, silence and parenthood? In the
prefatory list of corroborations of the self-evident proposition that people cry
for the loss of friends and kindred, Tristram instances Niobe, who grieved for
her children even when she was turned to stone. On the other hand, it is possible that Tristram is wickedly literalising Warburton's allegory of Job, not
only by having Walter complain of the difficulty of keeping one stone on
another (architecturally speaking) – thus representing the difficulties faced
by the Jews in raising the walls of Jerusalem – but also by turning his wife
into a stone image expressive of the idolatry of the Jewish women that kept
their men from rebuilding the holy city. The coincidence of the satiric touch
and the elegiac strain need not exclude each other, however, any more than
in other scenes of death and ruin where laughter and pathos are combined.
Mrs Shandy's crumbling figure blends the comic and the tragic in an extensive pattern of allusion and counter-allusion.

Tristram prefaces his father's tour of the fragments with a parody of it, using a battery of largely classical authorities to justify the proposition that weeping is a sign of grief. Like Addison, Dennis and Smith, we have seen Tristram equalling his contempt for the easy commonplaces of classical and neoteric rhetoric with an admiration for a scriptural sublime that is awkward and always close to silence. In this case the parody pointedly conceals the preferred examples, of which Job is the chief. But it is likely that the quoted case of Agrippina's noisy grief for her dead son is quietly contrasted with the grief of Sisera's mother, whose silence, terminating the Song of Deborah, was praised by Lowth as a tacit insinuation of 'the fatal disappointment of female hope' more powerful than any words could be (Judges, 5:28–31; Lowth, p. 149). The only scriptural example in Tristram's catalogue – of David weeping for Absolom – has its counterpart in the story, also from the second Book of Samuel, of a mother's grief silently expressed: Rizpah makes a mute appeal to David for the burial of her sons by spreading sackcloth 'upon the rock' and then just waiting (II Samuel, 21:10). Rizpah mourning the loss of her children against the rock and Niobe weeping herself into stone are parallel instances that cast some light on Mrs Shandy's silent transformation into a marmoreal figure of ellipsis.

Her posture at the door ('her head a little downwards, with a twist of her neck') is a subdued example of the serpentine line which, together with the reference to the classical statue of the listening slave, puts her inside the Hogarthian economy of more and less, particularly its illustration in *The Statuary's Yard* (plate 2), the companion plate to *The Country Dance* in the *Analysis of Beauty*. At its simplest level, Mrs Shandy's disintegration to the accompaniment of her husband's quotations rehearses in the sphere of consolation the same contrast between written rules and natural statues that are found in the picture of Henry Cheere's yard. But if the curve of her neck and torso is read simultaneously with her cracking fabric, she makes a comically expanded picture of Hogarth's own emblem of the spiral round a cone, the twenty-sixth of the figures bordering this plate. J. Hillis Miller locates the origin of this emblem in the ancient simulacrum of Venus, an obtruncated pyramidal cone. He suggests that Hogarth's spiral is the sign of desire around the sign of the female, except that the latter, in being both inanimate and incomplete, signifies also the absent female attributes of 'breast, waist, hip, and thigh'.[46]

It is more consistent with my argument to suppose that the combination of curve and stone in Mrs Shandy anticipates Jenny's ringlet, where the spiral sign of physical beauty encloses the emptiness into which it will disappear. The resemblance between the two tableaux is strengthened by stone. The rubies round Jenny's neck, stones as precious as the hours and days that are

46 'Narrative Middles: A Preliminary Outline', p. 378.

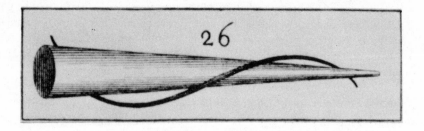

Plate 2 Hogarth's illustration 'The Statuary's Yard' from his *Analysis of Beauty* (1753), with an enlargement (above) of one of the details – an eel coiled around a cone – sketched by Hogarth in the margins.

passing, are indices of value, just as her lock of hair is an index of transience. The sapphire of Mrs Shandy's eye, 'a thin, blue, chill, pellucid chrystal' confronting Walter at the beginning of the ninth volume, has much the same function as all of the stones women use or turn into, which is to represent the loss of fleshly connexions and silently to remind a man that they are worth mourning. Paradoxically, stone softens scenes where women are close enough to death to have seemed to have helped it on. Their mute appeal ('**** ** ** *** ******; ____**** ** ****' (*TS*, 7.29.518)) is not necessarily an allurement to a man to risk the *petit mort* of carnal concupiscence, but more like an epitaph, composed of stone, flesh and the gestures of a grieving mother, that hovers between the worlds of the living and the dead and embraces, as the Shandean sublime always does, the borders of silence and the beginnings of eloquence.

These speculations may be carried further by specifying more clearly the faults of Walter's consolation. We have said that his aim is to divide the animate from the inanimate by means of Homenastic discourse: that is, language which expels both flesh and figure. His speech is structured exactly like the bad narratives of *Don Quixote* – Sancho's story of the goats and Cardenio's tale of his betrayal – because it operates by soritic overlapping and demands a contract of non-interruption ('Do not, I beseech thee, interrupt me at this crisis'). And, like Sancho's tale of the tally of the goats, all it provides is a repetition of an identical statement, 'All must die', variegated with illustrations of how things – buildings, towns and people – come to dust. Again, Montaigne offers an instructive parallel. In his essay 'Of Vanity' he quadrates the present ruin of France by civil war ('evident threats of alteration of Ruine'), the ruins of Rome ('Palaces in rubbish and Statues both of Gods and Men defac'd'), the fragments of his essays ('the frequent *Breaks*, and short *Paragraphs* . . . broke and dissolved the Attention'), and the disorder of his own mind, which he sets out as follows:

I moreover fear, in these Ravings of mine, the Treachery of my Memory, lest by Inadvertence it should make me write the same Thing Twice . . . These are common Thoughts, and having peradventure conceiv'd them an hundred times, I am afraid I have set them down some where else already. Repetition is every where troublesome . . . but 'tis ruinous in Things, that have only a superficial and transitory shew.

(*Essays*, III, 244, 249, 297)

This extraordinarily condensed account of the compulsion to repeat shows how ruin on ruin needs a figured relation if it is not to dominate the mind as repetition. Walter's sorites, taken by Toby for the ravings of temporary distraction, are echoed in the sheer nonsense of Tristram's fiddle-playing, 'Diddle diddle, diddle, diddle, diddle diddle', the repeated sounds of a failure to locate the 'ruin' on ruin or the 'breach' on breach. In its 'constant repetition of some remarks, some complaint, or song' (Burke, p. 74), Walter's iteration of the self-evident resembles that of Burke's madman, just as Montaigne's worries about repetition anticipate Mrs Radcliffe's about tautology.

The myth chosen by Freud as representing most aptly the elements of the repetition compulsion – Aristophanes' tale in the *Symposium* of the original double creatures from whose splitting sexual difference and desire derive – comes to Sterne in two forms. One is the badge in Gargantua's cap, which shows such a creature in its pristine condition, in appearance resembling the twined Ovidian bodies that eunuch Montaigne. The other is a miscellaneous poem from Swift's and Sheridan's collections of 'nauseous equivocals' called *The Original of Punning*. Aristophanes' *androgynos*, the original eight-limbed, two-headed monster, appears here as 'a PUN of flesh and blood; / A double two-faced living creature'. It leads a merry punning life of it until Jove, annoyed by the success of its double entendres, slices it in two. But,

> When the thing was split in twain
> Why then it PUNN'D as much again.[47]

If the poem is translated into the terms we have been using, Jove slices his creature in two for the sake of literal, unequivocal language, and subordinates flesh to an exemplary manifestation of prescriptive power. The cruelty of the cut corresponds to the creator's refusal to take the blame for what he has made, which is really a double evasion of responsibility when we consider that punning, being a register as well as a cause of violence, points to some kind of originary damage inflicted by the father on the 'androgynos'. In any event, the creature has the wit to transform cut on cut into multiplying figures of paranomasia, as Montaigne does with 'stone' or Tristram with 'breach'. Its puns upon puns give it the consolation of all pleonasms, which is to make the less-than-entire collaborate with the twice-as-much, privation with excess, the dwindling accident with the swelling design. Very economically the fable illustrates how the turn of the sublime Swift characterises as 'translated upon translation' and 'quotation upon quotation' develops an extra twist in its encounter with the violence of the univocal and self-identical father, to whose ear these tactical reconstitutive doublings sound like the babble of repetition. Between Jove's begetting of the live pun in a primordial act of violence and his subsequent step to reduce it to a single sex and unforked tongue, Walter's career as father is briefly but exactly delineated: all the way from his impatience with the accidental ambiguities of the conception to the the hopeless symbolism of putting his damaged child into breeches.

In this Scriblerian version of the myth the father wants to separate figure from flesh, the textual from the living part, in order to keep it quiet and free from ambiguity. The extra element of stone has to wait for Freud's reading. In *Beyond the Pleasure Principle* Freud theorises the uncanny as a desire to return

---

47 *The Art of Punning; or, The Flower of Languages*: in *The Works of Jonathan Swift*, ed. Thomas Roscoe, 2 vols. (London: Henry Bohn, 1851), II, 413.

to the primordially familiar state of an inanimate existence – death in short
– and he takes the symptom of this desire to be a compulsion to repeat. In
trying to mark more exactly this locus of the uncanny, the boundary between
life and death, he speculates on the primal scene of living matter as a transformation from stone to quivering flesh, effected by 'a force of whose nature we
can form no conception' which causes the new organism such horrible pain
that its first instinct is to cancel itself out.[48] It is then, in the catastrophic first
moments of being, that 'these splintered fragments of living substance' evolve
a drive transmitted to all their progeny 'to restore an earlier state of things',
a desire, manifest in various forms of indirect activity, 'to die . . . in [their]
own fashion' (BPP, pp. 332, 331, 312). Freud interprets Aristophanes' story
of the double creatures as the sole mythic representation of this desire.
Organic life is bounded by the inanimate from which it sprang and to which
it longs, sometimes deviously, to return. The degree of obliquity is determined
by the amount of inanimate material the organism can incorporate in its
life process. Freud refers to this as a 'crust' or 'shield', the scar tissue remaining from the shocks at first sustained by the living splinter which inhibits the
impact of subsequent ones: 'Its outermost surface ceases to have the structure
proper to living matter, becomes to some degree inorganic and thenceforward
functions as a special envelope or membrane resistant to stimuli' (BPP, p.
298). Here, with the saving blend of the animate and the inanimate, we can
locate in Freud's speculative biology the Scriblerian fleshly pun. Both
organisms are shielded by the scars of their first wounds, and the traces of
stone in the living flesh make them equivocal emblems of the desire to survive
and the longing to be extinct: the androgynos has to be cut again before it will
reproduce. Their oblique motions of body and tongue conciliate the rival
demands of their constituent flesh and stone, and violent coercion causes them
to be doubly oblique as they move to sustain the added threat of stone, or
death, with a corresponding charge of flesh, or life. The resemblance between
this perverse living fragment, the Scriblerian living pun and Tristram himself,
is hard to miss; but Mrs Shandy, who mingles flesh with stone as her Jove-like
husband tries to pare away indefinite flesh from questions of life and death
so that nothing is left but stone, belongs with them. A living monument of
splintering shock, a pun of animate and inanimate tissue, she stands as a
silent defalcating alternative to the cuts her husband is repeatedly making.

In Beyond the Pleasure Principle the role of the incisive father is taken by Freud
himself. First he asks, 'Shall we follow the hint given us by the poet-
philosopher and venture upon the hypothesis that living substance at the time
of its coming to life was torn apart into small particles, which ever since
endeavoured to reunite through the sexual instincts?' Then he mimics the

---

48 Sigmund Freud, Beyond the Pleasure Principle, in On Metapsychology: The Theory of Psychoanalysis,
ed. Angela Richards (Harmondsworth: Pelican Freud Library, 1984), XI, 311. Further
references are cited as BPP.

decisive act of the inconceivable natural force by cutting his newly conceived hypothesis in two: 'But here, I think, the moment has come for breaking off' (*BPP*, p. 332). The symptoms of repetition that accompany such gestures make their way into Freud's text, despite its being devoted to the very topic of repetition. 'We shall be compelled to say that *"the aim of all life is death"* and, looking backwards, that *"inanimate things existed before living ones"* ' (*BPP*, p. 311). The statement he is *compelled* to make is, he fears, a *repeated* one ('I have no doubt that similar notions . . . have already been put forward repeatedly' (p. 309 n.1)) about the *repetition compulsion*.[49] Burke falls into the same tautology when extending his remarks on repetition to the colonnade, where pillar after pillar 'repeats impulse after impulse, and stroke after stroke'. Suddenly alarmed, he retreats from repetition with an acknowledgment that he has already been guilty of it: 'To say a great deal therefore upon the corresponding affections of every sense, would tend rather to fatigue us by an useless repetition, than to throw any new light upon the subject' (Burke, pp. 141–2). The only light to be thrown on repetition is repetition. In an essay entitled *Repetition* Kierkegaard reminds his reader, 'I must ever be repeating that it is with reference to repetition that I say all this.'[50] It is safe to say that repetition upon repetition is precisely what breach on breach, the consoling pleonasm, is not.

The relation of repetition to stone – Burke's colonnade, Freud's inanimate substance, Walter's and Montaigne's fragments of antiquity, Job's rock – is always mediated by a creator (Godhead, parent, inconceivable force, author) whose function is either to facilitate the progress of tautology towards unequivocal ruin or to impede it with a redemptive equivoke. Mrs Shandy, who interposes her petrifying body between her husband's repetitions and her son's corpse, adopts that most primitive and enigmatic form of such an equivoke. Even the most ingenious commentary cannot assimilate it directly to the variety of pleonastic figures we have seen arrayed against repetition and tautology. Apart from her brief defence of the replenishing power of love, and her quiet enthusiasm for a match between Toby and Mrs Wadman, Mrs Shandy herself has nothing to say. One final obliquity will help. Again, the hint is given by Neil Hertz and it involves the great autobiographical enterprise of 'the Sterne of poetry', *The Prelude*.[51] In it Hertz identifies a number of

---

49 See Neil Hertz, 'Freud and the Sandman', in *The End of the Line*, pp. 97–121.
50 Soren Kierkegaard, *Repetition: An Essay in Experimental Psychology*, trans. Walter Lowrie (Oxford: Oxford University Press, 1941), p. 33.
51 See Alan B. Howes, *Sterne: The Critical Heritage* (London: Routledge and Kegan Paul, 1974, p. 378. He quotes an anonymous contributor to the *Gentleman's Magazine*: 'Wordsworth may in some respects be termed the Sterne of poetry. He has, like his predecessor, endeavoured to extract sentiment where nobody else ever dreamt of looking for it, and has often exalted trifles into a consequence which nature never intended them to occupy.' Wordsworth himself confessed, 'God knows my incursions into the field of modern literature, excepting in our own language three volumes of *Tristram Shandy*, and two or three papers of the *Spectator*, half subdued – are absolutely nothing.' *Letters*, ed. Ernest de Selincourt (Oxford: Clarendon Press, 1967), I, 56.

images typical of the sublime 'end of the line' mode where 'a practically (but not quite) dispensable "subject" confront[s] a split or doubled "object" ' (Hertz, *The End of the Line*, p. 222). In the work of George Eliot, Flaubert and Courbet the split object is a formation of flesh, water or rock folded into itself so as to appear as darkness upon darkness – those *redoublements d'obscurité* mentioned before – and the almost dispensable subject is a character who adopts a spectator's or reader's position vis-à-vis these pleonasms of darkness. Wordsworth's encounter with the blind beggar, whom he sees as divided between the emblematic fixedness of face above and the written label below, and the Boy of Winander, who sees heaven received into the bosom of the lake, are two examples Hertz finds in *The Prelude*.[52] A third comes in the second book, when Wordsworth says that to remember his childhood is to be 'conscious of myself, / And of some other being' (II, 32–3). Without a pause he realises the metaphor of self-division in the image of the 'grey stone / Of native rock' (II, 33–4) the Stone of Rowe that used to stand in the market square, and upon which the old woman for whom it was named would arrange her wares. When he returns to visit this monument of childhood joys, 'I found that it was split and gone to build/ A smart assembly-room' (II, 38–9). Hertz's reading of Wordsworth's reading of his two selves is that the abjection of the mother-figure – her metamorphosis into a stone that is split and then lost – is the price paid in mutilation and sacrifice for the successful self-location of the 'subject'-reader. To this extent the end of the line is the most exigent form of the figurative reconstitution allowed by violent scenarios of the sublime.

It is not quite like this in *Tristram Shandy*. Mrs Shandy's petrifaction and splitting marks her entry into her son's text as a consoling and obscurely exemplary figure at a crisis in which he finds it difficult to locate himself. The damage she sustains is already a figurative response to Bobby's loss, the assimilation of flesh to stone that re-equivocalises the division made by Walter's repetitive quotations. She is Tristram's writing in the rock, a sort of human epitaph. The only other character to do anything like Mrs Shandy is Yorick. 'A plain marble slabb' bears the last three words of his story, and in his subsequent resurrections some of his puns have the authentic flavour of the stone. His last, the answer he makes to Mrs Shandy's final question ('L—d, what is all this story about?'), comprehends the context of her first query in a metafictional joke ('A COCK and a BULL') that unites them in sceptical amusement at the expense of men and stories that pretend to be quite entire. Of course there is another, non-marmoreal and Homenastic side to

52 There are many others: The prospect from Snowdon of the sea surmounted by a sea of mist, for example, or his emblem of the French Revolution, 'The budding rose above the rose full blown.' The disfigured corpse that rises from the lake and reminds Wordsworth of books he has read, or the mouldered gibbet with the ghostly writing on the turf beneath, incorporate the specifically textual element in these superimpositions, most fully explored in the confrontation with the beggar.

Yorick which expresses itself in the desire for literal statements and in the point-blank rhetoric of the thing itself. But the Yorick who is sacrificed so that Tristram, and behind him Sterne, can get a chance to publish the true state of cases relating to him and them, is close both to Mrs Shandy and to the other stone-girt mother, the imprisoned Agnes Sterne. Reticence, tact, an inability or a reluctance 'to set a story right with the world' (*TS*, 4.27.324) is characteristic of all three. Mrs Sterne left no account at all of her story. Mrs Shandy squeezes the tale of her disappointments into the two 'Amens' of her last dialogue with her husband, which, like Yorick's inscription, redouble a sort of epitaph into an elegiac echo. The two mothers and the jester are objects divided betwen the *poco piu* which, as Hogarth says, completes the statue, finishes the work in stone, and the *poco meno* which conserves life and flesh by keeping something back. They ask for spectators and readers who can construe a text in stone without the ghastly finality Sterne and Tristram first planned for Yorick's, or which Walter, heaping up possible epitaphs, seems to intend for Bobby's.

Whether the text 'Alas, poor YORICK!' is surmounted by the winged skull common on eighteenth-century headstones, Tristram does not say; but in its doubled form of epitaph and elegy it sends a reverberation from the senseless stone to the ghost who '*still walks*' (*TS*, 2.17.143) paradigmatic of good graveyard reading. The stone, a sort of '*kolossos*' which, like the hobbyhorse itself, substitutes for what is missing, organises a set of ambivalences summarised by Ronald Paulson as 'a filling of absence, a surrounding of emptiness . . . a symbol of both fullness and emptiness'.[53] Not only is Yorick present and absent, he is also real and textual, articulate and silent, a male with motherly attributes, a face with a name and a disfigured skull. The arrangement of these ambivalences is always the same and corresponds both to the Hogarthian pleonasm of the cross-section on top of the whole story and to the beggar's face above the text in *The Prelude*. The beggar's pallid and immobile countenance, so fixed and eyeless it looks like a death's head, combined with the text of his history beneath, forms an object whose split character is only just discernible by the 'subject' as something more than an epitaph. The bone-cleaving flesh of Job's face, as he calls for his words to be written in rock, challenges his readers to the same apprehension of a bare difference between readable flesh and readable stone. The remnant of life –

53 The *kolossoi* were stone slabs set up by the Greeks as memorials for the missing dead whose corpses could not be interred. The *kolossos* does not represent the dead; it is their double or substitute, embodying 'in permanent form in stone . . . not the image of the dead man but his life in the beyond', an ambiguous intimation of presence and absence: J.-P. Vernant, *Myth and Thought among the Greeks* (London: Routledge and Kegan Paul, 1983), pp. 306–11. Vernant's researches provide the basis for Derrida's speculations on the sublime as a critical orientation of the body towards stone, *The Truth in Painting*, trans. Geoffrey Bennington (Chicago: University of Chicago Press, 1987), p. 141. See Ronald Paulson, 'The Aesthetics of Mourning', pp. 166–7.

the face not quite a skull – is poised above the written record which can so easily be absorbed into stone to become the last word of a full account whose death-drawn limits are supposed to set you straight with the world. The same arrangement of minimal life upon imminent death marks Yorick's horseriding and the explanation of his double existence on and off the page to the Count de B****. The narrow difference between his face and the *memento mori* formed by his horse's head and by the other Yorick's skull is like the minimal difference between the inscription and its repetition, or between stone and ghost: it is just enough to allow two readings, one on top of the other. Tristram responds to this ambivalence when he thinks of Yorick's reserve and says, 'All I blame and alternately like him for was that singularity of his temper which would never suffer him to take pains to set a story right with the world, however in his power' (*TS*, 4.27.324). Like the slab, which makes a joke out of the difference between the three words of quotation and the three hundred of the full account, dying in a joke is a contribution to the primitive equivocal economy of the animate. It goes for nothing if, like Walter's incorporation of Niobe among the fragments, it is incapable of a double inflection and a double response.

As a character with a posthumous existence, always to be scrutinised (after the black page at least) through the medium of stone, Yorick embodies in slightly more readable form the mixed consistency of Mrs Shandy. He emphasises the punning side of it, particularly in the scenes surrounding Tristram's circumcision where cut flesh, inanimate material, and large amounts of text require proper orientation; he also serves to make reading an important item in the scenes of instruction of the book, since from its outset he is both cynosure, always being studied and interpreted, and critic. More clearly than Mrs Shandy, he also exhibits the perversity of Freud's living splinter by acting contrary to the lessons he illustrates, and by seeming to seek the opposite of what he desires. So the particles of Homenas found in Yorick, like the bits of Eve in Mrs Shandy and the elements of Walter at his worst in Tristram, preserve the roughness of split objects, without which they would turn into smooth, sentimental paste. Yorick's point-blank rhetoric, then, which pushes his audience to the limit, his occasional dwarfishness in borrowing, the self-approval of his reflections upon morality, his early preference for calling plums, plums; all this adds a sibilance to his epitaph ('Alass poor Homenas!') which it would be a mistake to miss. Indeed, when Homenas falls from his pulpit and, brittle with his own frigidity, shatters into pieces, he is the bathos of whatever sublime inheres in the lapideous condition of Mrs Shandy and Yorick; but that sublime is sustained (like the living splinter) by endlessly incorporating its opposite and renewing, as Hartley would say, the sense of its inconsistency.

This onward ambivalence of the Shandean sublime accounts for the paradoxical alliance of natural variety, or the life-principle, with the death-drive. This is first illustrated by Yorick when on horseback he unites and reconciles 'two incompatible movements', imitating Nature from whose wise and wonderful mechanism flow uniformly 'different and almost irreconcileable effects' (*TS*, 1.10.20; 6.17.436). In their jolliest and most fully achieved form these reconcilations (analogous to the 'tune' Longinus Rabelaicus wants to make out of the proper and the improper) are the puns he makes out of his infirmities; but at their starkest and most ill-digested, that is when Death and Nature are at their most inconsistent, they form the contradictions of his life, the Homenas and the genial jester all in one.

It is something like that ambivalence Tristram responds to, except that his motive for alternately blaming and liking Yorick arises in this case not from his enjoyment of inconsistency but from his earnest wish that the whole of Yorick's story might be told. This wish, as we saw earlier, is inherited from a living and a literary source: from Laurence Sterne who saw a way to publish his own injuries by disguising them as Yorick's, and from *Hamlet*, where the eponymous hero speaks through the skull of the dead jester. Twice Tristram intervenes between Sterne and his fictional *alter ego* to put the record straight and to restore their reputations, names and faces in the sight of the world; here, where he unveils the conspiracy mounted against Yorick, and after the sermon-reading, where he justifies Sterne's theft of 'The Abuses of Conscience' on grounds of 'perfect charity' and adds, with the familiar hesitancy about acts of publication, 'I declare I would not have published this anecdote to the world——nor do I publish it with an intent to hurt his character and advancement in the church;——I leave that to others;——but I find myself impelled by two reasons, which I cannot withstand' (*TS*, 2.17.143). The first is the laying of Yorick's restless ghost; the other is the advertisement of *all* Yorick's sermons for publication and sale – whether in charity or for profit is not stated.

If these gestures of recuperation are spelt into a plan, Yorick is to be successively reduced from flesh to bone, then from bone to stone; for to convert him from ghost to text is to sink the minimal difference between the real Yorick and the silent Shakespearean death's head into pure skull and then to hide it forever under its marble slab (not at all what Yorick had in mind, we can assume, when he asked Eugenius, 'I beseech thee to take a view of my head' (*TS*, 1.12.31)). In disfiguring the man he was promising to keep in countenance, and to do it by a bargain that does away with ambivalence for the sake of a whole story with a clear message, Tristram behaves like his father, who defaces Bobby with his fragments of antiquity, or Jove, who maims his progeny so that they can mean something sensible. In Grey's account of Job, this is the sacrifice Job is prepared to make of himself in order to render a readable text of his life to God. The movement from a mixed case to a purely inanimate one is common to them all. It isn't hard to fit Sterne's wish-fulfilment into the scheme. As Yorick's death proves to be the *sine qua non* of Tristram's right to publish, so the transformation of the imprisoned Agnes into stone itself – a dead mother beneath her slab – is the condition of Sterne's self-vindication. Yorick, Sterne's substitute and her fictional victim, is really her fellow-sufferer, which explains why the jester and the other abjected mother, Mrs Shandy, have stone in common.

It also explains why Tristram's pride in his writing is proportionate to his belief that neither parent has had a part in his begetting. To be equivocally generated in the sense of coming about as an association of associations, combined rather than conceived, is agreeable to the double principle and solves the problem of the inheritance of impuissance. But to carry the conceit to the point where Tristram conceives himself as parentless, 'as if Nature had plaistered [him] up' (*TS*, 5.11.367) like other creatures of the Nile, is to forsake the examples of joint-consistency set by his mother and Yorick. The delusion of self-generation empowers him to write and read nothing but his own whole story and to literalise the pun on *Life*. Here Tristram loses the grip on the double principle and starts to treat himself as he treated Yorick, and the result is the allegorisation of his story, with Death and Nature personified as two separate principles at the beginning of the seventh volume. When he is arrested by Death the bailiff on Nature's suit, Tristram pleads with his creditor, 'Do stop that death-looking, long-striding scoundrel of a scare-sinner', and he makes a promise, 'I have no debt but the debt of NATURE, and I want but patience of her, and I will pay her every farthing I owe her' (*TS*, 7.7.487). It is exactly what one would expect to hear from a living splinter that seeks to die in its own fashion; and significantly it is the female principle – a creditor now instead of a debtor – that grants his wish. The rest of the volume is an account of how Tristram regains his 'crust', being mutilated just enough ('Behold these breeches!') to regain the obliquity of motion, thought and pen that lets him tell his story his own way (*TS*, 9.25.633). The way he chooses is the one that reinstates reticence as a narrative value and that re-unites the animate and the inanimate in his *Life*, so that he has enough stone in him to read gravestones in an animated and animating way. It seems right that Yorick and Mrs Shandy should have the last word on this readjustment. Christopher Smart shall have the last word on these words, since he understood enough about size (being a little fellow but no Homenas), filial piety, 'crust' and the sublime to frame his sense of the consolatory virtues of the pleonasm in a pleonasm: 'For tall and stately are against me, but humiliation on humiliation is on my side.'

Index